Rwanda

THE BRADT TRAVEL GUIDE

Philip Briggs and Janice Booth

Bradt Travel Guides, UK
The Globe Pequot Press Inc, USA

First published in 2001 by Bradt Travel Guides Ltd,
19 High Street, Chalfont St Peter, Bucks SL9 9QE, England
web: www.bradt-travelguides.com
Published in the USA by The Globe Pequot Press Inc, 246 Goose Lane,
PO Box 480, Guilford, Connecticut 06437-0480

British Library Cataloguing in Publication Data
A catalogue record for this book is available from the British Library
ISBN 1 84162 034 3

Library of Congress Cataloging-in-Publication Data
Booth, Janice
    The Bradt travel guide. Rwanda / Janice Booth and Philip Briggs.
    p.cm.
    Includes bibliographical references and index.
    ISBN 1-84162-034-3
    1. Rwanda—Guidebooks. I. Title: Rwanda. II. Briggs, Philip. III.
    Title.
DT450.13.B66 2001
916.757104'4—dc21

                                                                2001023498

Photographs
Ariadne Van Zandbergen

Illustrations Annabel Milne
Maps Steve Munns

Typeset from the author's disc by Wakewing
Printed and bound in Italy by Legoprint SpA, Trento

Authors

JANICE BOOTH

Janice's career has encompassed professional stage management, amateur archaeological excavation, charity work, writing short stories, poetry, newsletters and articles, selling haberdashery in Harrods, translating documents about African agriculture, travelling whenever possible, and compiling logic problems for puzzle magazines. She has been editing Bradt travel guides since first meeting Hilary Bradt on a bus on the Seychelles in 1996. Her first visit to Rwanda was in March 2000; she was so captivated by the country and impressed by its potential for tourism that she faxed Hilary from Kigali to propose a Bradt guide to Rwanda – and ended up co-writing it. Fortunately Philip Briggs was available to cover the national parks and wildlife… and the result is the book that you are now reading.

PHILIP BRIGGS

Philip is a travel writer and tour consultant specialising in sub-Saharan Africa. Born in Britain and raised in South Africa, Philip first travelled in East Africa in 1986, and since 1990 he has divided his time equally between travelling in Africa and writing about it. He is the author of Bradt guides to South Africa, Tanzania, Uganda, Ethiopia, Malawi, Mozambique and Ghana, as well as a South African-published guide to Kenya, and has contributed to eight other travel guides covering diverse parts of Africa. In collaboration with his wife, the photographer Ariadne Van Zandbergen, Philip has contributed more than 50 articles to magazines such as *Travel Africa*, *Africa Environment & Wildlife*, *Africa Birds & Birding* and *Wanderlust*. Email: philari@hixnet.co.za.

DIVISION OF LABOUR

Philip has written everything connected with natural history: geography, wildlife, and the national parks and reserves and other lakes/forests, together with their surroundings and access towns.

Janice has written Chapters 1, 5 and 6 (except where otherwise attributed) and Appendix 1, and co-ordinated all chapters.

The rest, unless specifically attributed, is a joint effort.

Contents

Acknowledgements		**VI**
Introduction		**VII**
Prologue		**IX**

PART ONE   PRACTICAL INFORMATION   I

Chapter I   Background Information   3
Natural history 3, History 5

Chapter 2   Planning and Preparation   25
When to visit 25, Getting there and away 25, Red tape 30,
Packing 31, Money 35, Itinerary planning 36

Chapter 3   Health and Safety   37
Health 37, Safety 48

Chapter 4   Travelling in Rwanda   49
Tourist information and services 49, Public holidays 49,
Money 50, Getting around 51, Local tour operators 55,
Accommodation 55, Eating and drinking 55, Language 57,
Hassles 59, Foreign representation in Rwanda 62, Media
and communications 63, Shopping 66, Arts and
entertainment 66, Photographic tips 66

Chapter 5   Culture and People   69
Religion 69, The arts 70, People 73, MC tells her story 82,
Becoming involved 84, Investing in Rwanda 90

PART TWO   THE GUIDE   93

Chapter 6   Kigali   95
Getting there and away 96, Getting around 96, Where to
stay 97, Where to eat and drink 102, Nightlife 103,
Practical information 103, What to see and do in Kigali
107, Excursions from Kigali 112

Chapter 7   Southwest Rwanda   115
The road from Kigali to Butare 115, Butare 122, Butare to
Nyungwe Forest 129, Nyungwe Forest National Park 130,
The southern Lake Kivu shore 146

Chapter 8   **Northwest Rwanda**   159
              Ruhengeri 159, The Volcanoes National Park 169,
              Byumba 184, Gisenyi 184

Chapter 9   **Eastern Rwanda**   191
              Rwamagana 193, Kayonza 193, Lake Muhazi 193,
              Nyagatare 195, Kibungo 196, Rusumo Falls 197, Akagera
              National Park 197

Epilogue   213

Appendix 1   **Language**   215

Appendix 2   **Contact Addresses**   219

Appendix 3   **Further Reading**   220

Index   226

LIST OF MAPS

Akagera National Park	198	Lakes Burera & Ruhondo	166
Butare	124	Northwest Rwanda	158
Cyangugu	148	Nyungwe National Park	138
Eastern Rwanda	192	Ruhengeri	160
Gisenyi	186	Rwanda	inside front cover
Kibuye	154	Southwest Rwanda	116
Kigali city centre	98	Volcanoes National Park	170
Kigali environs	108		

Acknowledgements

So many people in Rwanda helped us in their different ways, and all of them contributed those most valuable of inputs: enthusiasm and encouragement. Florence Nkera of Alliance Express helped to set the whole thing in motion and has been a solid rock of support throughout. Among the many people in the President's Office and other government departments who generously gave us their time, expertise and practical assistance, Patricia Kanyiginya has been smoothing the way for us quietly and efficiently since the very beginning. Beth Payne provided a variety of useful information, as did Liz Williamson of the DFGF and Ania Dudziec; Michel Kayihura checked some of the material; Gaston Gatare of Swift Tours & Travel contributed historical anecdotes. Marie Chantal Uwimana coped with last-minute requests for missing facts and provided background data. Guide Patrick Katabarwa and driver Jean-Pierre Kayinamura took good care of Philip and Ariadne as they travelled around. Dorette Boshoff and David Hartley shared their impressions of Rwanda with us. Other people found time in their busy schedules to write material for the guide – their authorship is indicated. Many individuals – too many to name here – also helped us by performing a number of other services.

THE BRADT STORY
Hilary Bradt

The first Bradt travel guide was written by Hilary and George Bradt in 1974 on a river barge floating down a tributary of the Amazon in Bolivia.

Since winning *The Sunday Times* Small Publisher of the Year Award in 1997, we have continued to fill the demand for detailed, well-written guides to unusual destinations, while maintaining the company's original ethos of low-impact travel.

If you experience anything which you would like to share with us, or if you have any amendments to make to this guide, please write; all your letters are read and passed on to the author. Most importantly, do remember to travel with an open mind and to respect the customs of your hosts. Happy travelling!

19 High Street, Chalfont St Peter, Bucks SL9 9QE, England
Tel: 01753 893444 Fax: 01753 892333
Email: info@bradt-travelguides.com Web: www.bradt-travelguides.com

Introduction

Philip Briggs

Rwanda, it has to be said, would probably not feature prominently on many people's holiday wish list. Try telling a few friends that you're thinking of visiting this small Central African country, and you'll see what I mean!

Rather like Uganda and the Amin regime of the 1970s, or Ethiopia and the mid-1980s famine, Rwanda today is almost exclusively associated with the genocide that occurred there in 1994. In the course of a few months it is estimated that up to one million Rwandans – an eighth of the population – were killed by their fellow countrymen in an orchestrated bout of 'ethnic cleansing'. Another two million fled across the borders to rudimentary refugee camps. The incomprehensible brutality of these killings and the abject misery of the refugee camps, all beamed across the world courtesy of satellite television, rapidly changed Rwanda from a rather obscure African country into a byword for human atrocity every bit as chilling as Hiroshima, or Auschwitz, or Siberia. Not, as I say, the most superficially appealing holiday destination.

And yet it hasn't always been this way. In the 1980s, Rwanda really was just another obscure African country, one which had certainly had its ups and downs since independence, but no more so than most of its neighbours. And, while most Westerners had barely heard of Rwanda before the genocide, a great many were familiar with the country's most celebrated inhabitants: the mountain gorillas of the Virunga Mountains. It was on the Rwandan slopes of the Virungas that the late Dian Fossey studied gorilla behaviour for almost 20 years, and on these very same bamboo-covered slopes that the acclaimed movie *Gorillas in the Mist* was shot on location in 1988.

Only ten years ago Rwanda was known in travel circles as *the* place to track mountain gorillas. Within ten years of the first habituated gorilla group being opened to tourist visits, gorilla-based tourism had become one of the country's three leading earners of foreign revenue. And, all things being equal, that should have been only the beginning: following the release of *Gorillas in the Mist* and the establishment of trails through the magnificent Nyungwe Forest, Rwanda in the late 1980s seemed set to take off as a major tourist destination. But in fact the political situation, shaky since independence in the 1960s, was deteriorating. As the reports of violence increased, so tourism declined. And then came the horror of 1994.

In the restless eyes of the mass media, the Rwandas of this world, along with the Ugandas and the Ethiopias, are deemed newsworthy only when things go wrong. A messy civil war, a few tourists killed, a demonstration gone out of control, a genocide, and the whole world watches. And yet the moment calm returns, the cameras move off, leaving us with a residual image of violence that may persist for decades. You don't believe me? Mention Uganda to a few people, and see how often the first thing mentioned is Idi Amin – a man who was ousted from power before Thatcher and Reagan won their first elections. So it is with the genocide in Rwanda, which subsided in 1995 – recent history, for sure, but history all the same.

The genocide is over, but the gorillas are still there in their misty mountain home, and Rwanda today is still Africa's premier gorilla tracking destination. That, alone, is sufficient reason to visit Rwanda: as anybody who has looked into the liquid brown eyes of a wild mountain gorilla will confirm, this is quite probably the single most awesome and emotional animal encounter to be had in a continent known for its peerless wildlife.

Gorilla tracking, which re-started in 1999, is Rwanda's main tourist draw card, the one absolute must-do that is already luring backpackers across the border from neighbouring countries; in early 2001 at least two prominent tour operators with years of experience in East Africa are organising trips there. But there are also all Rwanda's other natural wonders which once made the country such a popular tourist destination: the mountain-ringed inland sea that is Lake Kivu; the immense Nyungwe Forest with its chimpanzees, monkeys and rare birds; the wild savannah of Akagera National Park – and above all, perhaps, some of Africa's most consistently memorable scenery, an endless succession of steep cultivated mountains that have justifiably earned Rwanda the soubriquets 'Land of a Thousand Hills' and 'Switzerland of Africa'.

'But is it safe?' I hear you ask. Well, such things are difficult to quantify, but our impression is that Rwanda is as safe as anywhere in Africa, more so, in fact, than many places which routinely attract thousands of tourists monthly. Crime levels are low, stability is high, and – a factor not to be underestimated – the incidence of malaria in main tourist centres is negligible. Realistically, the biggest risk, as in so many parts of Africa, is somewhat less exotic – a car accident. Furthermore, this is an ideal time to visit Rwanda independently – package tourism is still in its infancy, costs are low, gorilla permits are still easy to obtain at short notice, and most parts of the country are still sufficiently untouristed to create the feeling of being well away from the crowd.

There may be some who feel ethically uneasy about the idea of holidaying in a country so recently emerged from a genocide. However, economic growth helps to forge political stability, and for Rwanda the importance of tourism as an economic stimulant cannot be overstated. Few could travel through Rwanda and not be conscious of the terrible brutality that stained its soil only six years ago – even if they knew nothing of it beforehand, genocide memorial sites at Nyamata, Murambi and elsewhere provide gut-wrenching testament to the horrors suffered by so many Rwandans. But these very same sites also highlight the commitment by the government and the man in the street that the events of 1994 should be neither forgotten nor repeated. Rwanda today is astonishingly open about its recent past. It is also, in my experience, among the most polite, safe and welcoming of African nations. You won't regret visiting it!

Prologue
Janice Booth

Back in the 1970s and 1980s, I worked for a Belgian charity which was providing sponsorships for Rwandan refugee children exiled in Uganda, so that they could continue their schooling. They – or their parents – had fled to Uganda to escape the outbreaks of unrest and violence that had dogged Rwanda since the early 1960s. This was largely a scheme of one-to-one sponsorship: individuals in Europe or elsewhere helped individual children. I was never in Uganda; I worked from home in London. My job was to recruit sponsors in Europe, to process information for them and to pass on their donations.

During that time, a 20-year-old Rwandan Tutsi wrote to me announcing firmly that he had decided we would be friends. Goodness knows how he had found my address. I was sceptical, as this kind of approach often precedes various requests for help; but in fact he took the friendship seriously, writing a short letter to me at least once a year to tell me his news. I was 18 years older, almost his mother's age. He and his brother had slipped over the border when they were teenagers in order to complete their education and get some qualifications, living as best they could, while the rest of his family stayed in Rwanda – he received little news of them during that time.

Peter – as he called himself while he was in Uganda – trained in electrical engineering after finishing his schooling, and returned home to Rwanda (while his brother stayed to study and work in Uganda) as soon as he had gained his diploma. I remember his first delighted letter from his home country: 'Janice, now I have a *family* again!' He got a job, working for a large company. Things were certainly tough for him, as they were for many Tutsis in Rwanda at the time, but he never asked for help. There was violence and there was discrimination – he wrote to me sadly: 'You know, Janice, this is Africa, and we are the wrong tribe.' He loved Rwanda – his homeland – very deeply.

As the years passed, he gradually drew me closer to his family. In the violence of 1990 he was thrown into prison and then fled to a neighbouring country for a while, so we passed letters via a friend. While he was away he asked me to encourage his younger sister, who was doing her final secondary exams, so I exchanged letters with her too. When his mother died, he commented: 'Perhaps you two could have been sisters.' In 1992 he sent me a photo of himself with four of his siblings – the first I'd seen since an old black-and-white passport photo sent many years before. On the back of the photo he wrote their names. Then he and a group of friends set up a small aid project, to help needy youngsters and people alone in hospital. He told me: 'We are doing better now, so we can give some help.'

In 1993 he wrote to let me know he was getting married, described his bride and sent me an invitation, not really expecting me to accept. (I had always said it was too far, and travel too expensive.) However, I suddenly wanted very much to be there, so, without telling him, I bought my air ticket – but then violence flared again and I feared a foreign guest might cause him problems, so I cancelled. We exchanged long letters afterwards (he sent a photo of himself and his bride) and at the New Year. He always believed that we would meet one day. 'Janice,' he asked me once, 'How do you see it when we meet? What will we say?' I replied that I thought we would probably just talk about an assortment of things for a very long while, as old friends do when they have been apart.

In April 1994, when the Rwandan President's plane was shot down, I heard about it on the news early the following morning – and knew in my bones that this would be the trigger. I found and dialled the number of the company where Peter was working, hoping to be able to warn him – but at the other end the phone just rang, unanswered. The killing had already begun. After our 17 years of correspondence, I never heard from him again.

One of my reactions to the genocide, apart from obvious horror at the pictures filling our television screens, was anger: anger at the waste, at the pointless loss of life, at the reduction to statistics of what had once been human beings. Anger at their anonymity in death, as if they had never existed. I wrote a dozen or so letters to people through whom I hoped to get news of Peter but mostly no-one answered – probably they had died too – or else they had no information. Rwanda was in chaos: the whole population on the move, refugees streaming from border to border, families split up, thousands of children orphaned. And I was powerless to help.

Time passed and my anger faded, but the wastefulness of it all still hammered at my mind. I wanted to tell Peter's story, so that at least he would have a small 'memorial'. In the autumn of 1999, the WEXAS *Traveller* magazine ran a travel-writing competition and I entered a piece about Peter. To my amazement, it scooped first prize – which, to my very great delight, meant that his story would be published and widely read. He was no longer just one of the anonymous victims.

Writing the piece for *Traveller* brought back all my memories of our correspondence. Somehow, I had to find out what had happened, so I decided to visit Rwanda – an unknown country for me – to try to track down any members of Peter's family who might have survived. I had no idea what I would find there. The media were painting a picture of a dangerous place, still violent, war-damaged, beset by suffering. In February 2000 I bought my air ticket.

I had so little information. Beyond my three photos (the old passport snap of Peter, the one of his siblings and the one of him with his wife) I had nothing, except the names of the two brothers and two sisters on the back of the family photo, and the name of the brother who had been with him in Uganda. Here luck took over. Although I had not kept any of my sponsorship files, some of the children's names had stuck in my mind – and I had read (because I was reading everything about Rwanda that I could lay my hands on) that some people with similar names were now working in the new Rwandan administration. Taking a chance, I wrote to one of them, explaining why I was coming. Immediately I got a phone call from someone in his office, asking me to contact her when I arrived so that she could try to help. She also booked accommodation for me in Kigali so that I had a base.

I gave her the name of a former headmaster from the refugee schools in Uganda at the time of the sponsorships – a friend of mine at home knew he worked somewhere in the education department but had lost his address. She tracked him down and he came to see me in Kigali. I gave him the names of Peter's siblings and he promised to do what he could to trace them, but obviously it would take a few days. So I decided to switch into tourist mode and discover the country that Peter had loved so much.

From the moment of my arrival in Rwanda I had felt at ease. Obviously the media reports were unduly negative – Kigali was a safe city, the services worked, people were friendly. I got to grips with the public transport system of minibus-taxis, which covered every part of the country, and I began to explore.

I was captivated. This country which I had seen only through horrific TV reports was stunningly beautiful: green, hilly and intensively cultivated, with far-reaching views. Every bus-ride was a pleasure as the panoramas unfolded. I visited the gorillas in the Volcanoes National Park (a tough climb, but worth every scratch and slither for the privilege of an hour spent in their company), I went to Butare and its absorbing museum, and I went to Kibuye where Peter had been working. He had described the little lakeside town as being peaceful and beautiful – which indeed it is. Hotels and guesthouses throughout the country were comfortable and I was able to wander without being hassled, which is not always the case for a lone, female traveller. The tourist structures dating from before the genocide (prior to the 1990s Rwanda earned more from tourism than from any other exports except coffee and tea) were still in place – more or less – and being refurbished fast. The national parks were accessible, varied and full of interest. For the independent traveller who prefers wildlife and local culture to 'packaged' entertainments, it seemed a terrific destination.

When I got back to Kigali I faxed Hilary Bradt, saying that she should absolutely consider producing a guide to Rwanda. She was persuaded. Philip Briggs and I have written it. And you are now reading page XI... When you have explored Rwanda fully by reading the rest of the book, you'll find the continuation of Peter's story in the *Epilogue*.

DEDICATION

To Chantal and Sandra, who are a part of Rwanda's future

Part One

Practical Information

THE REPUBLIC OF RWANDA AT A GLANCE
Geography
Land area 26,340 km² (less than half the land area of Scotland)
Location 120km south of the Equator in the Tropic of Capricorn
Capital Kigali
Rainfall Annual average 900–1,600mm; rainy seasons March–May
and October–December
Average temperature 24.6–27.6°C; hottest August and September
Altitude From 1,000 to 4,500m above sea level; highest point is Mt
Kalisimbi (4,507m)
Terrain Mostly grassy uplands and hills; relief is mountainous with
altitude declining from west to east
Vegetation Ranges from dense equatorial forest in the northwest to
tropical savannah in the east
Land use 47% cropland, 22% forest, 18% pasture, 13% other
Natural resources Some tin, gold and natural gas
Main exports Coffee and tea
National parks Volcanoes Park (northwest); Nyungwe Forest
(southwest); Akagera Park (east)

Human statistics
Population Approximately 8.01 million; 54% female, 46% male
Density 290 per km²
Life expectancy at birth Women 50.1 years, men 48.1 years
Religion Roman Catholic (majority), Protestant, Muslim, traditional
Language Kinyarwanda. French, English and Swahili are also spoken
Education Primary, secondary, technical/vocational, higher/university
Income per capita (1999) Rural US$105; urban US$1,569

Politics/administration
Government The broad-based Government of National Unity, with
three branches: executive, legislative and judicial.
President Major General Paul Kagame
Prime Minister Bernard Makuza
National flag Red (for the blood shed for independence), yellow
(representing peace) and green (symbolising the nation's agriculture).
Administrative divisions 12 prefectures, divided into 92 communes

Practical details
Time GMT + 2 hours
Currency Rwandan franc
Main health risk Malaria
Electricity 230/240 volts at 50Hz
International telephone country code 250
Airport Kigali International Airport
Nearest seaports Mombasa (1,760km); Dar es Salaam (1,528km)

Background Information

Rwanda is a land-locked country in Central Africa. Also known as the 'Land of a Thousand Hills', Rwanda has five volcanoes, 23 lakes and numerous rivers. The country lies 1,270km west of the Indian Ocean and 2,000km east of the Atlantic – literally in the heart of Africa.

NATURAL HISTORY
Philip Briggs
Geography
Rwanda's mountainous topography is a product of its position on the eastern rim of the Albertine Rift Valley, part of the Great Rift Valley which cuts through Africa from the Red Sea to Mozambique. The country's largest freshwater body, Lake Kivu, which forms the border with the DRC, is effectively a large sump hemmed in by the Rift Valley walls, while its highest peaks – in the volcanic Virunga chain – are a result of the same geological process which formed the Rift Valley 20 million years ago. The Rift Valley escarpment running through western Rwanda also serves as a watershed between Africa's two largest drainage systems: the Nile and the Congo.

Western and central Rwanda are characterised by a seemingly endless vista of steep mountains, interspersed with several substantial lakes whose irregular shape follows the mountains that surround them. Much of this part of the country lies at elevations of between 1,500 and 2,500m. Only in the far east of the country, along the Tanzania border, do the steep mountains give way to the lower-lying, flatter terrain of the Lake Victoria Basin. The dominant geographical feature of this part of the country is the Akagera River and associated network of swamps and small lakes running along the Tanzania border. Much of this ecosystem is protected within Akagera National Park.

Vegetation
In prehistoric times, as much as a third of what is now Rwanda was covered in montane rainforest, with the remainder of the highlands supporting open grassland. Since the advent of iron-age technology and agriculture some 2,000 years ago, much of Rwanda's natural vegetation has been replaced by agriculture, a process that has accelerated dramatically in the last 100 years. The only large stand of forest left in Rwanda today is Nyungwe, in the southwest, though several other small relic forest patches are dotted around

the country, notably Cyamudongo and Mukura Forests. Patches of true forest still occur on the Virungas, though most of the natural vegetation on this range consists of bamboo forest and open moorland. Outside of Nyungwe (soon to be designated a national park) and the Virungas, practically no montane grassland is left in Rwanda; the highlands are instead dominated by the terraced agriculture that gives the Rwandan countryside much of its distinctive character. The far east of Rwanda supports an altogether different vegetation: the characteristic African 'bush', a mosaic of savannah woodland and grassland dominated by thorny acacia trees.

Fauna

Rwanda naturally supports a widely varied fauna, but the rapid human population growth in recent decades, with its by-products of habitat loss and poaching, has resulted in the extirpation of most large mammal species outside of a few designated conservation areas. Rwanda today has three main conservation areas: the Volcanoes Park, Akagera Park and Nyungwe Forest. Each of these protects a very different ecosystem and combination of large mammals, for which reason greater detail on the fauna of each reserve is given under the appropriate regional section. Broadly speaking, however, Akagera supports a typical savannah fauna dominated by a variety of antelope, other grazers such as zebra, buffalo and giraffe, the aquatic hippopotamus, and plains predators such as lion, leopard and spotted hyena.

Nyungwe Forest and the Volcanoes Park probably supported a similar range of large mammals 500 years ago. Today, however, the faunas differ, mostly as a result of extensive deforestation on the lower slopes of the Virungas. The volcanoes today support bamboo specialists such as golden monkey and mountain gorilla, as well as relic populations of habitat-tolerant species such as buffalo and elephant. The latter two species are probably extinct in Nyungwe (buffalo were hunted out 25 years ago, while elephant spoor has not been detected since a dead elephant was found in late 1999), but this vast forest still supports one of Africa's richest varieties of forest specialists, ranging from 13 types of primate to golden cat, duiker and giant forest hog. Despite the retreat of most large mammals into reserves, Rwanda remains a rewarding destination for game viewing: the Volcanoes Park is the best place in the world to track mountain gorillas, while Nyungwe offers visitors a good chance of seeing chimpanzees and 400-strong troops of colobus monkeys – the largest arboreal primate troops in Africa today.

Rwanda is a wonderful destination for birdwatchers, with an incredible 670 species recorded in an area which is smaller than Belgium and has less than half the land surface of Scotland. Once again, greater detail is supplied in regional chapters, but prime birdwatching destinations include Nyungwe (275 species including numerous forest rarities and 24 Albertine Rift endemics) and Akagera (savannah birds, raptors and waterbirds). Almost anywhere in the country can, however, prove rewarding to birders: an hour in the garden of one of the capital's larger hotels is likely to throw up a variety of colourful robin-chats, weavers, finches, flycatchers and sunbirds.

HISTORY
Earliest times
Even back in the **ice age**, Rwanda was showing its typically green and fertile face; a part of the Nyungwe Forest remained uncovered by ice, so that animal and plant life could survive there. Excavations undertaken from the 1940s onwards identified several **early iron-age** sites in Rwanda and neighbouring Burundi, yielding fragments of typical 'dimpled' pottery (see *Africa in the Iron Age*, Roland Oliver & Brian M Fagan, Cambridge University Press 1975). At Nyirankuba in what is now Butare prefecture, a site of **late stone-age** occupation (without pottery) underlay a later occupation level containing both pottery and iron slag. Iron-smelting furnaces at two other sites in southern Rwanda (Ndora and Cyamakusa) gave radio-carbon datings of around AD200–300. Oliver & Fagan (above) describe these furnaces as being some 5ft in diameter, built of wedge-shaped bricks. Other sites in the area of Rwanda, Burundi and Kivu show late stone-age occupation sites underlying early iron-age occupation. The early iron-age pottery was later succeeded by a different and coarser type, apparently made by newcomers from the north who were cattle-raisers – but archaeological investigation in Rwanda has been sparse, and there must be much still awaiting discovery. Some artefacts are displayed in the National Museum in Butare.

The 'mountains of the moon' mentioned by the Alexandrian geographer Ptolemy in around AD150, and at the time believed to be the source of the Nile, may – but then again may not – have been the Virunga peaks in Rwanda's northwest. This claim is sometimes made, but seems geographically unlikely.

Rwanda's earliest inhabitants were pygmoid **hunter-gatherers**, ancestors of the *Twa* (the name means, roughly, 'indigenous hunter-gatherers'), who still form part of the population today and are still known for their skill as potters. Gradually – the dates are uncertain, but probably before about 700BC – they were joined by Bantu-speaking **farmers**, who were spreading throughout central Africa seeking good land on which to settle. Fertile Rwanda was a promising site. The arrival of these incomers, known as *Hutus*, was bad news for the Twa; now a minority, they saw some of their traditional hunting grounds cleared to make way for farming, and retreated further into the forests. Then iron-age technology developed tools – such as hoes – which enabled the farmers to grow more crops than were needed for subsistence and thus to trade.

Next came the **cattle-raisers**, taller and lankier people than either the pygmoid Twa or the sturdy farmers, who may have come from either the north or the northeast. With only oral tradition to guide us, there's no hard historic evidence for the timing of their arrival – some say before the 10th century AD, others after the 14th. Gradually, whether by conquest or by natural assimilation, a hierarchy emerged in which the cattle-raisers (known as *Tutsis*, meaning 'owners of cattle') were superior to the farmers and a master/client relationship known as *ubuhake* developed. Then most of Rwanda was a monarchy ruled by a Tutsi king or *Mwami* – although there remained outlying areas where the farming groups did not accept his authority.

Note The three groups are more correctly called Batwa, Bahutu and Batutsi, while individuals are a Mutwa, a Muhutu and a Mututsi. However, we have opted for the forms Twa, Hutu and Tutsi because outside Rwanda they are commonly used. The plural of Mwami (sometimes spelt Mwaami) is Bami. The language spoken by all three groups is Kinyarwanda.

The kingdoms of Rwanda

Rwanda has a rich oral history, which was maintained primarily by members of the Rwandan royal court. According to this history the founder of Rwanda's ruling dynasty, Abanyiginya, was not born naturally like other humans, but was born from an earthenware jar of milk. The grandmother of Rwandans lived in heaven with Nkuba (thunder) who was given the secret of creating life. He made a small man out of clay, coated him with his saliva, and placed him in a wooden jar filled with milk and the heart of a slaughtered bull. The jar was constantly refilled with fresh milk. At the end of nine months the man took on the image of Sabizeze. When Sabizeze learned of his origin, he was angry that his mother had revealed the secret and decided to leave heaven and come to earth. He brought with him his sister Nyampundu, his brother Mututsi, and a couple of Batwa. Sabizeze was welcomed by Kabeja who was of the Abazigaba clan and king of the region (in the present-day Akagera National Park). Sabizeze then had a son named Gihanga who was to found the Kingdom of Rwanda. A Rwandan historian, Alexis Kagame, estimates that Gihanga ruled as King of Rwanda in the late 10th or early 11th century.

Before the arrival of Europeans, Rwandans believed they were the centre of the world, with the grandest monarchy, the greatest power and the highest civilisation. Their king or *mwami* was the supreme authority and was magically identified with Rwanda. There was a strong belief that if the ruling monarch was not the true king, the people of Rwanda would be in danger. The well-being of Rwanda was directly linked to the health of the king. When he became old, the prosperity of Rwanda was compromised. Only when the ageing ruler died and a new, stronger king was enthroned did the country re-stabilise.

The centralised control by the king was balanced by a very powerful queen mother and a group of dynastic ritualists called the *abiiru*. The queen mother could never come from the same family clan as the king and rotated among four different family clans. The *abiiru*, who were also drawn from four different clans, could reverse the king's decisions if they conflicted with the magical Esoteric Code, protected and interpreted by the *abiiru*. They also governed the selection and installation of a new king. Any member of the *abiiru* who forgot any portion of his assigned portion of the Esoteric Code was punished severely. Members of the *abiiru* and other custodians of state secrets who revealed the secrets of the Royal Court were forced to drink *igihango*, a mixture which contained a magical power to kill traitors or anyone who failed in his duty. While the king could order the death of a disloyal member of the *abiiru*, he was required to replace the traitor with a member from the same family clan.

Rwanda's dynastic drums, which could be made only by members of one family clan from very specific trees with magical elements, had the same dignity as the king. The genitals of the enemies of Rwanda killed by the king hung from the drum. The capture of a dynastic drum from an enemy country normally signified annexation, with the group whose drum was stolen losing all faith in itself. This tradition is shared among all Bantu-speaking peoples in Africa. When Rwanda's royal drum *Rwoga* was lost to a neighbouring kingdom by King Ndahiro II Cyaamatare in the late 15th century, Rwanda was devastated. *Rwoga* was eventually replaced by *Karinga*, the last dynastic drum, when King Ruganzu II Ndori regained Rwanda's pride through his military exploits. The fate of *Karinga* is unknown. It is reported to have survived the colonial period, but disappeared during the first years of Rwanda's independence.

The origin of the division between Tutsis and Hutus is still being debated, but oral history portrays a feudal society with one group, the Tutsis or cattle herders, occupying a superior status within the social and political structure, and the other group, the Hutus or peasant farmers, serving as the serfs or clients of a Tutsi chief. The hunter-gatherer Twa were potters and had various functions at the royal court – for example, as dancers and music makers.

The complex system known as *ubuhake* provided for protection by the superior partner in exchange for services from the inferior: *ubuhake* agreements were made either between two Tutsis, or between a Tutsi and a Hutu. While *ubuhake* was a voluntary and revocable private contract between two individuals, with subjects able to switch loyalty from one chief to another, a peasant could not easily survive without a patron. Cattle could be acquired through *ubuhake* as well as by purchase, fighting in a war, or marriage. A Hutu who acquired enough cattle could thus become a Tutsi and might take a Tutsi wife, while a Tutsi who lost his herds or otherwise fell on hard times might become a Hutu and marry accordingly. A patron had no authority over a client who had gained cattle, whether Hutu, Tutsi or Twa. Whereas Hutus and Tutsis could and did sometimes switch status, a Twa seldom became a Tutsi or Hutu. In the rare instances when this did occur, it would be because the king rewarded a Twa for some act of bravery by granting him the status of a Tutsi. He would then be given a Tutsi wife and a political post within the royal court. Meanwhile the three groups spoke the same language (Kinyarwanda, a language in the Bantu group), lived within the same culture and shared the same recent history.

Rwandan nobles were experts in cattle-breeding and an entire category of poetry was devoted to the praises of famous cows. Cattle were bred for their beauty, rather than utility. Between AD1000 and 1450 herders in the Great Lakes region invented no fewer than 19 words for the colourful patterns of their animals' hides. As elsewhere in Africa, cattle were closely associated with wealth and status.

AD1000–1894

Whatever the exact timespan may have been, Rwanda (or the larger part of it) was ruled over by a sequence of Tutsi monarchs, each with his various political skirmishes, battles and conquests. Oral tradition shows us a colourful bunch of characters: for example, Ndahiro II Cyaamatare who catastrophically lost the Royal Drum; Mibambwe II who organised a system of milk distribution to the poor, ordering his chiefs to provide jugs of milk three times a day; and Yuhi III Mazimpaka, the only king to compose poetry – and to go mad. From the 17th century onwards the rulers seem to have become more organised and ambitious, using their armies to subjugate fringe areas. The royal palace was at Nyanza – and can still be seen, carefully reconstructed, today.

The *mwami* was an absolute monarch, deeply revered and seen to embody Rwanda physically. The hierarchy beneath him was complex and tight-knit, with different categories of chief in charge of different aspects of administration. His power covered most of Rwanda, although some Hutu enclaves in the north, northwest and southwest of the country clung to their independence until the 20th century. The country was divided into a pyramid of administrative areas: in ascending order of size, from base to apex, these were the immediate neighbourhood, the hill, the district and the province. (These are echoed in today's administrative pyramid of cellule, sector, commune and prefecture.) And through this intricate structure ran the practice and spirit of *ubuhake*, the master/client relationship in which an inferior receives help and protection in return for services and allegiance to a superior.

Beneath the *mwami*, power was exercised by various chiefs, each with specific responsibilities: *land chiefs* (responsible for land allocation, agriculture and agricultural taxation), *cattle chiefs* (stock-raising and associated taxes), *army chiefs* (security) and so on. While Hutus might take charge at neighbourhood level, most of the power at higher administrative levels was in the hands of Tutsis.

Since our only source of information about these early days is oral tradition, which by its nature favours the holders of power, we cannot be certain to what extent the power structure was accepted by those lower down the ladder, to what extent they resented it and to what extent they were exploited by it. But, whether harsh, benevolent or exploitative (or possibly all three), it survived, and is what the Europeans found when they entered this previously unknown country.

Rwanda had remained untouched by events unfolding elsewhere in Africa. Tucked away in the centre of the continent, the tiny kingdom was ignored by slave traders; consequently Rwanda is one of the few African countries that never sold its people, or its enemies, into slavery. There is no record of Arab traders or Asian merchants, numerous in other parts of East and Central Africa, having penetrated its borders, with the result that no written language was introduced and oral tradition remained the norm until the very end of the 19th century.

The Kingdom of Rwanda was isolationist and closed to foreigners (also to many Africans) until the 1890s. The famous American explorer, Henry Stanley, had attempted to enter several times but was forced to retreat under arrow attack. Trade with neighbouring countries was extremely limited and Rwanda had no monetary system.

German East Africa

Unlike most African states, Rwanda and Burundi were not given artificial borders by their colonisers – they had both been established kingdoms for many centuries. At the Berlin Conference of 1885, they – under the name of Ruanda-Urundi – were assigned to Germany as a part of German East Africa, although at that stage no European had set foot there. The first to do so formally was the German Count Gustav Adolf von Götzen on May 4 1894 (an Austrian, Oscar Baumann, had previously entered privately from Burundi in 1892 and spent several days in the south of the country). Von Götzen entered Rwanda by the Rusumo Falls in the southeast and crossed the country to reach the eastern shore of Lake Kivu. En route he stopped off at Nyanza where he met the *mwami*, King Rwabugiri – apparently causing consternation among the watching nobles when he, a mere mortal, shook the sovereign by the hand. They feared that such an affront might cause disaster for the kingdom. At this stage the *mwami* had no idea that his country had officially been under German control for the past nine years.

Von Götzen subsequently became Governor of German East Africa, into which Ruanda-Urundi was formally absorbed in 1898. At this time the kingdom was larger, stretching as far as Lake Edward in the north and beyond Lake Kivu in the west; it was reduced to its present area at the Conference of Brussels in 1910. The Germans were surprised to find that their new colony was a highly organised country, with tight, effective power structures and administrative divisions. They left these in place and ruled through them, believing that support for the traditional chiefs would render them and their henchmen loyal to Germany. Meanwhile various religious missions, Roman Catholic at first and then Protestant, began setting up bases in Ruanda-Urundi and establishing schools, farms and medical centres. In 1907 the colonisers opened a 'School for the Sons of Chiefs' in Nyanza, as well as providing military training.

Allowing for the blurring caused by intermarriage and the switching of status between Tutsi and Hutu, the power structures encountered by the colonisers were linked – and this proved to be a matter of great anthropological fascination – to three very visibly different groups of inhabitants: the tall, lanky Tutsi chiefs and nobles; the shorter, stockier Hutu farmers (who formed the majority); and the very much smaller Twa. The Duke of Mecklenburg, visiting the country in 1907, noted:

> The population is divided into three classes – the Watussi, the Wahutu, and a pygmy tribe, the Batwa, who dwell chiefly in the bamboo forests of Bugoie, the swamps of Lake Bolero, and on the island of Kwidschwi on Lake Kiwu.

> The Watussi are a tall, well-made people. Heights of 1.80, 2.00 and even 2.20 metres are of quite common occurrence, yet the perfect proportion of their bodies is in no wise detracted from....The

primitive inhabitants are the Wahutu, an agricultural Bantu tribe, who, one might say, look after the digging and tilling and agricultural economy of the country in general. They are a medium-sized type of people...

Ruanda is certainly the most interesting country in the German East African Protectorate – in fact in all Central Africa – chiefly on account of its ethnographical and geographical position. Its interest is further increased by the fact that it is one of the last negro kingdoms governed autocratically by a sovereign sultan, for German supremacy is only recognised to a very limited extent. Added to this, it is a land flowing with milk and honey, where the breeding of cattle and bee-culture flourish, and the cultivated soil bears rich crops of fruit. A hilly country, thickly populated, full of beautiful scenery, and possessing a climate incomparably fresh and healthy; a land of great fertility, with watercourses which might be termed perennial streams; a land which offers the brightest of prospects to the white settler.

In 1911–12 the Germans joined with the Tutsi monarchy to subjugate some independent Hutu principalities in the north of the country which had not previously been dominated. Their inhabitants, who had always been proud of their independence, resisted vigorously, overrunning much of what are now Ruhengeri and Byumba prefectures before they were defeated and brought under the *mwami's* control. Their resentment and deep sense of grievance were to endure for the next half-century.

Germany had little time to make its mark in the colonies; in 1916 Belgium invaded Ruanda-Urundi and occupied the territories until the end of World War I; Belgium was subsequently officially entrusted with their administration under a League of Nations mandate in 1919, to be confirmed in 1923.

The Belgian era

In its adjoining colony of the Congo, Belgium had full control, but for Ruanda-Urundi it remained responsible first to the League of Nations and then (after 1945) to the United Nations Organisation. Annual reports had to be submitted and no important changes could be made without agreement from above. Despite these constraints, and despite the fact that Ruanda-Urundi had far less potential wealth than the Congo, Belgium took its charge seriously, and by the time of independence some 40 years later its material achievements (in terms of increased production; public services such as roads, schools and hospitals; and buildings and administrative infrastructures) were considerable. In terms of human beings it did far less well, as later events demonstrated.

Priorities

Rwanda had always been subject to periodic famines, to such an extent that some were named and absorbed into history as milestones of time: such-and-such a child was born 'just after the Ruyaga famine' (1897), or a man died 'just before the Kimwaramwara famine' (1906). Most had climatic origins, but some which occurred around the time of the Belgian takeover (in 1916/17 and 1917/18) could also be blamed on World War I, as precious foodstuffs were shipped overseas to feed the troops. At the same time the new Belgian authorities commented that the local chiefs made little attempt to prevent the famines recurring, or to get emergency relief to the worst-hit areas. They therefore set about implementing a strict overall food strategy to make supplies less precarious.

The peasant farmers were first of all encouraged (by field workers) to maximise their production using traditional methods. They were then given help to improve their existing techniques, for example by using higher-yielding varieties of their normal crops. From 1924 the cultivation of food crops was made compulsory, including foreign species such as manioc and sweet potatoes. Next the distribution channels were upgraded, with a new road network and the development of markets and co-operatives. Storage facilities were set up; high-grade seed was distributed; the use of manure and fertiliser was promoted; the problem of erosion (caused by over-use of vulnerable land) was tackled; farmers were required to set aside a small emergency hoard of beans, peas or cereals each year; and various new types of stockbreeding were initiated. Factories and processing plants were built. Finally, the farmers were encouraged to grow crops (especially coffee) for export, so that they could earn cash with which to buy extra food in times of hardship.

These measures – not easily implemented, because of the farmers' understandable initial resentment and resistance to change – proved more or less successful, helped by a regulated but controversial and sometimes harsh policy of forced labour (*uburetwa*). Famine did recur in 1942–44 and resulted in thousands of deaths, but this could be blamed partly on the appropriation of manpower and the lack of efficient machinery caused by World War II. By the time of independence, large areas of farmland had been better protected against erosion and per-hectare crop yields had risen substantially. This agricultural improvement, together with material provisions such as roads and buildings, was probably colonisation's most helpful input to Rwanda. Its contribution to the relationship between the country's long-term inhabitants was less positive.

Power structures

Like the Germans before them, the Belgians decided to retain and use the existing power structures, but unlike their predecessors they then proceeded to undermine the authority of the *mwami* and his chiefs and to forbid some of their traditional practices, introducing their own Belgian experts and administrators at every level. This interference did not make for easy collaboration. In any case the *mwami* in power at the time of Belgian accession, Mwami Musinga, was hostile to colonisation and also resented the missionaries, since their innovations undermined the established order and worked against the subjugation of Hutus. In 1931 he was forced by the Belgians to abdicate in favour of his son, the more amenable and Westernised Mwami Mutara Rudahigwa. Until well into the 1950s, although the traditional structures keeping them in a subservient position were somewhat weakened, the Hutus still got a bad deal and remained 'second-class citizens' in almost all respects. So both Hutus and Tutsis – and indeed the minority Twas too, because they received virtually no recognition or privilege – reacted to colonisation with varying degrees of grievance.

Education

The Germans had established a few government schools in Rwanda and the Belgians followed suit, but the main source of education was always the Church. In the 1930s, the Catholic Bishop Léon Classé, who had arrived in Rwanda almost 30 years earlier as a priest and worked his way up through the hierarchy, entered into an agreement with the Belgian administration by which the Catholic Church took over full responsibility for the educational system. He may not have been entirely without financial motive: the government then subsidised the church to the tune of 47 francs per pupil and 600 francs per qualified teacher.

The Church broadened its curriculum to cover more secular subjects such as agronomy, medicine and administration; however, the main beneficiaries of the increased educational possibilities were still largely Tutsis, although Hutus were not entirely neglected and many attended primary school. Some did make good use of the limited educational openings available to them but could not easily progress beyond a certain level. Of those who trained in the Catholic seminaries (which they could enter more easily than secular educational institutions) some went on to become priests, while others switched back to secular careers. Less than one-fifth of the students attending the Groupe Scolaire in Butare from 1945 to 1957 – and emerging as agronomists, doctors, vets and administrators – were Hutus. The School for the Sons of Chiefs originally opened by the Germans in Nyanza had a minimum height requirement which effectively reserved it for Tutsis.

In 1955, there were some 2,400 schools of various types and levels (the majority were primary) in Rwanda, with around 215,000 pupils. Of the 5,500-odd teachers, over 5,000 were Rwandan.

Categorisation

Size mattered. Like the Germans before them, the Belgians were intrigued by the sharply differing physical characteristics of their colony's inhabitants, and enthusiastically measured, recorded, compared and commented on the facial and bodily proportions of Rwanda's three indigenous groups. For the more timid of the Rwandans, this 'attack' with calipers, measuring tapes, scales and other paraphernalia proved a fearsome ordeal. So man dehumanises his brothers…

Most tellingly, in the early 1930s the Belgians embarked on a census to identify all indigenous inhabitants, on the basis of these physical characteristics, as either Hutu, Tutsi or Twa, and in 1935 issued them with identity cards on which these categories ('ethnic groups' or, in French, 'ethnies', although the accuracy of this term is debatable) were recorded. If, even after strenuous measuring, someone's ethnie was not immediately clear, having been blurred by intermarriage or a change of status, those who were reasonably wealthy and/or had more than ten cattle were generally recorded as Tutsis. Identity cards – and the habit of classification they engendered – were still in use at the time of the genocide in 1994, providing an extra pointer (if one were needed) as to who should or should not die.

In 1945 the United Nations Organisation was created, with its charter promising the colonised peoples of the world justice, protection and freedom. Formerly a League of Nations mandate, Ruanda-Urundi now became a UN Trust Territory and Belgium was responsible to the UN's trusteeship council, which was to preside over all colonies' transition to independence. In 1948 a UN mission visited Ruanda-Urundi, and its report was critical of the administration, particularly regarding the inferior status of the Hutus and Twa by comparison with the Tutsis. All too often, compulsory labour was harshly enforced, and the educational system remained heavily biased in favour of Tutsis, although many priests and missions were starting to veer more towards the Hutus.

At the same time, the observers were surprised by the completeness and intricacy of the social and political hierarchy which, if used properly, would offer a sound framework for democratic development. All the necessary command structures were in place, but badly oriented.

Subsequent visits gave rise to similarly critical reports. The Belgians introduced elections at local and administrative levels – which Tutsis won, except in the far north where resentment still smouldered after the 1912 defeat. Throughout Africa, colonies were becoming restless and the scent of independence was in the air, but in Ruanda-Urundi far too little preparation had yet been made, in terms both of political awareness and practical training. Nothing was ready.

The run-up to independence
From about 1950, as the numbers of educated Hutus increased, the Hutu voice grew stronger. Hutu leaders such as Grégoire Kayibanda began to demand recognition for the majority. In 1954 the system of *ubuhake* was officially abolished, although in reality it lingered for a few more years. In 1957 the Superior Council of Rwanda (which had a huge Tutsi majority) called for independence preparations to be speeded up.

In 1956, Mwami Rudahigwa had called for total independence and an end to Belgian occupation. Just before another UN visit in 1957, a *Hutu Manifesto* drawn up by a group of Hutu intellectuals was presented to the Vice Governor-General, Jean-Paul Harroy. It challenged the whole structure of Rwanda's administration, called for political power to be placed in the hands of the Hutu majority, pointed out injustices and inequalities, and proposed solutions. Little official action was taken.

The Catholic Church, now pro-Hutu, encouraged Grégoire Kayibanda and his associates to form political parties: APROSOMA (*Association pour la Promotion Sociale des Masses*) was openly sectarian, championing Hutu interests strongly, while RADER (*Rassemblement Démocratique Rwandais*) was more moderate. Whereas Tutsis, comfortably in a position of power, were calling for immediate independence without any changes to the system, Hutus wanted change first (to a more democratic system, recognising the fact that they were the majority) and *then* independence. For whatever reasons and after whatever deliberations, Belgium, having supported the powerful Tutsi minority throughout colonisation, now switched its allegience to the Hutu majority, ostensibly in the name of fairness and democracy.

The wind of independence was blowing strongly in colonial Africa. More political parties sprang up. UNAR (*Union Nationale Rwandaise*) was formed by the proponents of immediate independence under the Rwandan monarchy, while PARMEHUTU (*Parti du Mouvement de l'Emancipation Hutu*) was established under the guidance of the Catholic Church by those favouring delayed independence. MSM (*Mouvement Social Muhutu*) was created by Grégoire Kayibanda to support Hutu interests, while UNAR (*Union Nationale Rwandaise*) was a pro-monarchy and anti-Belgian party.

In July 1959 the Mwami Rudahigwa died in hospital, in circumstances that may or may not have been suspicious. Rumours of Belgian involvement were rife and tension grew. He was succeeded by one of his brothers. There were arrests and some sporadic small-scale violence – which erupted on a larger scale on November 1, when a Hutu sub-chief belonging to the PARMEHUTU party was attacked and beaten in Gitarama by young members of UNAR. Within 24 hours, highly organised Hutu gangs were out on the streets of towns and villages throughout the country, burning, looting and killing. Then Tutsis began to retaliate. Within about a fortnight things were calm again – around 300 had died, and 1,231 (919 Tutsis and 312 Hutus) were arrested by the Belgian authorities. The country was placed under military rule headed by the Belgian Colonel Guy Logiest, who quickly began replacing Tutsi chiefs with Hutus. He was strongly pro-Hutu, claiming to be righting the injustices of colonisation, and played a virtually unconcealed part in anti-Tutsi attacks.

It is worth remembering that this was the first organised violence between the two groups, and it happened little more than 40 years ago. Those who speak of a long-drawn-out feud originating before colonisation are mistaken. But the revolution had begun, Tutsis started to flee the country in large numbers, and outbursts of violence continued.

The PARMEHUTU party won hastily manipulated elections in 1960. Belgium, the reins of power slipping rapidly from its grasp, organised a referendum on the monarchy under the auspices of the United Nations. In January 1961, Rwanda's elected local administrators were called to a public meeting in Gitarama, Grégoire Kayibanda's birthplace. They and a massed crowd of some 25,000 declared Rwanda a republic – and the United Nations had little option but to accept this ultimatum. However, the 1960 elections were not recognised by the UN so more were held in September 1961, under UN supervision. Again they were won by PARMEHUTU, with Grégoire Kayibanda at its head. Later that year, some 150 Tutsis were killed in the Butare area, 5,000 homes were burned and 22,000 people were displaced. In July 1962 Rwanda's independence was finally confirmed with Kayibanda as its new president, heading a republican government. The university town of Astrida, so named after Queen Astrid of Belgium, reverted to its local name Butare. Violence against Tutsis continued; by now about 135,000 had fled as refugees to neighbouring countries and the number was growing. Among those who left in 1960 was a three-year-old child named Paul Kagame, of whom much more was to be heard later.

It is true that Belgium emerged from the fiasco with little credit. But it is equally true that, even without colonisation, some kind of revolution would inevitably have occurred sooner or later, for the tightly stratified hierarchy of the 19th century could not have held firm indefinitely against the pressures, promises and potentials of the modern world.

1962–1994

The situation became yet more tangled and yet more sensitive. Since this is a guidebook rather than a historical treatise, readers who want a fuller picture than is given below will find several good sources in *Appendix 3*, page 220. John Reader's *Africa* (Penguin, 1998) is particularly recommended, as is Gérard Prunier's *The Rwanda Crisis – History of a Genocide* (Hurst, 1998). They (among others) have been used as sources in this chapter.

Once in power, the government sought to reinforce its supremacy. 'Quotas' were introduced, giving the Tutsis (who were a minority of about 9% of the population) a right to only 9% of school places, 9% of jobs in the workforce and so on. Small groups of Tutsi exiles in neighbouring countries made sporadic commando-style raids into Rwanda, leading to severe reprisals. In late 1963, up to 10,000 Tutsis were killed. The pattern of violence continued.

In 1964 the Fabian Society (London) published a report entitled *Massacre in Rwanda*, commenting on events since 1959. Also – chillingly, in view of what happened 30 years later – a report entitled *Attempted Genocide in Rwanda* appeared in the March 1964 issue of *The World Today* (vol 20, no 3).

In 1965 Kayibanda was re-elected president and Juvenal Habyarimana was appointed Minister of Defence. In 1969 Kayibanda was again re-elected and PARMEHUTU was renamed the MDR (*Mouvement Démocratique Républicain*). But Kayibanda's regime was becoming increasingly dictatorial and corrupt. The 'quotas' and other 'cleansing' measures began to be enforced so rigidly that even Hutus became uneasy. In 1973, ostensibly to quell violence following a purge of Tutsis from virtually all educational establishments, Major General Juvenal Habyarimana toppled Grégoire Kayibanda in a military coup.

In 1975, a single party, the MRND (*Mouvement Révolutionnaire et National pour le Développement*), was formed. For a while, there were signs of improvement, although this tends to be forgotten in the light of subsequent events. Despite initial optimism and a period of relative stability, however, the regime eventually proved little better than its predecessor. Some educational reforms were undertaken, with the object of 'Rwandanisation' – revaluing Kinyarwanda and Rwandan culture. Habyarimana was reconfirmed as president in 1978, 1983 and 1988 – unsurprisingly, since he was the only candidate. The Hutu/Tutsi conflict was to some extent replaced by conflict between Hutus from the south and those from the north (Habyarimana was a northerner, so was accused of favouring 'his own'). Meanwhile, in the international sphere, rising oil prices and falling commodity prices were bringing the country's economy close to collapse and, among all but the privileged elite, dissatisfaction grew.

In 1979 a group of Rwandan exiles in Uganda established the RRWF (Rwandan Refugee Welfare Foundation) which in 1980 became RANU (Rwandan Alliance for National Unity), whose name explains its aim. In 1981, in Uganda, one Yoweri Museveni, later to become Uganda's president, started a guerrilla war against the oppressive regime of Dr Milton Obote – among his men were two Rwandan refugees, Paul Kagame and Fred Rwigima. Obote was hostile to the Rwandan refugees in Uganda and political youth groups were encouraged to attack them and their property. As a result of such attacks in 1982–83, there was massive displacement of the refugees in southern Uganda and large numbers tried (or were forced) to return to Rwanda. The Rwandan government quickly closed its borders with Uganda and confined those who had already entered to a small and inhospitable area in the north, where many of the young and the old died of hunger and disease.

In 1986, in Uganda, Yoweri Museveni's National Resistance Army (which contained a number of Rwandan refugees) overthrew Obote, and Museveni assumed power. In 1987 RANU was renamed the RPF (Rwandan Patriotic Front), and was supported not only by exiled Tutsis but also by a few prominent Hutus opposed to Habyarimana's regime.

In 1987/8, a military coup in Burundi and consequent ethnic tensions caused a wave of Burundian refugees to flood into Rwanda. In 1989 the price of coffee, Rwanda's main export, collapsed, causing severe economic problems. Censorship rules were flouted, new politically oriented publications emerged and reports of corruption and mismanagement appeared openly. In July 1990, under pressure from Western aid donors, Habyarimana conceded the principle of multi-party democracy and agreed to allow free debate on the country's future. In practice, little changed.

Then, on October 1 1990, the RPF (led by Major General Fred Rwigyema), invaded the northeast of Rwanda from Uganda, with the stated objective of ending the political stalemate once and for all and restoring democracy. French, German and Zairean troops were called in to support the Rwandan national army and the incursion was soon suppressed; but the government now took the RPF threat seriously. Habyarimana enlarged the Rwandan army from around 5,000 in 1990 to about 24,000 in 1991 and 35,000 in 1993. Various overseas countries (France, South Africa, the US) provided arms. Additionally, the 1990 RPF invasion was followed by severe reprisals: thousands of Tutsi and southern Hutu were arrested and held in prison for some months. Several were tried and sentenced to death but the sentences were not carried out, although, as one of those arrested later wrote, 'many died of the hunger and the beatings'. Sporadic unrest continued throughout the country.

Political solutions were sought, both nationally and internationally, with several Western countries now involved. In November 1990 Habyarimana agreed to the introduction of multi-partyism and the abolition of 'ethnic' identity cards, but nothing was implemented. The Rwandan army began to train and arm civilian militias known as *interahamwe* ('those who stand together'). It was later estimated that up to 2,000 Rwandans (Tutsis or anti-government Hutus) were killed by their government between October 1990 and December 1992.

The RPF – now led by Major Paul Kagame, since the charismatic Rwigema had died in the October 1990 invasion – continued its guerrilla raids, striking at targets countrywide. By the end of 1992 it had expanded to a force of almost 12,000 and was growing rapidly. Its stated aim was always to bring democracy to Rwanda rather than to claim supremacy. Meanwhile, French troops were supporting the government forces. In the face of increasing violence, international pressure was applied more strongly and the Arusha Agreement (so named because it was drawn up in Arusha, Tanzania) committed Habyarimana to a number of reforms, including the establishment of the rule of law, political power-sharing, the repatriation and resettlement of refugees, and the integration of the armed forces to include the RPF. A 70-member Transitional National Assembly was to be established. The Agreement was signed in August 1993 and should have been implemented within 37 days, overseen by a United Nations force. But the process, unpalatable to both Tutsi and Hutu hardliners, stalled. Hostilities deepened. Radio stations poured forth inflammatory propaganda. Rwanda's *Radio-Télévision Libre des Mille Collines*, in particular, insistently and viciously identified Tutsis as 'the enemy', in dehumanising and vilifying terms. Scattered outbursts of violence rumbled on.

On October 21, the Hutu President of neighbouring Burundi, Melchior Ndadaye, elected only a few months previously, was killed in a military coup, fuelling ethnic tensions in Rwanda. The UN began sending UNAMIR (UN Assistance Mission for Rwanda) forces to the country. Politics were deadlocked. A sense of impending danger grew and, by March 1994, vulnerable (or well-informed) citizens were starting to evacuate their families from Kigali.

On April 6 1994, a plane carrying Rwanda's President Habyarimana and Burundi's new President Cyprien Ntaryamira was shot down by rocket fire near Kigali airport. Both men died. The source of the attack has never been confirmed. Within hours, the killing began.

The genocide

It had been well planned, over a long period. Road-blocks were quickly erected and the army and *interahamwe* went into action, on a rampage of death, torture, looting and destruction. Tutsis and moderate Hutus were targeted. Weapons of every sort were used, from slick, military arms to rustic machetes. Orders were passed briskly downward from *préfecture* to *commune* to *secteur* to *cellule* – and the gist of every order was: 'These are the enemy. Kill.'

A painfully detailed account, which includes many eyewitness testimonies and brings home the full horror of the slaughter, is given in the 1,200 pages of

Rwanda – Death, Despair and Defiance (African Rights, London, 1995). In *A People Betrayed*, L R Melvern analyses the political and international background (Zed Books, London & New York, 2000), as does Gérard Prunier (*The Rwanda Crisis*, see *Appendix 3*). A condensed overview of events is given below.

In three months, up to a million people were killed, violently and cruelly. Barely a family was untouched. The international media suddenly found Rwanda newsworthy. Chilling images filled our TV screens and the scale of the massacre was too great for many of us to grasp. Amid the immensity came tiny tales of heroism: villagers who flatly disobeyed the order to kill; Hutus who hid their Tutsi neighbours, at great (often fatal) risk to their own lives, or who, while feigning to round them up for the killers, furtively led some to safety. But these glimpses of humanity were engulfed and lost in the great, surging tide of slaughter that spread across the country.

On April 8, just two days after the plane crash, the Rwandan Patriotic Front (RPF) launched a major offensive to end the genocide. As they advanced, they rescued and liberated Tutsis still hiding in terror from the killers. Meanwhile, however, a new Hutu government, based on the MRND and supporting parties, was formed in Kigali and later shifted to Gitarama.

The United Nations' UNAMIR force was around 2,500 strong at the time. They watched helplessly, technically unable to intervene as this would breach their 'monitoring' mandate. After the murder of ten Belgian soldiers the force was cut to 250. On April 30 the UN Security Council spent eight hours discussing the Rwandan crisis – without ever using the word 'genocide'. Had this term been used, they would have been legally obliged to 'prevent and punish' the perpetrators. Meanwhile tens of thousands of refugees were fleeing the country. In May the UN agreed to send 6,800 troops and police to Rwanda to defend civilians, but implementation was delayed by arguments over who would cover costs and provide equipment. The RPF army had taken control of Kigali airport and Kanombe barracks and was gaining ground elsewhere. In June, France announced that it would deploy 2,500 peacekeeping troops to Rwanda (*Opération Turquoise*) until the UN force arrived. These created a controversial 'safe zone' in the southwest.

On July 4 the RPF captured Kigali and set up an interim government. The remnants of the Hutu government fled to Zaire, followed by a further tide of refugees. The RPF continued its advance westward and northward. Many thousands of refugees streamed into the French 'safe zone' and still more headed towards Zaire, cramming into makeshift camps on the inhospitable terrain around Goma. The humanitarian crisis was acute, later to be exacerbated by disease and a cholera outbreak which claimed tens of thousands of lives.

On July 18 1994, the RPF announced that the war had been won, declared a cease-fire, established a broad-based Government of National Unity and named Pasteur Bizimungu as president. Faustin Twagiramungu was appointed prime minister. The following day, the new president and prime minister were sworn in, and RPF commander Major General Paul Kagame was appointed defence minister and vice president. By the end of July, the UN

Security Council had reached a final agreement about sending an international force to Rwanda. By the end of August *Opération Turquoise* was terminated and UN forces had replaced the French. Internationally, it had now been accepted that a 'genocide' had indeed taken place – and it was over. At sites of some of the worst massacres around the country, memorials now commemorate the dead and remind the world that such an atrocity must never, never be allowed to occur again.

The aftermath

The 70-member Transitional National Assembly provided for in the Arusha Agreement of 1993 finally became operational in December 1994. In November 1994, the UN Security Commission set up the International Criminal Tribunal for Rwanda (ICTR), whose brief is to prosecute those who were guilty, between January 1 and December 31 1994, of genocide and other violations of international humanitarian law; by the end of 1996 suspects were being brought to trial.

Sporadic bursts of violence were to continue for a further three years or so, with killings on both sides, as tensions in and around refugee settlements persisted and hard-line Hutus who had fled across the border mounted guerrilla raids. But the RPF army and the new government remained in control. UN forces left the country in March 1996. Refugees returned home, in massive numbers. Problems of insecurity posed by former Rwanda government forces and *interahamwe* troops caused Rwanda to become militarily involved with the Democratic Republic of the Congo (DRC).

In 1999, local elections were held at sector and cellule level, and the Lusaka Agreement, to end the war in the DRC, was signed.

In March 2000, President Pasteur Bizimungu resigned and in April Major General Paul Kagame was sworn in as the fifth president of Rwanda, exactly four decades after his flight as a three-year-old refugee.

In May 2000, Britain's Secretary of State for International Development, Clare Short, commented during an official visit to Rwanda:

> There has been important progress in Rwanda since I last
> visited....The challenges remain enormous. The levels of poverty are
> terrible, there has got to be very great progress on the economy and
> reconciliation needs to go forward and continue. There needs to be
> progress on the trials of those accused of genocide and on the
> implementation of Gacaca [see box on pages 22–3]. Obviously the
> establishment of the Constitutional Commission and the settlement
> of the new Constitution are absolutely essential for the future of the
> country. So there is a lot to do. But we in the UK are expecting
> continuing progress, our strong partnership with the government of
> Rwanda continues and we expect that our support for the
> government of Rwanda is likely to increase.

In July 2000, the Organisation of African Unity (OAU) recommended that the international community should make payments to the government and

SIX YEARS OF PROGRESS

The following report is extracted from the official Rwanda website,
www.rwanda1.com.

Six years ago, the Government of Rwanda began the difficult task of rebuilding the country. In 1994, at the end of the war, no schools, hospitals, factories or government departments were functioning. Public utilities such as telephones, electricity and water were also not functioning. There was total displacement of the population, both internally and externally. There was no Civil Service and the government's administrative capacity had collapsed. Civil servants had either been killed in the genocide or had fled the country. Genocide survivors were still scattered all over the country, and traumatised. The genocide had further polarised Rwandan society.

The first challenge that the government faced was to stabilise the country and create conditions that would enable the whole population to enjoy peace and security.

About three-and-a-half million Rwandan refugees have been repatriated and resettled. The process of reintegrating refugees and members of the former government army (Forces Armées Rwandaises, otherwise known as FAR) has further promoted reconciliation. About 15,000 elements of the ex-FAR have been integrated into the Rwandan national army at various command levels, as well as within the rank and file.In promoting reconciliation, a Unity and Reconciliation Commission (see box on page 78) has been established, to consolidate the government policy of redressing the legacy of divisive politics that has been prominent in Rwanda for many decades. The Commission continues to raise public awareness through civic education initiatives (*ingando*). Furthermore, there has been intensive dialogue on history among various sectors of the Rwandan population. This dialogue, which took place under the leadership of the President of Rwanda, touched on unity and reconciliation, justice, democratisation, security, and the economy.

The Government of National Unity has made progress in building the justice system from scratch. Following the enactment of the Genocide Law, trials have taken place to bring the genocide suspects to justice. Currently, there are over 120,000 suspects in overcrowded prisons. About 12 billion Rwandan francs are spent annually on looking after these prisoners. To deal with this caseload expeditiously, the government has initiated a participatory form of justice, Gacaca (see box on pages 22–3), which draws

people of Rwanda in reparation for the genocide. The seven-man international panel appointed by the OAU to investigate the genocide stated: 'In the name of both justice and accountability, reparations are owed to Rwanda by actors in the international community for their roles before, during and after the genocide.' One member of the panel, former Canadian Ambassador to the on the experience of traditional, pre-colonial Rwandan society. This will be operational in early 2001.

Through a Genocide Survivors' fund, the government provides support in education, shelter, health and income-generating activities for the most vulnerable amongst the survivors. About 5% of government revenue collected each year (approximately 4 billion Rwandan francs) is allocated to this fund. Donations from the public or private sector, as well as from the international community, are welcome.

A Human Rights Commission has been established to promote the rule of law and respect for the fundamental rights of the citizen.

On the political front, the Government of National Unity has made progress in maintaining the inclusiveness of the broad-based government as an indispensable component of the new political dispensation. A policy of decentralisation has been initiated, to involve people in grass-roots communities in decision-making. This will enhance their participation in activities to transform their poor conditions. Local elections have already taken place at cellule and sector levels. Elections at commune and prefecture levels will have taken place by the end of the year 2000.

A Legal and Constitutional Commission has been established, to consult all Rwandan citizens on what kind of constitution Rwanda should have at the end of the transition period.

Transparency and accountability within government institutions have been identified and promoted as critical ingredients necessary for effective and efficient government. To that effect, a number of institutions have been established, namely the National Examinations Board, the National Tender Board, the Auditor General's Office and the Rwanda Revenue Authority. In addition, the government will require public officials to declare their assets in accordance with a National Leadership Code of Conduct.

Economic recovery has been consistent since 1994 when the real GDP declined by 50% and inflation stood at 65% (inflation in 1998 was quoted at 4.1%).

Security has been restored to all 12 administrative prefectures of Rwanda. Undoubtedly, this is a peace dividend from Rwanda's involvement in the DRC.

Rwanda has been welcomed to join the East African Cooperation (EAC), in pursuit of greater co-operation and economic integration. Rwanda is also an active member of the Common Market for East and Southern Africa (COMESA).

United Nations Mr Stephen Lewis, commented, after undertaking the study: 'You never quite see the world in the same way again. ...It is remarkable how well [Rwanda] is doing despite a genocide just six years ago. It deserves massive assistance from the rest of the world, particularly from those countries who betrayed it when it needed the world most.'

GACACA – A RETURN TO TRADITIONAL JUSTICE

During the 1994 genocide in Rwanda, up to a million people died in only a hundred days. Since the government of National Unity assumed power in July 1994, thousands of the perpetrators – or suspected perpetrators – have been arrested and face trial, while others have already been convicted. The sheer weight of numbers awaiting trial – estimated at over 120,000 – means that prisons are overflowing, in many cases with people who have already waited six years for their cases to be heard, and even the most streamlined and well-equipped judicial system would take years to work through the backlog. Rwanda's criminal justice system is handicapped by poor infrastructures and the death of so many professionals during the genocide. Yet justice is a vital component of the reconciliation that the country seeks.

Therefore, the government has decided to return – to some extent – to a traditional form of justice, used in Rwanda in pre-colonial times, which involves the community. **Gacaca** (pronounced *Gachacha*, with a hard G) is based on the administrative structures already in place, the cellules, sectors, communes and prefectures, and on the categorisation of genocide suspects according to the crimes of which they are accused.

Categorisation

Category One suspects are those 'whose criminal acts place them among the planners, organisers, instigators, supervisors and leaders of the crime of genocide or of a crime against humanity; persons who acted in positions of authority at national, prefecture, commune, sector or cellule level, or in a political party, the army, religious organisations or in a militia and who perpetrated or fostered such crimes; notorious murderers who by virtue of the zeal or excessive malice with which they committed atrocities, distinguished themselves in their areas of residence or where they passed; and persons who committed acts of sexual torture or violence.' In other words this is the top category, and these suspects cannot be judged by the Gacaca courts; they fall within the official judicial system.

Category Two suspects are 'persons whose criminal acts or whose acts of criminal participation place them among the perpetrators, conspirators

Later the same year, the Rwandan government launched a census to determine the true and total number of genocide victims – irrespective of whether they were Hutus, Tutsis, Twa or foreigners. The results will be useful to the Gacaca trials and should make compensation claims easier to process.

Nothing is simple. As one genocide survivor wrote:

> I can only be reconciled with the people who killed my family if they come and ask me for forgiveness and they tell me the whole truth about how and where they killed them. It is very difficult to accept

or accomplices of intentional homicide or serious assault against the person causing death'. They can be tried by Gacaca courts at commune level.

Category Three suspects are those 'whose criminal acts or whose acts of criminal participation make them guilty of other serious assaults against the person'. These can be tried by Gacaca courts at sector level.

Category Four suspects are 'persons who committed offences against property' – and they can be tried by Gacaca courts at cellule level.

GACACA hierarchy

At **cellule** level (the lowest), the General Assembly of the Gacaca Court consists of all the inhabitants of the cellule over 18 years of age. The members of the General Assembly elect a Court Council. The main responsibilities of the General Assembly at this level are to compile a list of those who died in the cellule as a result of the 1994 genocide, as well as those who were raped and those who participated in those crimes; and to compile a list of those who moved away from their usual residential areas during the genocide. This court has the power to judge category four suspects.

At **sector, commune** and **prefecture** levels, the general assemblies consist of members representing the bodies lower in the hierarchy. Again, each general assembly elects a Court Council. Courts at sector level can try category three suspects; courts at commune level can try category two suspects; and courts at prefecture level (the highest) are competent to hear and pass judgement on appeals from the lower courts.

Monitoring and supervision

Gacaca courts and the Office of Public Prosecutions will maintain a close working relationship. The operation of Gacaca courts throughout the country will be monitored and supervised by a co-ordination department set up within the High Court. They will also come under scrutiny from human-rights organisations internationally, to ensure there are no abuses. A careful programme of 'sensitisation' is being undertaken beforehand, to prepare the public for the courts and for their own role in the procedure.

loss when you don't even know where the body is, or who committed the murder. In general, reconciliation would be possible only if justice prevails: those who carried out the genocide should be punished accordingly, and compensation given to the victims.

Orbit 78, VSO, London

Many of those now in the government and heading the public and private sectors had no previous experience of running a country or of top-level administration – and inevitably inexperience, no matter how good the intentions, can cause delays and mistakes. Also, the most able tend to become the victims of their own competence, as heavier responsibilities and workloads are heaped upon them.

As for the refugees, although indeed very large numbers have been successfully resettled, a survey carried out in July 2000 indicated that there were still 6,273 living in plastic tents, 62,123 in seriously damaged houses and 92,881 occupying houses illegally. (But the fact that the survey was carried out at all, and that its results were published openly, is also significant.)

Of course tensions still exist; of course the government has its critics, some of them vociferous; of course poverty persists; of course there are complaints of 'discrimination'; and of course many of Rwanda's inhabitants still struggle in conditions that are far from ideal. Human rights organisations point to some abuses, and there are problems of land allocation. Agriculture in some areas is lagging behind. The budget is seriously overstretched and the neediest are not always benefiting enough from the reforms. But can't the same be said of many other countries too?

Considering the size and resources of Rwanda, considering what happened there in 1994 and considering the inherent problems faced by almost *all* countries in sub-Saharan Africa, even without the aftermath of a genocide, the achievements of the past six years have been amazing, and based on a huge amount of energy, courage, goodwill and sheer hard work. Rwanda today is a vibrant and forward-looking country, well able to cope with the demands and technologies of the 21st century.

It deserves respect.

Planning and Preparation

WHEN TO VISIT

Rwanda can be visited at any time of year. The long dry season, June to September, is the best time for tracking gorillas and hiking in Nyungwe, since the ground should be dry underfoot and the odds of being drenched are minimal. The dry season is also the best time for travelling on dirt roads, and when the risk of malaria should be lowest. You might read or hear about a short dry season, which runs from December to early March. Rainfall figures indicate that this dry season cannot be relied upon: on average, Kigali receives more rain in January or February than in October or November. The wettest months are March to May, ideally to be avoided, although it is perfectly feasible to travel during this period.

One of the local tour operators explains:

> There are two annual rainy seasons: the big rains which last from mid-February to the beginning of June, and the small rains from mid-September to mid-December. Rainfall, especially over the mountains, is heavy during these two periods – particularly from March to May. As for the two dry seasons, the major one lasts from June to September and the shorter from December to February. However, the climate is not uniform throughout the country: it is generally dryer in the east than in the west and north. On occasion, the volcanoes of the north may be capped by snow, and evenings in Kigali can call for a sweater. Nevertheless, every season is good for swimming and tanning on the banks of Lake Kivu.

An advantage of travelling during the rainy season is that the scenery is greener, and the sky less hazy (at least when it isn't overcast), a factor that will be of particular significance to photographers. The wet season is also the best time to track chimps in Nyungwe, while the months of November to March will hold the greatest appeal for birders, as resident birds are supplemented by flocks of Palaearctic migrants.

GETTING THERE AND AWAY
By air

Rwanda's Alliance Express flies directly to Kigali from Entebbe (Uganda), Johannesburg (South Africa), Nairobi (Kenya) and Bujumbura (Burundi). It also runs connecting flights from London via Entebbe in partnership with British Airways.

Other direct flights to Kigali are run by Sabena Airlines from Brussels, Kenya Airways from Nairobi, Ethiopian Airlines from Addis Ababa, Air Tanzania from Dar es Salaam, and Air Burundi from Bujumbura.

Travellers from the Americas, Australasia and the rest of Europe will do best to aim for the connections via London, Brussels, Johannesburg, Nairobi and Entebbe.

The international airport lies 10km from central Kigali, and taxis are available to the city centre. An airport tax of US$40 is levied, theoretically now collected on the ticket at the time of issue so you don't need to hand over cash – but check this in case procedures change.

On no account neglect to **confirm your return flight at least three days in advance**, via an airline office or travel agent in Kigali. Unless you do this, there is – at least with some airlines – a serious risk of being 'bumped' at the last minute.

Air tickets

A number of travel companies are good sources of **cut-price tickets**, as well as offering various other services. The list below is not exhaustive but should give you a start.

UK

Bridge the World 47 Chalk Farm Rd, London NW1 8AN; tel: 020 7911 0900; email: sales@bridge-the-world.co.uk; web: www.b-t-w.co.uk

Flight Centre 64 Goodge St, London W1P 1FP; tel: (booking) 08705 666677; tel: (to find your nearest centre) 08708 999888; web: www.flightcentre.com. Flight Centre has several offices in London, also Edinburgh, Bristol etc. It offers cut-price airfares, visa and insurance services etc.

STA Travel 6 Wrights Lane, London W8 6TA; tel: 020 7361 6262; email: enquiries@statravel.co.uk; web (very comprehensive): www.statravel.co.uk. STA has branches around Britain and specialises in youth and student travel. The telesales number is 08701 600599.

Trailfinders 194 Kensington High St, London W8 7RG; tel: 020 7938 3939; web (very comprehensive): www.trailfinders.com

WEXAS 45–49 Brompton Rd, Knightsbridge, London SW3 1DE; tel: 020 7589 3315; web: www.wexas.com. There is an annual subscription to WEXAS (for current details email: mship@wexas.com or phone the number above) but it gives you access to a whole range of services including an excellent quarterly travel magazine.

Ireland

Trailfinders 4/5 Dawson St, Dublin 2; tel: 01 677 7888; web: www.trailfinders.com

Australia

Flight Centre Tel (booking): 1300 362 665; tel (to find your nearest office): 131600; web: www.flightcentre.com. See under UK, above.

Trailfinders 8 Spring St, Sydney 2000; tel: (02) 9247 7666; web: www.trailfinders.com. Also offices in Brisbane, Cairns, Melbourne and Perth.

Canada
Flight Centre Tel: 1888-WORLD-31; web: www.flightcentre.com. See under UK, above.

New Zealand
Flight Centre Southern Cross Building, High Street, Auckland; tel: 3005410; fax: 3005415; web: www.flightcentre.com. Offices throughout the country. See under UK, above.

USA
Council Travel Specialists in student and budget travel, with offices throughout the country; check web: www.counciltravel.com

Flight Centre Tel: 1877WORLD47; web: www.flightcentre.com. Two offices in LA. See under UK, above.

STA (see under UK, above) also has branches in a number of countries worldwide; check them out on website www.sta-travel.com.

Overland

Four countries border Rwanda: Tanzania to the east, Uganda to the north, the DRC to the west, and Burundi to the south. At the time of writing, the borders between Rwanda and the **DRC** are effectively a dead end, with the DRC embroiled in an ongoing civil war, though it is possible to cross into the DRC from Rwanda as a day trip from Gisenyi or Cyangugu on Lake Kivu.

Burundi, too, has been something of a travel dead-end of late, again due to a civil war which has not only posed a risk to travellers at times, but has also led the Tanzanian authorities to discontinue the leg of the Lake Tanganyika ferry between Kigoma (Tanzania) and Bujumbura (Burundi). Regular buses do link Kigali and Bujumbura, but at the time of writing one of these was recently attacked by rebels near Bujumbura, so there are temporary restrictions on this road. Check up on the current situation before travelling. The ferry on Lake Tanganyika (assuming it once again starts running the full length of the lake from Bujumbura to Mpulungu in Zambia) has long been the best way of crossing directly from the Great Lakes countries (Uganda, Rwanda and Burundi) to southern Africa.

Crossing to and from **Uganda** is a lot simpler. Direct buses and minibus-taxis connect Kampala and Kigali, taking 10–12 hours and costing around US$15. There are plenty of local minibus-taxis along the roughly 50km road between Kisoro in southwest Uganda and Ruhengeri in northwest Rwanda (an hour's trip, not allowing for changing vehicles and other delays at the Cyanika border post, which might add another hour to the journey). It is also easy to travel by minibus-taxi between Kabale, the largest town in southwest Uganda, and Kigali, though once again you might have to change vehicles at the border – this trip should take about five hours in total. After a trip to Rwanda in December 2000, Dorette Boshoff and David Hartley wrote: 'We both bought 15-day transit visas at the Kabale border – they cost US$35 for South African and British passports. We paid US$20 for vehicle insurance that was valid for the period of our stay.

Our vehicle has a carnet, which seemed to be standard procedure for the guys at customs, so we paid no other fees for the vehicle except insurance.'

Crossing between Rwanda and **Tanzania** is something of a slog, due to the poor state of roads and lack of large towns in northwest Tanzania. The Rusumo border post lies about 160km from Kigali, roughly a four-hour trip by minibus-taxi, with the possibility of staying the night en route at the town of Kibungo, 60km from the border. The closest Tanzanian town to the border is Ngara, which is connected to Rusumo by occasional minibus-taxis taking about six hours, and has a few small guesthouses. From Ngara, daily buses to Mwanza on Lake Victoria take 12–18 hours depending on the condition of the road. Mwanza is a large port with a full range of accommodation and other facilities, including thrice-weekly rail links to Dar es Salaam on the coast and daily buses to Arusha in northeast Tanzania. A rail link between Rwanda and Tanzania is optimistically planned, but don't count on it being up and running in the near future.

Tour operators
UK
Reef & Rainforest Tours Ltd 1 The Plains, Totnes, Devon TQ9 5DR; tel: 01803 866965; fax: 01803 865916; email reefrain@btinternet.com; web: www.reefrainforest.co.uk. They currently run annual two-week tours (in 2001 and 2002 they're in August) covering all three of Rwanda's national parks, and other tourist attractions throughout the country. They plan to start tailor-made tours in 2001.
Discovery Initiatives Ltd 51 Castle St, Cirencester, Gloustershire GL7 1QD, England; tel: 01285 643333; fax: 01285 885888; email: enquiry@discoveryinitiatives.com; web: www.discoveryinitiatives.com. They run nine-day 'gorilla conservation in action' tours which offer gorilla tracking in Rwanda's Volcanoes Park and the Ugandan parks, as well as visits to local Rwandan communities and a day exploring Kigali.
Volcanoes Safaris Web: www.volcanoessafaris.com. *UK office:* PO Box 16345, London SW1X 0ZD; tel: 020 7235 7897; fax: 020 7235 1780; email: ukinfo@volcanoessafaris.com. *Uganda office:* 27 Lumumba Av, Nakasero Hill, PO Box 22818, Kampala; tel: 41 346464/5; fax: 41 341718; mobile: (0)75 741718; email: sales@volcanoessafaris.com. *Rwanda office:* Hotel des Mille Collines, Kigali; tel: 76530; fax: 76541; mobile: 0853 6908. *USA & Canada:* PO Box 58, Whitby, Ontario L1N5R7, Canada; tel: toll free 1-888-AFRICAN 237-4226; fax: 1-905-666-9231; email: alliance@baxter.net. This well-established operator runs regular safaris from Kigali for gorilla tracking in the Volcanoes National Park as well as parks in Uganda. They also arrange tailor-made Rwanda tours, starting from either Kigali or Kampala.

South Africa
Wild Frontiers PO Box 844, Halfway House 1685, South Africa; tel: 011 702 2035; fax: 011 468 1655; email: wildfront@icon.co.za; web: www.wildfrontiers.com. This is the only South African company with significant experience of Rwanda. This highly regarded operator has its own ground operation in Uganda, and a decade of hands-on experience in East Africa generally, making it a good first contact for setting up trips to Rwanda from anywhere in the world.

Uganda
See Volcanoes Safaris and Wild Frontiers, above.

USA/Canada
See Volcanoes Safaris and Wild Frontiers, above.

RED TAPE

Check well in advance that you have a valid **passport**, and that it won't expire within six months of the date you intend to leave Rwanda. Should your passport be lost or stolen, it will generally be easier to get a replacement if you travel with a photocopy of the important pages.

Visas are required by all visitors except nationals of the USA, Tanzania, Uganda, Burundi and the Democratic Republic of Congo, and cost US$35 upwards depending on the place of issue. For air travellers, visas may by now be issued at Kigali Airport on arrival, but check this beforehand. If you're coming overland, you'll probably do best to buy your visa in a neighbouring country: there are embassies or high commissions in Bujumbura (Burundi), Kampala (Uganda) and Dar es Salaam (Tanzania), as well as in Nairobi (Kenya). Further afield, there are embassies or high commissions in Brussels, Bonn, Paris, London, Ottawa, Washington DC, Cairo etc. See list below. Nationals of countries without an embassy can obtain a visa on arrival by prior arrangement with their hosts, who can arrange a *facilité d'entrée.*

If there is any possibility that you'll want to drive or hire a vehicle while you're in the country, do organise an **international driving licence** (any AA office in a country in which you're licensed to drive will do this for a nominal fee), which you may be asked to produce together with your original licence. You may sometimes be asked at borders for an **international health certificate** showing you've had a yellow fever shot.

For **security** reasons, it's advisable to detail all your important information on one sheet of paper, photocopy it, and distribute a few copies in your luggage, your money-belt, and amongst relatives or friends at home: the sort of things you want to include on this are travellers' cheque numbers and refund information, travel insurance policy details and 24-hour emergency contact number, passport number, details of relatives or friends to be contacted in an emergency, bank and credit card details, camera and lens serial numbers etc. We also email this information to ourselves immediately before we leave, so it is stored in our in-tray throughout our travels.

Rwandan embassies and consulates abroad

Belgium 1 Av des Fleurs, 1150 Brussels; tel: (0032) 02 763 07038; fax: 763 07053

Burundi 24 Av de la République Démocratique du Congo, BP 400 Bujumbura; tel: (257) 226865; fax: 223255; email: arbuja@cni.cbinf.com

Canada 121 Sherwood Drive, Ottawa, Ontario KIY 3V1; tel: (1-613) 722 7921; fax: 722 4052

China Hsieu Shaouei Bei Yie, Beijing; tel: (861) 065 321820; fax: 065 322006; email: ambarwda@public3.bta.net.cn

Ethiopia Africa Av, PO Box 5618 Addis Ababa; tel: (251) 1 61 0300; fax: 01 610411
Germany Beethovenallee 72, 53173 Bonn; tel: (049 228) 367038; fax: 351922; email:
ambrwabonn@aol.com
India B 112 Neet Bash, New Delhi 110016; tel: (972 3) 6913419; fax: 6568085
Kenya Kilimani, Kahahwe Rd, PO Box 30.619, Nairobi; tel: (00 254) 2575977; fax:
2575976
South Africa 35 Marais St, Brooklyn, Pretoria; tel: (027 12) 460709; fax: 460708;
email: rwasap@rwanda.co.za
Switzerland Rue de la Serviette 93, CH-1202 Geneva; tel: (41 22) 9191000; fax:
9191001
Tanzania 32 Ali Hassan Mwinyi Rd, PO Box 2918 Dar es Salaam; tel: (255 51)
115889; fax: 115888
Uganda 2 Nakaima Rd, PO Box 2468 Kampala; tel: (256 41) 343662; fax: 244405;
email: rwanda@swiftuganda.com
United Kingdom 58–59 Trafalgar Square, London WC2N 5DX; tel: (44 020) 7930
2570; fax: 7930 2572; email: ambarwanda@compuserve.com
United States 124 East 39th St, New York, NY 10016; tel: (1 212) 679 9010; fax: 679
9133. Also 1724 New Hampshire Av NW, Washington DC 20009; tel: (1 202) 232
2882; fax: 232 4544

For updates and additions, refer to website www.rwanda1.com/government.

PACKING

In 1907, when the Duke of Mecklenburg set off on an expedition through
Rwanda with a group of scientific researchers, he carried (or rather his team of
bearers carried) numerous cases of soap, candles, rope and cigars, as well as
such items as salt, wire, beads and woollen blankets to barter with the natives.
You could probably cut down on this a little.

In fact there are two simple rules to bear in mind when you decide what to
take with you to Rwanda, particularly for those using public transport. Rule
one is to bring with you *everything* that you could possibly need and that might
not be readily available when you need it. Rule two is to carry as little as
possible. Somewhat contradictory rules, you might think, and you'd be right –
so the key is finding the right balance, something that probably depends on
personal experience as much as anything. Worth stressing is that most genuine
necessities are surprisingly easy to get hold of in the main centres in Rwanda,
and that most of the ingenious gadgets you can buy in camping shops are
unlikely to amount to much more than deadweight on the road. If it came to
it, you could easily travel in Rwanda with little more than a change of clothes,
a few basic toiletries and a medical kit.

Carrying your luggage

Visitors who are unlikely to be carrying their luggage for any significant
distance will probably want to pack most of it in a conventional suitcase. Make
sure it is tough and durable, and that it seals well, so that its contents will
survive bumpy drives and boisterous baggage handlers at airports. A lock is a

good idea, not only for flights but for when you leave your case in a hotel room – in our experience, any theft from upmarket hotels in Africa is likely to be casual, and a locked suitcase is unlikely to be tampered with.

If you are likely to use public transport, then a backpack is the most practical way to carry your luggage. An internal frame is more flexible than an external one. Once again, ensure your pack is durable, that the seams and zips are properly sewn, and that it has several pockets. If you intend doing a lot of hiking, you definitely want a backpack designed for this purpose. On the other hand, if you'll be staying at places where it might be a good idea to shake off the sometimes negative image attached to backpackers, then there would be obvious advantages in using a suitcase that converts into a backpack.

Before I started travelling with piles of Ariadne's camera equipment, my preference was a robust 35cl daypack. The advantages of keeping luggage as light and compact as possible are manifold. For starters, you can rest it on your lap on bus trips, avoiding complications such as extra charges for luggage, arguments about where your bag should be stored, and the slight but real risk of theft or damage if your luggage ends up on the roof. A compact bag also makes for greater mobility, whether you're hiking or looking for a hotel in town. The sacrifice? Leave behind camping equipment and a sleeping bag. Do this, and it's quite possible to fit everything you truly need into a 35cl day pack, and possibly even a few luxuries – I refuse to travel without binoculars, a bird field guide and at least five novels, and was still able to keep the weight down to around 8kg. Frankly, it puzzles me what the many backpackers who wander about with an enormous pack and absolutely no camping equipment actually carry around with them! If your luggage won't squeeze into a daypack, a sensible compromise is to carry a large daypack in your rucksack. That way, you can carry a tent and other camping equipment when you need it, but at other times reduce your luggage to fit into a daypack and leave what you're not using in storage.

Travellers carrying a lot of valuable items should look for a pack that can be easily padlocked. A locked bag can, of course, be slashed open, but in Rwanda you are more likely to encounter casual theft of the sort to which a lock would be real deterrent.

However you travel, a small day pack will be useful for gorilla tracking and other walks, and to stow any breakable goods on your lap during long drives – anything like a walkman or camera will suffer heavily from vibrations on rutted roads.

Camping equipment

There are few opportunities for camping in Rwanda, and the financial advantages are limited since affordable accommodation is generally available. Balanced against that, for those without transport, the campsite at Nyungwe is a far more convenient base for walks than the resthouse, and a tent will be essential for hiking in off-the-beaten-track areas (camping is also the only option within Akagera National Park).

For backpackers who decide to carry camping equipment, the key is to look for the lightest available gear. It is now possible to buy a lightweight tent weighing little more than 2kg, but make sure that the one you choose is mosquito proof. Other essentials for camping include a sleeping bag and a roll-mat, which will serve as both insulation and padding. You might want to carry a stove and Camping Gaz cylinders (not readily available in Rwanda). A box of firelighter blocks will get a fire going in the most unpromising conditions. It would also be advisable to carry a pot, plate, cup and cutlery.

Clothes

Try to keep your clothes to a minimum, especially if you are travelling with everything on your back. Bear in mind that you can easily and cheaply replace worn items in markets. In my opinion, the minimum is one or possibly two pairs of trousers and/or skirts, one pair of shorts, three shirts or T-shirts, one light sweater or similar, one heavy sweater or similar, a waterproof jacket during the rainy season, enough socks and underwear to last five to seven days, one solid pair of shoes or boots for walking, and one pair of sandals, thongs or other light shoes.

When you select your clothes, remember that jeans are heavy to carry, hot to wear, and slow to dry – but excellent wear for gorilla tracking and other forest walks. In other situations, light cotton trousers are preferable. Skirts are best made of a light natural fabric such as cotton. T-shirts are lighter and less bulky than proper shirts, though the top pocket of a shirt (particularly if it buttons up) is a good place to carry spending money in markets and bus stations, since it's easier to keep an eye on than a trouser pocket. A couple of sweaters or sweatshirts will be necessary in places such as Nyungwe, which get chilly at night.

Socks and underwear *must* be made from natural fabrics. Bear in mind that re-using sweaty undergarments will encourage fungal infections such as athlete's foot, as well as prickly heat in the groin region. Socks and underpants are light and compact enough that it's worth bringing a week's supply. As for footwear, only if you're a serious off-road hiker should you consider genuine hiking boots, since they are very heavy whether on your feet or in your pack. A good pair of walking shoes, preferably made of leather with good ankle support, is a good compromise. For gorilla tracking, a pair of old gardening gloves can be handy when you're grabbing for handholds in thorny vegetation.

Another factor in selecting your travel wardrobe is local sensibilities. In Rwanda, which is predominantly Christian, this isn't the concern it is in several other parts of Africa, but travellers are nevertheless advised to dress relatively modestly. For women, the ideal garment is a knee-length skirt, though long trousers – while unconventional female wear in Rwanda – are most unlikely to give offence. For men, shorts are not unacceptable, but few local men wear them and it is considered more respectable to wear trousers. Walking around in a public place without a shirt is dodgy.

Many Africans think it is insulting for Westerners to wear scruffy or dirty clothes in their country, reasoning that we wouldn't dress like that at home. It is difficult to explain that at home you also wouldn't spend a morning slithering around the muddy Virungas in your last clean outfit! If you're travelling rough, you're bound to look a mess at times, but it's worth trying to look as spruce as possible.

Other useful items

Most backpackers, even those with no intention of camping, carry a **sleeping bag**. I've never seen the necessity for this, particularly in Rwanda. You might meet travellers who, when they stay in local lodgings, habitually place their own sleeping bag on top of the bedding provided. Nutters, in my opinion: I'd imagine that a sleeping bag placed on a flea-ridden bed would be unlikely to provide significant protection – it would be more likely to become flea-infested itself.

I wouldn't leave home without **binoculars**, which some might say makes *me* the nutter. Seriously, though, if you're interested in natural history, it's difficult to imagine anything that will give you such value-for-weight entertainment as a pair of light, compact binoculars, which these days needn't be much heavier or bulkier than a pack of cards. Binoculars are essential if you want to get a good look at birds (Africa boasts a remarkably colourful avifauna even if you've no desire to put a name to everything that flaps) or to watch distant mammals in game reserves. For most purposes, 7x21 compact binoculars will be fine, though some might prefer 7x35 traditional binoculars for their larger field of vision. Serious birdwatchers will find a 10x magnification more useful.

Some travellers like to carry their own **padlock**. This is useful if you have a pack that is lockable, and in remote parts of the country might be necessary for rooms where no lock is provided. If you are uneasy about security in a particular guesthouse, you may like to use your own lock instead of, or in addition to, the one provided. Although combination locks are reputedly easier to pick than conventional padlocks, I think you'd be safer with a combination lock in Rwanda, because potential thieves will have far more experience of breaking through locks with keys

Your **toilet bag** should at the very minimum include soap (secured in a plastic bag or soap holder unless you enjoy a soapy toothbrush!), shampoo, toothbrush and toothpaste. This sort of stuff is easy to replace as you go along, so there's no need to bring family-sized packs. Boys will probably want a **razor**. Girls should carry enough **tampons** and/or **sanitary pads** to see them through at least one heavy period, since these items may not always be immediately available. If you wear **contact lenses**, be aware that the various fluids are not readily available in Rwanda, and, since many people find the intense sun and dust irritate their eyes, you might consider reverting to glasses. Nobody should forget to bring a **towel**, or to keep handy a roll of **loo paper**, which although widely available at shops and kiosks cannot always be relied upon to be present where it's most urgently needed. A lot of washbasins in Rwanda are plugless, so one of those 'universal' rubber plugs that fit all sizes of plughole can be useful.

Other essentials include a **torch**, a **penknife** and a compact **alarm clock** for those early morning starts. If you're interested in what's happening in the world, you might also think about taking a **short-wave radio**. Some travellers carry **games** – most commonly a pack of cards, less often chess or draughts or travel Scrabble. A light plastic **orange-squeezing device** gives you fresh orange juice as an alternative to fizzy drinks and water.

You should carry a small **medical kit**, the contents of which are discussed in the chapter on health, as are **mosquito nets**. For those who wear **glasses**, it's worth bringing a spare pair, though in an emergency a new pair can be made up cheaply (around US$10) and quickly in most Rwandan towns, provided that you have your prescription available.

MONEY
Organising your finances
There are three ways of carrying money: hard currency cash, travellers' cheques, or a credit card. My advice is to bring all you will possibly need in the combination of cash and travellers' cheques, but if possible also carry a credit card for an emergency. I would strongly urge all but the most denominationally chauvinistic of backpackers to bring their cash and travellers' cheques in the form of US dollars, and to learn to think and budget in this currency.

From the point of view of security, it's advisable to bring the bulk of your money as travellers' cheques, which can be refunded if lost or stolen. It is best to use a widely recognised type such as American Express and Thomas Cook, and to keep your proof of purchase separate from the cheques, as well as noting which cheques you have used, in order to facilitate a swift refund should you require one. Buy your travellers' cheques in a healthy mix of denominations, since you may sometimes need to change a small sum only. On the other hand, you don't want an impossibly thick wad of cheques. For a trip to one country, I'd take five US$20 cheques and the remainder of my money in US$100 cheques. Whatever your bank at home might say, currency regulations and other complications make it nearly impossible to break large denomination travellers' cheques into smaller ones, so don't bring denominations larger than US$100.

You should also bring some hard currency cash, since you may meet situations where travellers' cheques won't be accepted. Whether you elect to bring all or most of your money in cash is a personal decision. Cash fetches a considerably better exchange rate than travellers' cheques, and it can be changed with far less fuss and outside of banking hours – none of which will be much consolation should it be stolen! Whatever you do, note that large denomination bills such as US$100 and US$50 fetch a better rate than smaller ones, but also that US$100 bills printed before 1992 may be refused on account of the number of forged old bills floating around East Africa.

Carry your hard currency and travellers' cheques, as well as your passport and other important documentation, in a money belt – one that can be hidden beneath your clothing rather than the sort of fashionable, externally worn codpiece which may serve as a beacon rather than protection. Your money belt should be made of cotton or another natural fabric, and everything inside the belt should be wrapped in plastic to protect it against sweat.

You might want to bring a credit card as a fallback, but be conservative in your assumptions about where and how you'll be able to use it – see page 51 for more details. In an emergency you can get cash transferred from your home to Kigali via Western Union or Moneygram; see page 51.

An airport departure tax of US$40 is levied on international flights out of Kigali. Before you pay it, check whether it has already been included in the price of your ticket.

Budget planning

Any budget will depend so greatly on how and where you travel that it is almost impossible to give sensible advice in a general travel guide. As a rule, readers who are travelling at the middle to upper end of the price range will have pre-booked most of their trip, which means that they will have good idea of what the holiday will cost them before they set foot in the country. Pre-booked packages do vary in terms of what is included in the price, and you are advised to check the exact conditions in advance, but generally the price quoted will cover everything but drinks, tips and perhaps some meals.

For budget travellers, Rwanda is not the cheapest country in Africa, but it's damn close to it – and after Ghana it offers the best value for money of any country I've visited in the last couple of years. Throughout the country, a soft drink will cost you around US$0.30 and a 700ml beer less than US$1 in a local bar, more in a hotel or restaurant that caters primarily to Westerners. A meal in a local restaurant will cost US$1–2 while a meal in a proper restaurant might cost US$4 upwards to US$10. Budget accommodation will probably average out at about US$5 per head, often for a self-contained room with a hot shower or bath. Public transport is cheap – typically about US$1 per 50km – and distances are relatively small. Taking the above figures into account I think that budget travellers could scrape by in most parts of Rwanda on around US$10–15 per day for one person or US$20 per day for two. Double this amount, and within reason you can eat and stay where you like. The above prices assume an exchange rate of around 400 Rwandan francs per dollar. They will increase if the franc grows stronger, as may well happen.

The above calculations don't allow for more expensive one-off activities, such as gorilla tracking (US$250 per person, payable in cash) or visiting the other national parks (not expensive unless you hire a vehicle). If you want to keep to a particular budget and plan on undertaking such activities, you would be well advised to treat your day-to-day budget separately from one-off expenses.

ITINERARY PLANNING

Rwanda is so small, and all parts of it are so easily accessible from Kigali, that you needn't engage in any complicated planning. Your first port of call should be Kigali, to gather information and to get your **gorilla-viewing permits** from the ORTPN (see page 49). It's sensible not to rush off to the gorillas immediately; take a few days to get the feel of the country and to acclimatise, because the trek can be quite strenuous and the altitude can take you unawares.

The best **map** available outside the country is currently International Travel Maps' *Rwanda and Burundi*, scale 1:400,000, which is published in Canada – ISBN 09211463669. Good bookshops should be able to order it for you.

Useful **websites** for information on Rwanda are www.rwandemb/org (of the Rwandan Embassy in Washington) and www.rwanda1.com, which give relevant addresses and contact details and have numerous links. Also see *Further Reading*, page 225. The international country telephone code for Rwanda is 250.

Health and Safety

HEALTH

With thanks to Dr Jane Wilson-Howarth and Dr Felicity Nicholson

Rwanda itself isn't a particularly unhealthy country for tourists and you'll never be far from some kind of medical help. The main towns have hospitals (for anything serious you'll be more comfortable in Kigali) and all towns of any size have a pharmacy, although the range of medicines on sale may be limited. In Kigali, the pharmacy in Boulevard de la Révolution is open 24 hours.

Rwanda is divided into 11 health regions, and further into 40 health districts, with almost one hospital per district. There are 340 health centres, averaging more than two per commune. Each health centre covers an average of 23,000 people. It is generally staffed by one or two nurses, supported by medical assistants. In rural areas traditional medicine is also widely used. The above figures look promising, but in fact the severe shortage of qualified personnel caused by the targeting of professionals during the genocide has not yet been remedied.

The guidelines below relate to tropical Africa in general, since travellers may well want to spend time in more than one country.

Before you go

As you should for any trip to a tropical or remote area, visit your doctor about eight weeks before leaving for Rwanda to discuss your plans and requirements. Preparations to ensure a healthy trip to anywhere in Africa should include checks on your immunisation status: it is wise to be up to date on tetanus (ten-yearly), polio (ten-yearly), diphtheria (ten-yearly), hepatitis A and typhoid. For many parts of Africa, immunisations against yellow fever, meningococcal meningitis and rabies are also needed.

In countries (including Rwanda) where yellow-fever vaccination is recommended, it is wise to carry the international certificate with you, as you may be required to show it on arrival. This also applies if you are arriving from another country where yellow fever is a risk. The certificate is not valid until ten days after your vaccination, so make sure you have this done in good time. This potentially lethal virus (its mortality rate can be up to 50%) is spread by mosquito bites and is currently on the increase worldwide, so keep your vaccination up to date.

Certain countries in sub-Saharan Africa also require a certificate of vaccination for cholera. In the UK this vaccine is no longer given as it is ineffective, but certificates of exemption can be acquired from immunisation centres. Currently this is not necessary for Rwanda, but seek up-to-date information before you travel.

Particularly if you'll be passing through other African countries, it's wise to be immunised against hepatitis A (eg: with havrix monodose or avaxim). One dose of vaccine lasts for one year and can be boosted to give protection for up to ten years. The course of two injections costs about £100. The vaccine can be used even close to the time of departure. Hepatitis A vaccine is always preferable to gamma globulin, which gives immediate but short-term partial protection, since there is a theoretical risk of CJD (the human form of mad cow disease) with this blood-derived product.

The newer typhoid vaccines last for three years and are about 75% effective. They are advisable unless you are leaving within a few days for a trip of a week or less, when the vaccination would not be effective in time.

Vaccinations for rabies are advised for travellers visiting more remote areas. Ideally three injections should be taken over a period of four weeks, at 0, 7 and 28 days. The timing of these doses does not have to be exact and a schedule can be arranged to suit you (see *Rabies*, below).

Hepatitis B vaccination should be considered for longer trips (two months or more), or if you'll be working with children or in situations where contact with blood is increased. Three injections are ideal: they can be given at 0, 4 and 8 weeks prior to travel or, if there is insufficient time, then on days 0, 7–14, then 21–28. At the time of writing, the only vaccine licensed for the latter more rapid course is Engerix B. The longer course is always to be preferred as immunity is likely to be longer lasting.

A BCG vaccination against tuberculosis (TB) is also advisable for trips of two months or more. This should be taken at least six weeks before travel.

Malaria prevention

This is probably the greatest health risk to travellers in Rwanda, although it is less prevalent there than in some other African countries. There is no vaccine against malaria, but using prophylactic drugs and preventing mosquito bites will considerably reduce the risk of contracting it. Seek professional advice to ascertain the preferred anti-malarial drugs for Rwanda at the time you travel. Mefloquine (Lariam) is the most effective prophylactic agent for most countries in sub-Saharan Africa. If this drug is suggested then you should start taking it at least two and a half weeks before departure to check that it suits you. Stop immediately if it seems to cause depression or anxiety, visual or hearing disturbances, fits, severe headaches or changes in heart rhythm. Anyone who is pregnant, has been treated for depression or psychiatric problems, has diabetes controlled by oral therapy, or who is epileptic (or has suffered fits in the past) or has a close blood relative who is epileptic should not take mefloquine. The usual alternative is two tablets of chloroquine (nivaquine/avloclor) taken weekly, plus two tablets of proguanil (paludrine) taken daily. Although this is less effective, it is often used for trips of short duration (two weeks or less) or where there is no time to try mefloquine. In

Namibia and the game parks of South Africa this is the prophylactic regime of choice.

The antibiotic doxycycline (100mg daily) is considered by many to be better than the chloroquine-plus-paludrine regime in areas where resistance to these drugs is high. It need only be started one day before arrival. Unlike the other regimes, it may also be used by travellers with epilepsy, although anti-epileptic therapy may make it less effective. Also there is a possibility of allergic skin reactions developing in sunlight; this can occur in about 3% of users. The drug should be stopped if this happens. Women using the oral contraceptive should use an additional method of protection.

There is no malaria transmission above 3,000m; at intermediate altitudes (1,800–3,000m) the risk exists but is low.

In addition to taking anti-malarial medicines, it is important to avoid mosquito bites between dusk and dawn, which is when the *anopheles* (malaria-carrying) mosquito is most active. Pack a DEET-based insect repellent (eg: Repel, Autan, Jungle Jell or Cutters) and take either a permethrin-impregnated bednet or a permethrin spray so that you can treat bednets in hotels. Permethrin treatment makes even very tatty nets protective and mosquitoes are also unable to bite through the impregnated net when you roll against it. Putting on long clothes (including long-sleeved shirts or blouses) at dusk means you can reduce the amount of repellent needed; but be aware that malaria mosquitoes hunt at ankle level and will penetrate through socks, so apply repellent to your feet and ankles too. Travel clinics usually sell a good range of nets, treatment kits and repellents.

Important While you are away, assume that any high fever lasting more than a few hours is malaria, regardless of any other symptoms. Always seek medical help. And remember that malaria may occur anything from seven days into your trip to up to one year after leaving Africa. If symptoms appear after you have returned home, visit your doctor immediately, and mention that you have been travelling in a malarial area.

Travel clinics
UK
British Airways Clinics There are now 30 clinics throughout Britain and three in South Africa. Phone 01276 685040 (UK) for the address of your nearest one. Apart from providing inoculations and malaria prophylaxis, they sell a variety of health-related travel goods including malaria tablet memory cards, bednets and treatment kits.
Fleet Street Travel Clinic 29 Fleet St, London EC4Y 1AA; tel: 020 7353 5678
MASTA (Medical Advisory Service for Travellers Abroad) London School of Hygiene and Tropical Medicine, Keppel St, London WC1 7HT; tel: 0891 224100. This is a premium-line number, charged at 50p per minute. Readers with access to the internet may prefer to check their large website:
http://dspace.dial.pipex.com/masta/index.
Nomad Travel Pharmacy and Vaccination Centre 3–4 Wellington Terrace, Turnpike Lane, London N8 0PX; tel: 020 8889 7014

Trailfinders Immunisation Clinic 194 Kensington High St, London W8 7RG; tel: 020 7938 3999. Non-profit-making private clinic with a one-stop shop for health advice, vaccines and travel goods, visas and passport services and foreign exchange.

Irish Republic

Tropical Medical Bureau Grafton Street Medical Centre, Grafton Buildings, 34 Grafton St, Dublin 2. Tel: (353-1) 671 9200. This organisation has a useful website specific to tropical destinations: http://www.tmb.ie.

USA

Centers for Disease Control 1600 Clifton Road, Atlanta, GA 30333; tel: 877 FYI TRIP; 800 311 3435; web: www.cdc.gov/travel. This organisation is the central source of travel health information in North America, with a touch-tone phone line and fax service. Travelers' Hot Line: (404) 332 4559. Website (for East Africa): www.cdc.gov/travel/eafrica.htm. Each summer they publish the invaluable *Health Information for International Travel*, available from the Center for Prevention Services, Division of Quarantine at the above address.

Connaught Laboratories PO Box 187, Swiftwater, PA 18370; tel: 800 822 2463. They will send a free list of specialist tropical-medicine physicians in your state.

IAMAT (International Association for Medical Assistance to Travellers) 736 Center St, Lewiston, NY 14092, USA; tel: 716 754 4883. Consult website www.sentex.net/~iamat for details of other clinics in the US. A non-profit organisation which provides health information and lists of English-speaking doctors abroad.

Canada

IAMAT (International Association for Medical Assistance to Travellers) Suite 1, 1287 St Clair Avenue West, Toronto, Ontario M6E 1B8; tel: (416) 652 0137; web: www.sentex.net/~iamat.

TMVC (Travel Doctor Group) Sulphur Springs Rd, Ancaster, Ontario; tel: (905) 648 1112; web: www.tmvc.com.au.

Australia and New Zealand

TMVC (Travel Doctor Group) Web: www.tmvc.com.au. TMVC has several clinics in Australia and New Zealand, including: *Brisbane* Qantas Domestic Building, 5th floor, 247 Adelaide St, Brisbane 4000; tel: (07) 3221 9066; *Melbourne* 393 Little Bourke St, 2nd floor, Melbourne, VIC 3000; tel: (03) 9602 5788; *Sydney* Dymocks Building, 7th floor, 428 George St, Sydney, NSW 2000; tel: (02) 9221 7133; *Auckland* Canterbury Arcade, 170 Queen St, Auckland City; tel: 373 3531.

South Africa

TVMC (Travel Doctor Group) 113 DF Malan Drive, Roosevelt Park, Johannesburg; tel: +27 (011) 888 7488. Consult website www.tmvc.com.au for addresses of other clinics in South Africa.

Switzerland

IAMAT (International Association for Medical Assistance to Travellers) 57 Voirets, 1212 Grand Lancy, Geneva; web: www.sentex.net/~iamat

Travel insurance

Before you travel, make sure that you have adequate medical insurance – choose a policy which gives comprehensive cover for hospitalisation as well as for repatriation in case of an emergency. Nowadays the range of cover available is very wide – choose whatever suits your method of travel. Be aware (if you plan travelling by motorbike taxi in Rwanda) that not all policies cover you for this form of transport. Remember to take all the details with you, particularly your policy number and the telephone number that you have to contact in the event of a claim.

Personal first-aid kit

The more I travel the less I take. My minimal kit contains:

- a good drying antiseptic, eg: iodine or potassium permanganate (don't take antiseptic cream)
- a few small dressings (Band-Aids)
- sunscreen
- insect repellent; malaria tablets; impregnated bednet
- aspirin or paracetamol
- antifungal cream (eg: Canesten)
- Ciprofloxacin antibiotic (take 500mg twice a day for three days) or Norfloxacin for severe diarrhoea
- Tinidazole (2g taken in one dose then repeat seven days later) for amoebic dysentery or giardiasis
- another broad-spectrum antibiotic like amoxycillin (for chest, urine, skin infections, etc) if going to a remote area
- pair of fine-pointed tweezers (to remove hairy-caterpillar hairs, thorns, splinters etc)
- condoms or femidoms
- possibly a malaria treatment kit

Common medical problems
Travellers' diarrhoea

It remains true that at least half of those travelling to the tropics/developing world will suffer from a bout of travellers' diarrhoea during their trip; the newer you are to exotic travel, the more likely you will be to suffer. By taking precautions against travellers' diarrhoea you will also avoid typhoid, cholera, hepatitis, dysentery, worms, etc.

From food

Travellers' diarrhoea and the other faecal-oral diseases come from getting other peoples' faeces in your mouth. This most often happens from cooks not washing their hands after a trip to the toilet, but even if the restaurant cook does not understand basic hygiene you will be safe if your food has been properly cooked and arrives piping hot. The maxim to remind you what you can safely eat is:

PEEL IT, BOIL IT, COOK IT OR FORGET IT.

This means that fruit you have washed and peeled yourself, and hot foods, should be safe, but raw foods, cold cooked foods, salads, fruit salads which have been prepared by others, ice cream and ice are all risky, as are foods kept lukewarm in restaurant or hotel buffets. Self-service or buffet lunches and suppers are popular in Rwanda, so try to eat these when the food is hot and freshly cooked – for example a late buffet lunch eaten in mid-afternoon will have been sitting around a long while. If you are struck by travellers' diarrhoea, see box below for treatment.

From water

It is much rarer to get sick from drinking contaminated water but it does happen, so try to drink from safe sources. Tap water in Kigali is supposedly safe although the smell of chlorine may put you off. To make risky water safe it should be brought to the boil (even at altitude it only needs to be brought to the boil), passed through a good bacteriological filter or purified with iodine; chlorine tablets (eg: Puritabs) are also adequate although theoretically less effective, and they taste nastier. Micropur tablets are tasteless but take at least two hours to become effective. If you buy bottled water (which is widely available in Rwanda) make sure the seal is intact.

TREATING TRAVELLERS' DIARRHOEA

It is dehydration which makes you feel awful during a bout of diarrhoea and the most important part of treatment is drinking lots of clear fluids. Sachets of oral rehydration salts give the perfect biochemical mix to replace all that is pouring out of your bottom but they do not taste nice. Any dilute mixture of sugar and salt in water will do you good, so if you like Coke or orange squash, drink that with a three-finger pinch of salt added to each glass. Otherwise make a solution of a four-finger scoop of sugar with a three-finger pinch of salt in a glass of water. Or add eight level teaspoons of sugar (18g) and one level teaspoon of salt (3g) to one litre (five cups) of safe water. A squeeze of lemon or orange juice improves the taste and adds potassium, which is also lost during a bout of diarrhoea. Drink two large glasses after every bowel action, and more if you are thirsty. If you are not eating, then you need to drink three litres a day plus the equivalent of whatever is pouring into the toilet. If you feel like eating, take a bland, high-carbohydrate diet. Heavy, greasy foods will probably give you cramps.

If the diarrhoea is bad, or you are passing blood or slime, or you have a fever, you will probably need antibiotics in addition to fluid replacement. A three-day course of Ciprofloxacin 500mg twice daily (or Norfloxacin) is appropriate treatment for dysentery and bad diarrhoea. If the diarrhoea is greasy and bulky and is accompanied by 'eggy' burps, the likely cause is giardia. This is best treated with Tinidazole (2g in one dose repeated seven days later if symptoms persist).

Dengue fever

This mosquito-borne disease resembles malaria but there is no prophylactic available to deal with it. The mosquitoes which carry this virus bite during the daytime, so it is worth applying repellent if you see them around. Symptoms include strong headaches, rashes and excruciating joint and muscle pains with high fever. Dengue fever lasts for only a week or so and is not usually fatal. Complete rest and paracetamol are the usual treatment. Plenty of fluids also help. Some patients are given an intravenous drip to keep them from dehydrating.

Insect bites

It is crucial to avoid mosquito bites between dusk and dawn; as the sun is going down, don long clothes and apply repellent on any exposed flesh. This will protect you from malaria, elephantiasis and a range of nasty insect-borne viruses. Malaria **mosquitoes** are voracious, hunt at ankle-level, and can penetrate through socks. Sleep under a permethrin-treated bednet or in an air-conditioned room. During the day it is wise to wear long, loose (preferably 100% cotton) clothes if you are pushing through scrubby country; this will deter **ticks** as well as **tsetse flies** and day-biting *Aedes* mosquitoes which may spread dengue and yellow fever. Tsetse flies hurt when they bite and are attracted to the colour blue; locals will advise on where they are a problem and where they transmit sleeping sickness.

Minute pestilential biting **blackflies** spread river blindness in some parts of Africa between 190°N and 170°S; the disease is caught close to fast-flowing rivers since flies breed there and the larvae live in rapids. The flies bite during the day but long trousers tucked into socks will help keep them off. Citronella-based natural repellents do not work against them.

Tumbu flies or *putsi* are a problem in areas of eastern, western and southern Africa where the climate is hot and humid. The adult fly lays her eggs on the soil or on drying laundry and when the eggs come in contact with human flesh (when you put on clothes or lie on a bed) they hatch and bury themselves under the skin. Here they form a crop of 'boils' each of which hatches a grub after about eight days, when the inflammation will settle down. In *putsi* areas either dry your clothes and sheets within a screened house, or dry them in direct sunshine until they are crisp, or iron them.

Jiggers or **sandfleas** are another kind of flesh-feaster. They latch on if you walk barefoot in contaminated places, and set up home under the skin of the foot, usually at the side of a toenail where they cause a painful, boil-like swelling. These need picking out by a local expert; if the distended flea bursts during eviction the wound should be dowsed in spirit, alcohol or kerosene, otherwise more jiggers will infest you.

Bilharzia or schistosomiasis
With thanks to Dr Vaughan Southgate of the Natural History Museum, London
Bilharzia or schistosomiasis is a disease which commonly afflicts the rural poor of the tropics who repeatedly acquire more and more of these nasty little

QUICK TICK REMOVAL

African ticks are not the prolific disease transmitters they are in the Americas, but they may occasionally spread disease. Lyme disease, which can have unpleasant after-effects, has now been recorded in Africa, and tick-bite fever also occurs. The latter is a mild, flu-like illness, but still worth avoiding. If you get the tick off whole and promptly the chances of disease transmission are reduced to a minimum.

Manoeuvre your finger and thumb so that you can pinch the tick's mouthparts, as close to your skin as possible, and slowly and steadily pull away at right angles to your skin. This often hurts. Jerking or twisting will increase the chances of damaging the tick which in turn increases the chances of disease transmission, as well as leaving the mouthparts behind.

Once the tick is off, dowse the little wound with alcohol (local spirit, whisky or similar is excellent) or iodine. An area of spreading redness around the bite site, or a rash or fever coming on a few days or more after the bite, should stimulate a trip to a doctor.

worm-lodgers. Infected travellers and expatriates generally suffer fewer problems because symptoms will encourage them to seek prompt treatment and they are also exposed to fewer parasites. However, it is still an unpleasant problem that is worth avoiding.

The parasites digest their way through your skin when you wade, bathe or even shower in infested freshwater. Unfortunately many African lakes, rivers and irrigation canals, carry a risk of bilharzia. In Rwanda, the bathing areas of Lake Kivu are currently said to be safe.

The most risky shores will be close to places where infected people use water, where they wash clothes, etc. Winds disperse the cercariae, though, so they can be blown some distance, perhaps up to 200m from where they entered the water. Scuba-diving off a boat into deep offshore water, then, should be a low-risk activity, but showering in lake water or paddling along a reedy lake shore near a village carries a high risk of acquiring bilharzia.

Although absence of early symptoms does not necessarily mean there is no infection, infected people usually notice symptoms two or more weeks after penetration. Travellers and expatriates will probably experience a fever and often a wheezy cough; local residents do not usually have symptoms.

There is now a very good blood test which, if done six weeks or more after likely exposure, will determine whether or not parasites are going to cause problems, and then the infection can be treated. While treatment generally remains effective, it does fail in some cases for reasons that are not yet fully understood; retreatment seems to work fine and it is not known if some drug resistance is developing. Since bilharzia can be a nasty illness, avoidance is better than waiting to be cured and it is wise to avoid bathing in high-risk areas. Take local advice about this.

Avoiding bilharzia

If you are bathing, swimming, paddling or wading in freshwater which you think may carry a bilharzia risk, try to stay in no longer than ten minutes. Afterwards dry off thoroughly with a towel; rub vigorously. Avoid bathing or paddling on shores within 200m of villages or places where people use the water a great deal, especially reedy shores or where there is lots of water weed. Covering yourself with DEET insect repellent before swimming will help to protect you. If your bathing water comes from a risky source try to ensure that the water is taken from the lake in the early morning and stored snail-free, otherwise it should be filtered or Dettol or Cresol should be added. Bathing early in the morning is safer than bathing in the last half of the day. If you think that you have been exposed to bilharzia parasites, arrange a screening blood test (your GP can do this) *more* than six weeks after your last possible contact with suspect water.

Skin infections

Any mosquito bite or small nick in the skin provides an opportunity for bacteria to foil the body's usually excellent defences; it will surprise many travellers how quickly skin infections start in warm humid climates and it is essential to clean and cover even the slightest wound. Creams are not as effective as a good drying antiseptic such as dilute iodine, potassium permanganate (a few crystals in half a cup of water), or crystal (or gentian) violet. One of these should be available in most towns. If the wound starts to throb, or becomes red and the redness starts to spread, or the wound oozes, and especially if you develop a fever, antibiotics will probably be needed; flucloxacillin (250mg four times a day) or cloxacillin (500mg four times a day). For those allergic to penicillin, erythromycin (500mg twice a day) for five days should help. See a doctor if the symptoms do not start to improve in 48 hours.

Fungal infections also get a hold easily in hot moist climates so wear 100% cotton socks and underwear and shower frequently. An itchy rash in the groin or flaking between the toes is likely to be a fungal infection. This needs treatment with an antifungal cream such as Canesten (clotrimazole); if this is not available try Whitfield's ointment (compound enzoic acid ointment) or crystal violet (although this will turn you purple!).

Prickly heat

A fine pimply rash on the torso is likely to be heat rash; cool showers, dabbing (not rubbing) dry, and talc will help; if it's bad you may need to check into an air-conditioned hotel room for a while. Slowing down to a relaxed schedule, wearing only loose, baggy 100% cotton clothes and sleeping naked under a fan reduce the problem.

Sun damage

The incidence of skin cancer is rocketing as Caucasians are travelling more and spending more time exposing themselves to the sun. Keep out of the sun during the middle of the day and, if you must expose yourself, build up gradually from 20 minutes per day. Be especially careful of sun reflected off water and wear a T-shirt and lots of waterproof SPF 15 suncream when swimming; snorkelling often leads to scorched backs of the thighs so wear Bermuda shorts. Sun exposure ages the skin and makes people prematurely wrinkly; cover up with long loose clothes and wear a hat when you can.

Meningitis

This is a particularly nasty disease as it can kill within hours of the first symptoms appearing. The telltale symptoms are a combination of a blinding headache (light sensitivity), a blotchy rash and a high fever. Immunisation protects against the most serious bacterial form of meningitis (types A and C) and is recommended for Tanzania and Zanzibar. Other forms of meningitis exist (usually viral) but there are no vaccines for these. Local papers normally report outbreaks. If you show symptoms go immediately to a doctor.

Sexual risks

Travel is a time when we may enjoy sexual adventures, especially when alcohol reduces inhibitions. Remember the risks of sexually transmitted infection are high, whether you sleep with fellow travellers or with locals. About 40% of HIV infections in British heterosexuals are acquired abroad and AIDS is a serious problem in Rwanda. Use condoms or femidoms, preferably bearing the British kite mark and ideally bought before travel. If you notice any genital ulcers or discharge get treatment promptly.

Ebola

So far this has never occurred in Rwanda, but at the time of writing an outbreak in northern Uganda (the first one ever recorded there) had claimed almost a hundred lives. It is a rare, but deadly, highly contagious, virally induced disease which causes haemorrhagic fever. In the unlikely event of an outbreak, protective measures will be taken and you should follow whatever local advice is given.

Useful contacts

Central Hospital of Kigali Tel: 75555
King Faycal Hospital (Kigali) Tel: 82421

Animals
Rabies

Rabies can be carried by all mammals and is passed on to man through a bite or a lick of an open wound. You must always assume any animal is rabid (unless personally known to you). The closer the bite is to the face the shorter the incubation time of the disease, but it is always wise to get medical help as soon as possible. Remember, though, that it is never too late to bother. In the interim, scrub the wound with soap and bottled/boiled water, then pour on a strong iodine or alcohol solution. This helps stop the rabies virus entering the body and will guard against wound infections including tetanus. If you intend to have contact with animals and/or are likely to be more than 24 hours away from medical help, then pre-exposure vaccination is advised. Ideally three doses should be taken over four weeks. Contrary to popular belief these vaccinations are relatively painless! If you are exposed as described, then treatment should be given as soon as possible, but it is never too late to seek help as the incubation period for rabies can be very long.

Those who have not been immunised will need a full course of injections together with rabies immunoglobulin (RIG), but this product is expensive (around US$800) and may be hard to come by – which is a reason why pre-exposure vaccination should be encouraged in travellers who are planning to visit more remote areas. Tell the doctor if you have had pre-exposure vaccine as this will change the treatment you receive. Remember that if you do contract rabies, mortality is 100% and death from rabies is probably one of the worst ways to go!

Snakebite

Snakes rarely attack unless provoked and bites to travellers are unusual. You are less likely to get bitten if you wear stout shoes and long trousers when in the bush. Most snakes are harmless and even venomous species will only dispense venom in about half of their bites. If bitten, then, you are unlikely to have received venom; keeping this fact in mind may help you to stay calm. Many so-called first-aid techniques do more harm than good: cutting into the wound is harmful; tourniquets are dangerous; suction and electrical inactivation devices do not work. The only treatment is antivenom. In case of a bite which you fear may have been from a venomous snake:

- Try to keep calm - it is likely that no venom has been dispensed.
- Prevent movement of the bitten limb by applying a splint.
- Keep the bitten limb BELOW heart height to slow the spread of any venom.
- If you have a crepe bandage, bind up as much of the bitten limb as you can, but release the bandage every half hour.
- Evacuate to a hospital which has antivenom.

And remember:

- NEVER give aspirin; you may offer paracetamol, which is safe.
- NEVER cut or suck the wound.
- DO NOT apply ice packs.
- DO NOT apply potassium permanganate.

If the offending snake can be captured without risk of someone else being bitten, take it to show to the doctor – but beware, since even a decapitated head is able to dispense venom in a reflex bite.

Further reading

Self-prescribing has its hazards so, if you are going anywhere remoter than Rwanda, or if you like to have facts at your fingertips, then consider taking a health guide. For adults there is *Bugs, Bites & Bowels: The Cadogan Guide to Healthy Travel* by Jane Wilson-Howarth (1999); if travelling with children look at *Your Child's Health Abroad: A Manual for Travelling Parents* by Jane Wilson-Howarth and Matthew Ellis, published by Bradt Publications in 1998.

SAFETY
Big game
If you are venturing into the bush remember that it is inhabited by some threatening wildlife. The most dangerous species are the big primates and wild buffalo; hippos are dangerous if you happen to frighten them and you are between them and the safety of their waterhole.

Theft
The following security hints are applicable anywhere in Africa:

• Most casual thieves operate in busy markets and bus stations. Keep a close watch on your possessions in such places, and avoid having valuables or large amounts of money loose in your daypack or pocket.
• Keep all your valuables and the bulk of your money in a hidden money belt. Never show this money belt in public. Keep any spare cash you need elsewhere on your person – I feel that a button-up pocket on the front of the shirt is the most secure place as money cannot be snatched from it without the thief coming into your view. It is also advisable to keep a small amount of hard currency (ideally cash) hidden away in your luggage so that, should you lose your money belt, you have something to fall back on.
• Where the choice exists between carrying valuables on your person or leaving them in a locked room I would tend to favour the latter option (only one of the hundreds of thefts I've heard about in Africa have happened from a locked hotel room, and that was in Nairobi where just about anything is possible). Obviously you should use your judgement on this and be sure the room is absolutely secure. A factor to be considered is that some travellers' cheque companies will not refund cheques which were stolen from a room.
• Leave any jewellery of financial or sentimental value at home.

Useful contact
Police Tel: 08311117

Other hazards
People new to exotic travel often worry about tropical diseases, but it is accidents which are most likely to carry you off. Road travel isn't as dangerous in Rwanda as in some other African countries but still accidents aren't uncommon; so be aware and do what you can to reduce risks. For example, try to travel during daylight hours and refuse to be driven by anyone who is drunk. *Always* heed local advice about where you should (or should not) travel, or about areas where you should take particular care. At the time of writing, Rwanda is a relatively safe country – but, sadly, it has been seen elsewhere in the developing world that an increase in tourism can lead to an increase in opportunistic crime. Be as sensible in Rwanda as (I hope!) you would be in any other strange country about carrying your cash discreetly and not flaunting jewellery, and (particularly in towns) about where you walk after dark. Also be sensible in hotels and guesthouses: don't leave tempting items too readily accessible.

Travelling in Rwanda

TOURIST INFORMATION AND SERVICES

The **Office Rwandais du Tourisme et des Parcs Nationaux**, more commonly referred to as ORTPN (*Or-ti-pen),* doubles as both tourist office and national parks authority. The ORTPN offices in the airport arrivals hall and in central Kigali stock a fair range of booklets and maps, and are the best places to seek out current information relating to the national parks and other reserves. The office in central Kigali (Avenue de l'Armée, near its junction with Place de la Constitution) handles advance bookings and issues permits for gorilla-tracking in the Volcanoes National Park. Permits can sometimes – depending on availability – also be bought at the ORTPN office in Ruhengeri, but check this in Kigali first.

ORTPN can also provide details of hotels around the country, as well as lists of car-hire agencies in Kigali, tour operators, public transport and local events. It's best to call in personally, otherwise contact details are: ORTPN, BP 905 Kigali; tel: 76514/5 or 73396; fax: 76512; email: ortpn@ rwandatel1.rwanda1.com. Also see advertisement on page 92.

Two bookshops in central Kigali with a reasonable stock of guidebooks and maps, as well as a wide selection of background reading, are the **Librairie Caritas** near the GPO, and the **Librairie Ikirezi** in Avenue de la Paix. See advertisement on page 91. (Remember that in French *librairie* means bookshop; lending library is *bibliothèque.)*

Tour operators and travel agents (see pages 112–13) are also sources of local information.

PUBLIC HOLIDAYS

In addition to the following fixed public holidays, Rwanda recognises Good Friday and Easter Monday, which fall on different dates from one year to the next.

January 1	New Year's Day	August 15	Assumption Day
January 28	Democracy Day	September 8	Culture Day
April 7	Genocide Memorial Day	September 25	Republic Day
May 1	Labour Day	October 1	Heroes' Day
July 1	Independence Day	November 1	All Saints' Day
July 4	National Liberation Day	December 25	Christmas Day
August 1	Harvest Festival	December 26	Boxing Day

MONEY

The unit of currency is the Rwanda franc (Rfr). In December 2000, the exchange rate against the dollar varied from Rfr360 to Rfr440, depending on whether the transaction involved cash or travellers' cheques, and where it took place. In Rwanda more than most African countries, US dollars are by far the most widely recognised foreign currency, and, except in Kigali, US dollars cash are the only foreign currency likely to be exchangeable outside of banks.

If you intend visiting the mountain gorillas – and who in their right mind would not! – then bear in mind that your permit will cost US$250 which currently must be paid in US$ *cash*, so bring at least that much with you.

Foreign exchange

Foreign cash and travellers' cheques can be changed into Rwandan francs at any bank in Kigali. There are also several private bureaux de change (known locally as forex bureaux) in the capital, which generally offer better rates than banks against US dollars (and other currencies) cash, but don't handle travellers' cheques. Elsewhere in the country, there are very few forex bureaux, and bank rates tend to be poorer than in the capital.

Travellers' cheques can only be exchanged at banks. Even in Kigali, rates are very unfavourable and a hefty commission may be charged. In most other towns, there is at least one bank that accepts travellers' cheques, generally at lower rates than you'll get in Kigali, although it may need to contact its head office to find out the current rate. In some towns, notably Ruhengeri, there is nowhere to change travellers' cheques at all. Do always carry your proof-of-purchase receipt for the cheques, as banks may (or may not – it seems arbitrary) demand to see it. Theoretically this receipt should always be kept separately from your cheques. Wherever you go, carrying travellers' cheques in a currency other than dollars will only add to the confusion. Details of the situation in individual towns are given in the main body of the guide.

The best rates for US dollars cash anywhere in the country are offered by the private individuals who hang out around the main post office in Kigali. Their activities are technically illegal, but they operate in the open (and, conveniently, at times when banks are closed) and appear to be tolerated. The atmosphere when you're changing money here can be pretty fraught, with up to a dozen individuals breathing down your neck, so that being cheated or hustled is probably of greater concern than falling foul of the law, and you should always decide beforehand the minimum rate you're prepared to accept. Fortunately, the money changers in Kigali do have a reasonable reputation for honesty: they might well quote a sub-standard rate, but are unlikely to get into more elaborate con tricks. This could change, however, so keep your wits about you, and – once you've decided who to deal with – try to get the mob to disperse before you start the transaction.

In other towns, particularly those close to international borders, it is also possible to change US dollars cash on the street, at rates significantly better than those offered by the bank, but lower than the street rate in Kigali. As in Kigali, there is always a risk of being duped by street operators. One way around this is to ask the manager of your hotel to exchange your US dollars – you may lose slightly on the deal, as the hotel will effectively be acting as a broker, but it will save a lot of hassle.

To give an idea of comparative rates, in September 2000 the bank rate for US dollars cash was around Rfr410, the bank rate for travellers' cheques Rfr380–390 after commission, the street rate (cash) in Kigali up to Rfr455, and the street rate elsewhere in the country between Rfr420 and 440. Actual rates are bound to change during the lifespan of this book, but these figures do show that the rate for travellers' cheques in banks as against the best street rate for cash might differ by as much as 20%.

Banking hours are from approximately 08.00 to 12.00 and 14.00 to 17.00 Monday to Friday (some banks stay open longer), and 08.00 to 12.00 Saturday. Private forex bureaux may keep slightly longer hours than banks. Both are closed on Sundays and public holidays.

Credit cards

At the time of writing there are no facilities for drawing cash via credit or debit cards, although there are plans to phase this in eventually. Meanwhile, don't be misled by the gleaming ATMs you may see around the city – they accept only cards issued by a local bank (the BCDI). Some – at present only a very few – of the bigger hotels and restaurants may accept payment by Visa or MasterCard, but when I used this facility I got a poor rate, as for some reason the Rwandan francs were translated into Belgian francs before eventually being debited to my account in sterling.

Transfers from abroad

If your budgeting has fallen apart and you need a rescue transfer from home, there are Western Union facilities at the Banque Commerciale du Rwanda, and Moneygram facilities (accessed via any branch of Thomas Cook in the UK) at the Banque Continentale Africaine Rwanda, both in Boulevard de la Révolution in Kigali.

Prices in this book

Most services in Rwanda are best paid for in local currency. The exceptions are gorilla-tracking fees and some upmarket hotels, which charge in US dollars. Nevertheless, given the tendency for instability among African currencies, it is probably more reliable in the long term to quote prices at the US dollar equivalent. Throughout this guide, **prices are quoted in US dollars using an approximate exchange rate of Rfr400 per US$1**. Prices were correct as of September 2000, but may be subject to inflation during the lifespan of this edition.

GETTING AROUND
Self-drive

Most trunk roads in Rwanda are surfaced and in reasonable condition, including the main road from Kigali to Cyangugu via Butare; to Gisenyi via

APPROXIMATE DISTANCES BETWEEN MAIN TOWNS
(in kilometres)

	Kigali	Butare	Byumba	Gitarama	Kibungo	Kibuye	Gisenyi	Gikongoro	Ruhengeri	Cyangugu
Kigali		135	60	53	112	144	187	164	118	293
Butare	135		210	82	247	129	237	29	190	158
Byumba	60	210		128	187	219	173	240	104	349
Gitarama	53	82	128		165	91	177	112	108	221
Kibungo	112	247	187	165		256	299	277	230	386
Kibuye	144	129	219	91	256		108	258	199	130
Gisenyi	187	237	173	177	299	108		366	69	238
Gikongoro	164	29	240	112	277	258	366		220	128
Ruhengeri	118	190	104	108	230	199	69	220		307
Cyangugu	293	158	349	221	386	130	248	128	307	

Ruhengeri; to Rusumo via Kibungo; to Kibuye via Gitarama, and to the Uganda border via Byumba or Umutara. There are, however, potholed sections along all these routes which, together with the winding terrain and the tendency for Rwandans to drive at breakneck speeds and overtake on sharp corners, necessitate a more cautious approach than one might take at home.

The unsurfaced roads most likely to be used by tourists include the long stretch running parallel to Lake Kivu between Gisenyi, Kibuye and Cyangugu; the approach roads to Akagera National Park (and roads within the park); and approach roads to the Parc des Virungas and Lakes Burera and Ruhondo from Ruhengeri. In all cases, these roads are in fair condition, and should be 'do-able' in a saloon car during the dry season, though a 4x4 would certainly be preferable.

On all routes, be alert to cyclists swaying from the verge, and for livestock and pedestrians wandering blithely into the middle of the road, any one of which may force you to leave your lane at an inopportune moment. Putting one's foot to the floor and hooting like a maniac is the customary Rwandan approach to driving through crowded areas; driving rather more defensively than you would at home is a safer approach. Whatever else you do, avoid driving at night, when the general chaos is exacerbated by vehicles lacking headlights.

Several travel agencies in Kigali rent out saloons and 4x4s, with or without drivers. For details see *Chapter 6,* page 112–13. Further up-to-date listings are given in the tourism section of the Rwanda website www.rwanda1.com; also you can get details from ORTPN in Kigali. Rates vary according to whether you'll be driving outside Kigali, and whether fuel is included. A 4x4 can cost from US$100 to US$150 per day including driver, depending on its type/size.

Mountain biking

The relatively short distances between tourist centres and the consistently attractive scenery should make Rwanda ideal for travelling by mountain bike. These cannot easily be bought locally, so you would have to bring one with you (some airlines are more flexible than others about carrying bicycles; you should discuss this with them in advance). Buses will allow you to take your bike on the roof, though expect to be charged extra for this. Minor roads are variable in condition, but in the dry season you're unlikely to encounter any problems. Several of the more off-the-beaten-track destinations mentioned in this book would be particularly attractive to cyclists.

Hitching

This is an option on main routes, though you should expect to pay for lifts offered by Rwandans.

Public transport
Air

The only internal service is the flight between Kigali and Cyangugu, running twice weekly in both directions.

Boat and rail

There are no rail services in Rwanda (although a rail link with Tanzania is on the drawing-board), nor is there at present a functional ferry on Lake Kivu. It is, however, possible to travel between the main lake ports using small cargo boats, and to rent local dugouts for short excursions on the lake. Motor-boats are also available for hire on Lake Kivu – see *Kibuye* in *Chapter 7* and *Gisenyi* in *Chapter 8*. Small boats can be used to get around the smaller lakes, such as Burera and Ruhondo, by making an informal arrangement with the boat owner.

RWANDA: THE REALITY

One guidebook was so negative about Rwanda that it nearly stopped us from going. But we went along to see for ourselves and were astonished to find a most organised, friendly and positive community... A very small country indeed, with quite a few thousand people too many! But we had an amazing visit. Rwanda, especially because of its history and recent changes, positive reconciliation, etc, is totally different from the other countries in the region. I suppose the entire country is just one big paradox.

Dorette Boshoff and David Hartley, December 2000

Road

The main mode of road transport is shared **minibuses**, generally known as *minibus-taxis* or *taxi-minibuses*, which connect all major centres (and most minor ones) and leave from the town's minibus station (*gare taxi/minibus*) when they are full. No smoking inside is the rule. Departures continue throughout the day but it's best not to wait until too late, in case the last one proves to be full. Fares generally work out at around US$1 per 50km. Travel times along main surfaced roads typically average out at around 50km per hour, with frequent pauses to drop off passengers and negotiate roadblocks balanced against driving that verges on the manic between the stops. Overloading is not the problem it is in many African countries, nor are tourists routinely overcharged, though the latter does happen from time to time so check the fare with other passengers if it feels too high. You pay just before you alight rather than when you board, so there's the opportunity to see what other people are paying. On some routes **buses** are also available, which leave at fixed times. They are cheaper than minibuses but considerably slower and few travellers make use of them. In and around Kigali there's a network of urban minibuses, running on set routes through the capital and its suburbs.

In some larger towns you'll also find normal **taxis** – identifiable by a yellow or orange stripe round the side – known as *taxi-voitures* to distinguish them from taxi-minibuses. The same rules apply as in most African countries – agree a price in advance and haggle if it seems extortionate. Details appear under the relevant towns in *Part Two*.

Smokers beware – there's an unspoken non-smoking policy on public transport; the one man I saw having a quick drag, with his head stuck well outside the window, was getting disapproving looks.

Private minibuses

Between Kigali and Butare, and probably other main towns too by the time you read this, a few companies operate private minibuses to fixed timetables and with bookable seats. These start and finish at the company's offices rather than at the public minibus stations. The price is generally the same as for public minibuses. Details appear under the relevant towns in *Part Two*.

There are also privately owned minibuses which operate flexibly throughout the country, in much the same way as normal taxis, with passengers sharing the fare. If you're hitching, you may well come across these.

Two-wheeled taxis

In and around minibus-taxi stations you may find 'taxis' in the form of motorbikes (*motos*) or bicycles. They're handy for short distances – but be aware that your travel insurance may not cover you for accidents when on either of them, and you certainly won't be offered a safety helmet. Agree a price beforehand, and check with a passer-by if it seems excessive. If you've got a heavy bag, an alternative is to stick it on the saddle of the bicycle and walk alongside.

LOCAL TOUR OPERATORS

See the *Kigali* chapter (pages 112–13) for details of local tour operators who can fix up trips within the country for you.

ACCOMMODATION

There are hotels of international standard in Kigali and Gisenyi. Elsewhere, accommodation is restricted to mid-range hotels, geared to local businesspeople as much as to tourists, and cheaper local guesthouses. With a few exceptions, accommodation in Rwanda is good value for money when compared with that of other countries in the region. Where mid-range hotels are available – in Ruhengeri, Butare and the Lake Kivu resorts – rates generally work out at comfortably under US$30 for a clean double with en-suite hot bath. Budget accommodation mostly falls into the US$7–15 price range, and in many cases this will get you a very clean room with en-suite hot shower. In hotels of all standards, if you're staying for more than a few days you may be able to negotiate a lower rate.

Most accommodation establishments are recognisably signposted as a hotel, *logement,* guesthouse or similar, but some local places are signposted as *Amacumbi* – which literally means 'Place with Rooms' in Kinyarwanda. Note, too, that in the Swahili language – not indigenous to Rwanda but more widely spoken by locals than any other exotic tongue – a *hoteli* is a restaurant, which can create confusion when asking a non-French speaker for a hotel.

Few formal campsites exist in Rwanda. Some hotels will permit camping in the gardens, but at little saving over the price of a budget room. One place in Rwanda where camping is at present the only viable option is in Akagera National Park. At Nyungwe, the campsite is far more attractively located than the resthouse for travellers without a vehicle. A tent may also come in handy for travellers backpacking or cycling through relatively untouristed rural areas, where you are strongly advised to ask permission of the local village headman before setting up camp.

EATING AND DRINKING
Eating out

Kigali boasts a good range of restaurants representing international cuisines such as Indian, Italian, Chinese and French. In most other towns, a couple of hotels or restaurants serve uncomplicated Western meals – chicken, fish or steak with chips or rice. Possibly as a result of the Belgian influence, restaurant standards seem to be far higher than in most East African countries, and Rwandan chips are probably the best on the continent. Servings tend to be dauntingly large, and prices very reasonable – around US$5 for a main course.

Wherever you travel, local restaurants serve Rwandan favourites such as goat kebabs, grilled or fried tilapia (a type of lake fish), bean or meat stews. These are normally eaten with one of a few staples: *ugali* (a stiff porridge made with maize meal), *matoke* (cooking banana/plantain), *chapatti* (flat bread), and boiled potatoes (as in Uganda, these are somewhat mysteriously referred to as Irish potatoes) – not to mention rice and the ubiquitous chips. At local restaurants, you should be able to fill yourself adequately for US$2 or less.

Buffet or self-service meals are often offered in restaurants – and are said to originate from a period in the 1980s when the government decreed that civil servants should have shorter lunch breaks. As a result, enterprising restaurants dreamed up this way of enabling them to eat faster. Smarter restaurants, especially in Kigali, may be closed or take a while to rustle up food outside of normal mealtimes.

Unless you have an insatiable appetite for greasy omelettes or stale *mandazi* (deep-fried dough balls not dissimilar to doughnuts), breakfast outside of Kigali or the larger hotels can be a problematic meal. One area in which Rwanda is definitely influenced more by its anglophone neighbours than by its former coloniser is baking: in common with the rest of East Africa, the bread is almost always sweetish and monumentally stale. In such cases a bunch of bananas, supplemented by other fresh fruit, is about the best breakfast option: cheap, nutritious and filling.

Cooking for yourself
The alternative to eating at restaurants is to put together your own meals at markets and supermarkets. The variety of foodstuffs you can buy varies from season to season and from town to town, but in most major centres you can rely on finding a supermarket that stocks frozen meat, a few tinned goods, biscuits, pasta, rice and chocolate bars. If you're that way inclined, and will be staying in hotels rather than camping, bring a small electric immersion heater for use in your bedroom (sockets take standard continental two-pin plugs), plus some teabags or instant coffee, so you can supplement your picnic with a hot drink.

Fruit and vegetables are best bought at markets, where they are very cheap. Potatoes, sweet potatoes, onions, tomatoes, bananas, sugar cane, avocados, paw-paws, mangoes, coconuts, oranges and pineapples are seasonally available in most towns.

For hikers, about the only dehydrated meals available are packet soups. If you have specialised requirements, you're best doing your shopping in Kigali, where a wider selection of goods is available in the supermarkets; there are also a couple of excellent bakeries, with mouthwatering goodies hot from the oven.

Drinks
Brand-name soft drinks such as Pepsi, Coca Cola and Fanta are widely available, and cheap by international standards. Tap water is debatably safe to drink in larger towns, although the smell of chlorine may put you off; bottled mineral water is widely available if you prefer not to take the risk.

The most widely drunk hot beverage is tea (*chai* or *icyayi* in Swahili/Kinyarwanda). In rural areas, the ingredients are often boiled together in a pot: a sticky, sweet, milky concoction that definitely falls into the category of acquired tastes. Most Westernised restaurants serve tea as we know it, but if you want to be certain, specify that you want black tea. The milk served separately with it is almost always powdered, but of a type that dissolves well and doesn't taste too bad. Coffee is one of Rwanda's main cash crops, but you'd hardly know it judging by the insipid slop that passes for coffee in most restaurants and hotels. You're on safe if unexciting ground with instant coffee (ask for *Nescafé*); after a few days in the country we made a policy of checking whether coffee was of the brewed or instant variety before we ordered – if the former, we settled for tea.

The most popular alcoholic drink is beer, brewed locally near Gisenyi. The cheaper of the two local brands (and I thought the tastier) is *Primus*, which comes in 700ml bottles which cost anything from US$0.75 in local bars to US$2 in Kigali's swankiest hotels. The alternative is *Mutzig*, which tastes little different, costs about 30% more, and comes in 700ml or 350ml bottles. There's also the local banana beer, *urwagwa*.

South African and French wines are sold at outrageously inflated prices in a few upmarket bars and restaurants. Far more sensibly priced are the boxes of Spanish or Italian wine sold in some supermarkets. If you want to check out your capacity for locally brewed banana wine (also called *urwagwa*) before ordering it with a meal (at least one of the authors finds it delicious...!) most supermarkets and some small grocers/snackbars have bottles on sale. It comes in many varieties – some have honey added, and I've heard of a kind made in the northeast that contains hibiscus flowers. There's also a banana liqueur.

As for the harder stuff – *waragi*, a millet-based clear alcohol from Uganda, is available everywhere; you can either knock it back neat or mix it as you would gin. (In its undistilled form it could strip away a few layers of skin!) The illegal Rwandan firewater, *kanyanga*, is also available everywhere: treat with care.

LANGUAGE

The local language is Kinyarwanda, but almost all Rwandans speak at least one international language. In rural areas, this is most likely to be KiSwahili, a coastal Bantu language with strong Arabic influences which, thanks largely to the 19th-century slave caravans, has come to serve as the *lingua franca* of East Africa. Most educated Rwandans who were brought up within the country also speak passable to fluent French, but very few speak any English. By contrast, many returned long-term exiles were educated in Uganda, Kenya or Tanzania or another anglophone territory, and don't know any French, but do speak fluent English.

The upshot of this is that French speakers will have no difficulty getting by in the towns, and should always be able to find somebody who can speak French in rural areas. English speakers will struggle more, though particularly in Kigali and Ruhengeri they'll find that a fair number of people speak English. Travellers who know some Swahili will also find this very useful, particularly in rural areas. The potential for chaos is, of course, immense: in Ruhengeri, I regularly tried my faltering Swahili in a bar or hotel to no avail, followed up on this in my even more limited French, only to have the person I was addressing ask me whether perhaps I spoke English!

Both French and English are now taught from primary school onwards, with the aim of making Rwanda a trilingual country; however, *the* national language, spoken by everyone, remains Kinyarwanda, and for the sake of friendliness and courtesy you should try to take on board a few words. At the very least aim for *yégo* (yes), *oya* (no), *murakozé* (thank you), *muraho* (hello, good morning/afternoon), *bitesé?* (how are you?) and *byiza* (good). For me, an essential phrase in any language is 'What's your name?', to be used on children; their faces light up and they start to take you seriously! Then point to yourself and say your own name, and the introduction is complete. In Kinyarwanda it's easy – *Witwandé?* The above words are written phonetically – the value of consonants may change a bit in different parts of the country; for example 'b' may sometimes sound more like 'v' or 'w'. If you're linguistically ambitious, turn to the more comprehensive vocabulary in *Appendix 1*.

Place names

In Kinyarwanda, as in most African languages, place names are more or less phonetic, so that the town of Base, for instance, is pronounced *Bah-say*. While this might take some adaptation on the part of any English speaker, the transcription of place names in Rwanda displays some other quirks that I've not encountered anywhere, namely the occasional pronunciation of 'g' as 'j' (Kinigi, for instance, is pronounced Kiniji), and of an initial 'k' or 'cy' as 'ch' (Kigali = Chigali, Cyangugu = Changugu). Further complication is created by the African tendency to treat 'r' and 'l' as interchangeable, and the local custom of distinguishing certain towns from the synonymous region by adding the French word *ville* to the end of the town's name. Hence, when you hear a bus conductor yelling *Chigari-ville* at the top of his voice, he is in fact referring to the city of Kigali!

WHAT THE 'ELL...?

When I visited the old royal palace at Nyanza, a couple of local lads who spoke some French came to help interpret, as the woman at the gate knew only Kinyarwanda. They were proud of the history and wanted to give me full value, describing at length the background and customs of the king and his wives. Their accent made it hard for me to follow in detail. One of them kept talking about the *loi* (= law) and it was obviously of great importance; but I was baffled when he started on about *la laine* (= the wool). I hadn't been aware that knitting was an ancient Rwandan custom. Then light dawned. The *loi* was in fact the king, or *roi*; while the *laine* was his queen, or *reine*. So – watch out for the very common transposition of these consonants, not only in speech but in writing too.

Particularly when travelling in off-the-beaten-track areas, it can pay to recognise that the names of communes – the smallest administrative unit in the country – are often used interchangeably with town or village names. This can create confusion where a commune and its principal settlement have the same name, something that happened to us on the east side of Lake Burera, where it took me quite some time to understand why we were in Butaro and not in Butaro at the same time – Butaro is the name of both the commune and its administrative centre. The opposite thing happened to us when we crossed into the next commune: it was only after we passed through the area that I grasped that the town people referred to as Cewyu is actually called Kirambo, but is referred to by the name of the commune for which is serves as an administrative centre. The point is not that there are any hard and fast rules governing this sort of thing, rather that one should be alert to the fact that the names given on maps and in other secondary sources of information – this travel guide included – may not entirely coincide with local conventions.

HASSLES
Overcharging and bargaining
Tourists may sometimes need to bargain over prices, but this need is often exaggerated by guidebooks and other travellers. Hotels, restaurants and supermarkets generally charge fixed prices, and cases of overcharging in such places are too unusual for it to be worth challenging a price unless it is blatantly ridiculous. In other situations – mostly markets or in the street – you're bound to be asked a higher price than the vendor will expect, and a certain degree of bargaining is considered normal. It is, however, important to keep this in perspective. Some travellers, after a couple of bad experiences, start to haggle with everyone from hotel owners to old women selling fruit by the side of the road, often accompanying their negotiations with aggressive accusations of dishonesty. Such posturing may be the easiest way to find out whether you are being overcharged, but it is unfair on the majority of Rwandans who are forthright and honest in their dealings with tourists. There are better ways of handling the problem.

Minibus conductors may occasionally ask tourists for higher fares than normal. The way to counter this is to watch what other people are paying, or to ask a fellow passenger what the fare should be. The main instance where bargaining is essential is when buying handicrafts or curios. What should be understood, however, is that the fact that a curio seller is open to negotiation does not mean that he or she was initially trying to rip you off. Vendors will generally quote a starting-price knowing full well that you are going to bargain it down – they'd probably be startled if you didn't – and it is not necessary to respond aggressively or in an accusatory manner. It is impossible to say what size of reduction you should expect (some people say that you should offer half the asking price and be prepared to settle at around two-thirds, but my experience is that curio sellers are far more whimsical than such advice allows for). The sensible approach is to ask the

BARGAINING UPWARDS

The girl was pattering alongside me in the street, trying to persuade me to buy a pair of woven baskets. They were excellent quality, representing many hours of work, but would be awkward to fit into my rather small suitcase. I said, '*Non, merci.*' I'd seen the girl on other days, and normally this was enough to shake her off, but today she persisted. The price dropped lower and lower, until it was far below what was reasonable for the materials and craftsmanship. I looked at her and spotted the desperation in her face. I took her on one side (other vendors were buzzing around) and paid a fair – but still low – price, wondering whether I was a sucker. My doubt vanished when her smile of relief flashed out and she grabbed my hand in thanks, before hurrying off into the crowd. I saw her afterwards, on other days, and she always gave me a smile, but she never tried to push her wares again and nor did her fellow vendors treat me as a soft touch. Her desperation had been genuine.

price of similar items at a few different stalls before you actually contemplate buying anything.

In fruit and vegetable markets and stalls, bargaining is often the norm, even between Africans, and the most healthy approach to this sort of haggling is to view it as an enjoyable part of the travel experience. There will normally be an accepted price-band for any particular commodity. To find out what it is, listen to what other people pay (it helps if you know some Kinyarwanda) and try a few stalls – a ludicrously inflated price will drop the moment you walk away. When buying fruit and vegetables, a good way to feel out the situation is to ask for a bulk discount or a few extra items thrown in. And bear in mind that the reason why somebody is reluctant to bargain may be that they asked a fair price in the first place.

Above all, don't lose your sense of proportion. No matter how poor you may feel, it is your choice to travel on a tight budget. Most Rwandans are much poorer than you will ever be, and they do not have the luxury of choosing to travel. If you find yourself quibbling with an old lady selling a few piles of fruit by the roadside, stand back and look at the bigger picture. There is nothing wrong with occasionally erring on the side of generosity.

Theft

Rwanda, of all the African countries I've visited, is perhaps the most free of crime against tourists. Kigali is a very safe city, even at night, though it would probably be courting trouble to stumble around dark alleys with all your valuables on your person. Be aware, too, that this sort of thing can change very quickly: as recently as 1995, muggings and petty theft were practically unheard of in Malawi, but today you won't spend long in that country without meeting somebody who has been mugged or pick-pocketed. As tourism increases, so does opportunistic and petty crime. See the *Safety* section of *Chapter 3* (page 48) for a list of tips applicable to anywhere in Africa.

Begging

To anyone who knows Africa it should come as no surprise to see beggars on the streets; the surprise, in view of Rwanda's recent past, is that they aren't more numerous. Nor are they aggressive. For more about Kigali's street kids, see pages 79–81. The maimed, handicapped and very old tell an obvious story. I can't advise you what to do about them. It's true that if you give to one you risk being surrounded by a dozen – but sometimes it's hard to walk on by. Rwandans themselves often recommend that you give a few coins, because they and the country's budget have little enough to spare. I set aside a 'ration' of small notes each day – when they're used up, that's it. If you don't believe in handing over cash, *Chapter 5* lists some charities where your money will be well used.

Women travellers

I (Janice) experienced far less hassle and anxiety in Rwanda during my visits in 2000 than I have (as a lone female traveller) in very many other countries. I travelled all over the country by public transport feeling completely safe. There was a refreshing absence of 'smart Alecs' trying to engage me in dubious conversation. Once I was told rather brusquely to get off one minibus and catch another standing nearby; it turned out that the second was non-stop and they knew it would get me back to Kigali more quickly. I had the impression I was being 'looked after' because I was a woman on my own. (Having white hair helps, too!)

In one town, a young man (Congolese, as it turned out) overheard me asking directions to the guesthouse and spontaneously walked with me, chatting occasionally, to make sure I found it safely. Then he shook my hand and went off. Another time I left my unlockable duffel bag with a smiling girl in a small wooden drinks kiosk near a minibus stop while I explored a village; when I returned to collect it, it had been stowed safely in a corner and the girl's baby was gurgling happily on top. I felt a kind of 'sisterhood', particularly with village women – if I smiled it was always reciprocated, although often shyly, and I always asked a woman first if I needed help or directions.

In Kigali I spent a lot of time walking both in and outside the city centre and never felt threatened, although there are some poorer areas which (and a Rwandan woman friend agrees with me) become scarier after dark. This applies to men too, of course, but women are generally seen – rightly or wrongly! – as a target less likely to put up resistance. The rule here is to take the same sensible precautions you'd take in any capital city, and then relax.

As a matter of courtesy, watch what the local women wear and don't expose parts of yourself that they leave covered, particularly in village areas. In business areas people are smartly dressed; I was glad I'd brought a skirt and some crumple-free tops. Be sensitive to the fact that people here have suffered a great deal; if someone is reluctant to talk or to answer questions, don't push it.

You may not be as fortunate as I was. Nor do I suggest that you drop your guard and behave over-confidently. There can be bad apples in any barrel. Would-be Lotharios exist in any country and they tend to home in on female travellers. In fact, one night in Kigali a strange man did knock on my bedroom door at 11pm, but it turned out that he needed money to take a sick street kid to hospital (yes, honestly!).

I place Rwanda very high on the list of relatively hassle-free countries where good manners, honesty and trust are the order of the day – and of course this should be a two-way process.

Bribery and bureaucracy

For all you read about the subject, bribery is not the problem to travellers in Africa that it is often made out to be. Those who are most often asked for bribes are the ones with private transport; and even they only have a major problem at some borders and from traffic police in some countries (notably Mozambique and Kenya). If you are travelling in Rwanda on public transport or as part of a tour, or even if you are driving yourself, I doubt whether you need to give the question of bribery serious thought.

There is a tendency to portray African bureaucrats as difficult and inefficient in their dealings with tourists. As a rule, this reputation says more about Western prejudices than it does about Africa. Sure, you come across the odd unhelpful official, but then such is the nature of the beast everywhere. The vast majority of officials in the African countries I've visited – Rwanda included – have been courteous and helpful in their dealings with tourists, often to a degree that is almost embarrassing.

A factor in determining the response you receive from African officials – and those in Rwanda are unlikely to be an exception – will be your own attitude. If you walk into every official encounter with an aggressive, paranoid approach, you are quite likely to kindle the feeling held by many Africans that Europeans are arrogant and offhand in their dealings with other races. Instead, try to be friendly and patient, and remember that the person to whom you are talking does not speak English (or French) as a first language and may thus have difficulty understanding you. Treat people with respect rather than disdain, in Rwanda as elsewhere, and they'll tend to treat you in the same way.

FOREIGN REPRESENTATION IN RWANDA

Foreign embassies and consulates in Kigali (or in other East African countries, if there is none in Rwanda) are given below. International dialling codes are Rwanda 250; Kenya 254; Uganda 256.

Australia (Kenya) PO Box 39341 Nairobi; tel: (2) 445034, 445039; fax: 444718
Austria (Kenya) City House, Wabera St, PO Box 30560 Nairobi; tel: (2) 228281/2; fax: 331792
Belgium Rue de Nyarugenge, BP 81 Kigali; tel: 75551
Burundi 4 Rue Ntaruka, BP 714 Kigali; tel: 75512, 75718, 73465; fax: 76418

Canada 1534 Rue Akagera, BP 1177 Kigali; tel: 73210; fax: 72719
China 44 Bd de la Révolution, BP 1545 Kigali; tel: 75415; fax: 76442
Denmark (Uganda) 3 Lumumba Av, PO Box 11234 Kampala; tel: (41) 256687, 256783, 250938; email: denmark@emul.com
Egypt Av de l'Umuganda, BP 1069 Kigali; tel: 87560; fax: 87510
France Av Paul VI, BP 53 Kigali; tel: 75206, 75225; fax: 76957
Germany 8 Rue de Bugarama, BP 355 Kigali; tel: 75141, 75222; fax: 77267
India (Uganda) 11 Kyadondo Rd, PO Box 7040 Kampala; tel: (41) 257368, 242994; fax: 254943
Ireland (Uganda) Plot 12, Acacia Av, Kololo, Kampala; tel: (41) 2444348, 2444344; fax: 244353
Italy (Consulate) Bureau de la Coopération Italienne, Rue de l'Akagera, BP 2085 Kigali; tel: 78630; fax: 78851
Japan (Kenya) ICEA Building, Kenyatta Av, PO Box 60202 Nairobi; tel: (2) 2332955/6/7/8/9; fax: 216530
Libya Libyan People's Bureau, 8 Rue Cyahafi, BP 1152 Kigali; tel: 72294; fax: 72347
Netherlands (Kenya) Uchumi House, Nkrumah Av, PO Box 42537 Nairobi; tel: (2) 227111/2/3/4; fax: 334093
Norway (Uganda) Acacia Av Quarter, Kololo, PO Box 22770 Kampala; tel: (41) 343621, 346733, 346757, 340848; fax: 343936
Russian Federation 19 Av de l'Armée, BP 40 Kigali; tel/fax: 75286, 74818
South Africa (Uganda) 28 Nakasero Hill Lane, Nakasero, PO Box 22667 Kampala; tel: (41) 343543/4/6; fax: 343560
Sweden Av de la Paix, BP 2689 Kigali; tel: 72528, 72557, 72634; fax: 77932
Switzerland Swiss Agencies for Development and Cooperation, 38 Bd de la Révolution, BP 1257 Kigali; tel: 73534; fax: 72461
Tanzania Communications House, Av de l'Umuganda, BP 3973 Kigali; tel: 75656; fax: 75684
Uganda 13 Av de la Paix, BP 656 Kigali; tel/fax: 72115
United Kingdom Parcelle 1131, Bd de l'Umuganda, BP 576 Kigali; tel: 84098, 85771; fax: 82044
USA 55 Bd de la Révolution, BP 28, Kigali; tel: 75101/2/3; fax: 72128

For updates and/or additions, either ask ORTPN or check website www.rwanda1.com/government.

MEDIA AND COMMUNICATIONS
Newspapers and magazines
Rwanda has two weekly English-language newspapers: *The New Times* which supports the government and *Rwanda Newsline* which works hard at being independent. Imported dailies and weeklies from Uganda are also widely available on the streets of Kigali and Butare (but, oddly, not Ruhengeri). A very limited range of international papers can be bought at the kiosks of upmarket hotels such as the Mille Collines in Kigali. News magazines such as *Time* and *Newsweek* are available from street vendors and some bookshops.

MTN

MTN (the initials stand for Mobile Telephone Networks) is a GSM cellular network operator delivering world-class quality and service in South Africa and other African countries, including Rwanda (see *MTN Rwandacell*, below).

Mission statement

MTN's vision is: *'to become the leading telecommunications operator on the African continent. To improve telecommunications infrastructures and access throughout the countries in which we operate.'*

The vision is one of 'connectedness'. Towards the end of the 19th century, international postal services reduced the distance between people. Their champions believed that this would facilitate peace and understanding. The protagonists of telegraph and radio said the same. We could become cynical and view the state of the world as one of conflict and irreconcilable differences – one in which communication technology has not rid us of poverty, disease and war. On the other hand we could recognise the advances that have been made thanks to the technological, and subsequently social, 'connectedness' – new democracies, international cooperation in combating disease, increased transparency as a result of effective communication, etc.

For communication technologies to serve us, they need to be accessible and affordable. MTN realises that it cannot be *the* African Connection unless it addresses this challenge. Technology is converging around the consumer and the consumer is mobile. We look forward to taking these technologies into the future. Check us out on our website: www.mtn.co.za

MTN Rwandacell

MTN Rwandacell has been active in Rwanda's telecommunications sector since 1997. A network of dealers nationwide gives customers access to handsets, accessories, on-the-spot connection and a range of services such as *Voicemail*, *Faxmail* and *Call Wait & Hold*. Visitors to Rwanda can hire mobiles on arrival or have their own converted for use within the country.

Business and social contacts have been greatly facilitated – but the influence of MTN Rwandacell spreads further. It has sponsored educational establishments such as KIST, as well as helping several orphanages and local charities. It is one of the major corporate sponsors of the National Soccer Team; and enabled all Rwandan citizens to watch the 1999 CECAFA Cup free of charge. There can be no doubt of MTN Rwandacell's strong commitment to the future of Rwanda and of the Rwandan people.

Internet, email and fax

The electronic communications age is slowly establishing a foothold in Rwanda, with an increasing number of businesses having email addresses. The local servers tend to be slow, however, and subject to regular breakdowns. Public internet facilities are limited to a handful of cyber-cafés in Kigali, and a couple (not always operational, at the time of writing) in Butare. Judging by recent developments in neighbouring countries, it is simply a matter of time before reliable internet facilities become more widely available. Most hotels of mid-range and upwards have fax facilities, and in Kigali there's an efficient fax office at the main post office in Avenue de la Paix. Sending faxes here costs under US$4 to Europe and US$4.50 to the US; receiving a fax costs US$1. If you want someone at home to fax you there, the number is (250) 76574.

Telephone

Rwanda's telephone system is reasonably efficient. From overseas, it is definitely one of the easier African countries to get through to first time. The international code is 250. Because of the small size of the country, and limited number of phones, no area codes are in use.

In Kigali, international phone calls can be made from the central post office in Avenue de la Paix and from various other phone centres in the city. For calls within Rwanda the street kiosks and shops with public phones work well – calls are metered and you pay when you've finished, so there's no fussing with coins or tokens. Some of these can handle international calls too.

Cell phones (mobiles) have caught on in a big way in Rwanda. Cell-phone numbers can be recognised by an '08' prefix. Most cannot be accessed internationally. MTN RwandaCell, the country's very go-ahead supplier, is setting up dealers and service centres nationwide, and, since starting operations in Rwanda in 1998, has acquired almost as many subscribers as there are for non-mobile phones. On arrival at the airport, and in dealers such as Video Dreams (tel: 70953) opposite the Belgian School in Kigali, it's possible to buy a package to convert your own mobile (if compatible) for use in Rwanda.

Post

Post from Rwanda is cheap and reasonably reliable, but often very slow. The best place to arrange to collect Poste Restante is the main post office in Kigali. Address letters as follows:

> Philip Briggs
> Poste Restante
> Kigali (centre ville)
> Rwanda

(The 'centre ville' bit is because there's another main post office in Kigali, out in Kacyiru which is the government and business area, but it's less conveniently positioned for collecting mail.)

Yellow post-buses with *Iposita* on the side shuttle mail around Rwanda. Letterboxes outside post offices have a variety of appellations – sometimes

Boite aux Lettres, sometimes (eg: in Butare) *Box of Letters* and sometimes (as a Belgian/Flemish relic) *Brievenbus*.

Radio and television

The BBC World Service comes across loud and clear, on different frequencies according to the time of day. Local radio stations broadcast in Kinyarwanda, French, English and Swahili. TV is largely piped in from elsewhere; on the one occasion when I had a television in my hotel room, I was treated to a diet of all Michael Caine's worst movies.

SHOPPING

All basic requirements (toiletries, stationery, batteries and so forth) are available in Kigali, and, away from the capital, most towns of any size have a pharmacy as well as a reasonable supermarket or general store. In Kigali, the pharmacy in Boulevard de la Révolution is open 24 hours. Photographic equipment (film etc) is available in Kigali – try the photographic shop in Avenue de la Paix or the well-established Fotolab in Rue Kalisimbi, opposite the Isimbi Hotel – but may be scarcer (or out of date) in smaller places, so it's best to bring whatever you'll need.

For handicrafts you've a very wide range – wood carvings, weaving, pottery, baskets, clay statues, beadwork, jewellery, masks, musical instruments, banana-leaf products, batik – see *Handicrafts* in the Kigali chapter (page 109–10) and the Butare section (page 127) for more details. CDs or cassettes of Rwandan music make good gifts, as does local honey: buy it in a market and decant it into a screwtop soft-drinks bottle for travelling. In Kigali market you can buy candles of local beeswax. Locally made wines, spirits and liqueurs are heavier to carry but generally appreciated! For traditional musical instruments, you need a well-informed local advisor to help you to pick the best and most authentic.

Women can buy lengths of brightly dyed fabric in the market and have street dressmakers make up a garment on the spot; men can similarly kit themselves out with hand-tailored shirts. And just browsing in any large street market will give you dozens more ideas…

ARTS AND ENTERTAINMENT

Concerts (whether pop or classical) and displays of traditional dance are held from time to time in the various stadiums – check for details with the ORTPN (see page 49). The Centre for Franco-Rwandan Cultural Exchanges (see page 107) organises presentations of theatre, music, dance and cinema in its newly reopened theatre in Kigali – either contact the centre for its current programme or ask at the ORTPN.

PHOTOGRAPHIC TIPS

Ariadne Van Zandbergen
Equipment

Although with some thought and an eye for composition you can make nice photos with a 'point and shoot' camera, you need an SLR camera with one or more lenses if you are at all serious about photography. If you carry only one lens in Rwanda, a 28–70mm or similar zoom should be ideal. For a second lens, a 80–200mm or 70–300mm or similar will be excellent for candid shots and wildlife, and for varying your composition.

Film

Print film is the preference of most casual photographers, slide film of professionals and some dedicated amateurs. Slide film is more expensive than print film, but this is broadly compensated for by cheaper development costs. Most photographers working outdoors in Africa favour Fujichrome slide film, in particular Sensia 100, Provia 100 (the professional equivalent to Sensia) or Velvia 50. Slow films (ie: those with a low ASA (ISO) rating) produce less grainy and sharper images than fast films, but can be tricky without a tripod in low light. Velvia 50 is extremely fine-grained and shows stunning colour saturation; it is the film I normally use in soft, even light or overcast weather. Sensia or Provia may be preferable in low light, since 100 ASA allows you to work at a faster shutter speed than 50 ASA. Because 100 ASA is more tolerant of contrast, it is also preferable in harsh light.

For print photography, a combination of 100 or 200 ASA film should be ideal. For the best results it is advisable to stick to recognised brands. Fujicolor produces excellent print films, with the Superia 100 and 200 recommended.

Some basics

The automatic programmes provided with many cameras are limited in the sense that the camera cannot think, but only make calculations. A better investment than any amount of electronic wizardry would be to read a photographic manual for beginners and get to grips with such basics as the relationship between aperture and shutter speed.

Beginners should also note that a low shutter speed can result in camera shake and therefore a blurred image. For hand-held photographs of static subjects using a low magnification lens (eg: 28-70), select a shutter speed of at least 1/60th of a second. For lenses of higher magnification, the rule of thumb is that the shutter speed should be at least the inverse of the magnification (for instance, a speed of 1/300 or faster on a 300 magnification lens). You can use lower shutter speeds with a tripod.

Most modern cameras include a built-in light meter, and give users the choice of three types of metering: matrix, centre weighted or spot metering. You will need to understand how these different systems work to make proper use of them. Built-in light meters are reliable in most circumstances, but in uneven light, or where there is a lot of sky, you may want to take your metering selectively, for instance by taking a spot reading on the main subject. The meter will tend to under- or over-expose when pointed at an almost white or black subject. This can be countered by taking a reading against an 18% grey card, or a substitute such as grass or light grey rocks – basically anything that isn't almost black, almost white or highly reflective.

Dust and heat

Dust and heat are often a problem in Africa. Keep your equipment in a sealed bag, stow films in an airtight container (such as a small cooler bag), leave used films in your hotel room, and avoid changing film in dusty conditions. On rough roads, I always carry my camera equipment on my lap to protect against vibration and bumps. Never stow camera equipment or film in a car boot (it will bake), or let it stand in direct sunlight.

Light

The light in Africa is much harsher than in Europe or North America, for which reason the most striking outdoor photographs are often taken during the hour or two of 'golden light' after dawn and before sunset. Shooting in low light may enforce the use of very low shutter speeds, in which case a tripod (ideally) or monopod (lighter) will be required to avoid camera shake. Be alert to the long shadows cast by a low sun; these show up more on photographs than to the naked eye.

With careful handling, side lighting and backlighting can produce stunning effects, especially in soft light and at sunrise or sunset. Generally, however, it is best to shoot with the sun behind you. Because of this, most buildings and landscapes are essentially a 'morning shot' or 'afternoon shot', depending on the direction in which they face. When you spend a couple of nights in one place, you'll improve your results by planning the best time to take pictures of static subjects (a compass can come in handy).

When photographing people or animals in the harsh midday sun, images taken in light but even shade are likely to look nicer than those taken in direct sunlight or patchy shade, since the latter conditions create too much contrast. Fill-in flash is almost essential if you want to capture facial detail of dark-skinned people in harsh or contrasty light.

Protocol

Except in general street or market scenes, it is unacceptable to photograph people without permission. Expect some people to refuse or to ask for a donation. Even the most willing subjects will often pose stiffly when a camera is pointed at them; relax them by making a joke, and take a few shots in quick succession to improve the odds of capturing a natural pose.

Photographing gorillas

Gorillas are not an easy subject to photograph, and because you will spend only one hour with them, it's worth preparing properly. To be reasonably sure of making the most of the opportunity, carry an array of films from 100–1000ASA, which will cover most weather conditions (it is often rainy or overcast on the Virungas) and the possibility that the gorillas might be in the open or might stick to thick vegetation. Flash photography is not allowed. When exposing your pictures, be aware that the black coat might fool your camera into overexposing; rather take a reading against the green foliage (see *Some basics* above).

Culture and People

RELIGION

The Christian religions are a powerful force in Rwanda today, as witnessed by the great number of active churches throughout the country. Roman Catholicism leads the field with 65% adherence, followed by 9% for Protestantism. Pope John Paul II visited Rwanda in 1990. Some evangelical sects are now gaining ground. There is a small (1%) Muslim population, leaving a 25% following for minority and traditional beliefs, some of which may have absorbed traces of Christianity.

Traditional religion and beliefs

Rwandans traditionally believe in a supreme being called *Imana*. While *Imana*'s actions influence the whole world, Rwanda is his home where he comes to spend the night. Individuals hold informal ceremonies imploring *Imana*'s blessing. There is a tradition that, before retiring, a woman may leave a pitcher of water for *Imana* in the hope he will make her fertile.

Since words can have a magical impact, the name of *Imana* is often used when naming children, also in words of comfort, warnings against complacency, blessings, salutations, and during rites associated with marriage and death. Oaths take the form of 'May *Imana* give me a stroke', or 'May I be killed by *Imana*'. In instances when a long-desired child is born, people say to the new mother, '*Imana* has removed your shame.' Tales of *Imana* granting magical gifts to humans, who then lose these gifts through greed and disloyalty, are common.

There is a special creative act of *Imana* at the beginning of each person's life. Impregnation in itself would not be sufficient to produce a new human being. This is why the young wife, at evening, leaves a few drops of water in a jar. *Imana*, as a potter, needs some water to shape the clay into a child in her womb. Then after birth, *Imana* decides what life is to be for that individual: happy or unhappy. If, later on, a man is miserable, poverty-stricken or in bad health, it is said that he was created by *Ruremakwaci*, a name given to *Imana* when he does not create very successfully, when 'he is tired', or, for some inscrutable reason, decides that a certain destiny will be unhappy.

Rwandans traditionally believe that a life force exists in all men and animals. In animals this invisible soul disappears when the creature dies, but in humans it is transformed into *bazimu*, spirits of the dead who live in *Ikuzimu*, the underworld or the world below the soil. While the deceased kings of Rwanda constitute a kind of governing body in the underworld, there are no social distinctions. Life is neither pleasant nor unhappy. The *bazimu* continue the individuality of living persons and have the same names. Though non-material, they are localised by their activity. They do not drink, eat, or mate but their existence in other respects is similar to that in the world of the living. *Bazimu* return to the world, often to places where they used to live. Some may stay permanently in the hut where their descendants live or in the small huts made for them in the enclosure around the dwelling. *Bazimu* are generally bad. They bring misfortune, sickness, crop failure and cattle epidemics because they envy the living the cherished things they had to leave behind. Their power, actuated by the male spirits, or grandfathers, extends only over their own clan. The living members of a family must consult a diviner to discover the reason for the ancestor's anger. Respect to *bazimu* is shown principally by joining a secret cult group.

The cult of Ryangombe

Ryangombe is said to be the chief of the *imandwa*, Rwandans who are initiated into the cult of *Ryangombe*. According to Rwandan legend, *Ryangombe* was a great warrior who was accidentally killed by a buffalo during a hunting party. In order not to leave *Ryangombe*, his friends threw themselves on the bull's horns. *Imana* gave *Ryangombe* and his followers a special place, the Karisimbi volcano in the Virunga volcano chain, where they have a notably more agreeable afterlife than the other *bazimu*. The cult of *Ryangombe* became an important force of social cohesion, with Tutsi, Hutu and Twa being initiated into the cult. *Ryangombe* has said himself that he should be called upon by everybody. He is propitiated by the *babandwa*, a politico-religious fraternity, who perform rituals, chants and dances in his honour. They are not a permanent group and meet only once a year during July, at which time initiation takes place. During their festival the members of the fraternity paint themselves and decorate the spirit huts. A member of the group appears as the personification of the spirit of *Ryangombe,* carrying his sacred spear. After a ritual is performed, all members purify themselves at the stream. While the cult of *Ryangombe* is not common today, Rwandans can recall when their grandfathers or fathers participated in the *Ryangombe* festival and a popular Rwandan song recounts *Ryangombe*'s exploits as a warrior and lover.

THE ARTS
Literature

A written language was not introduced until the Europeans arrived in Rwanda at the end of the 19th century, so there is no great tradition of written literature. However, there is a wealth of oral literature in the form of myths, folk stories, legends, poetry and proverbs. These have passed on not only stories but also moral values and historical traditions from generation to generation. Before (and to some extent after) the arrival of the Europeans, the Mwami's court was a centre for training young nobles in various art forms, particularly the composition and performance of songs and poems dedicated to valour in warfare and the magnificence of their cattle.

The historian Alexis Kagame wrote extensively about oral poetry and recorded many poems in both Kinyarwanda and French. A display in Butare's National Museum (see pages 128–9) gives an idea of the intricacy of some poetic structures.

Music

Music is of great importance to all Rwandans, with variations of style and subject among the three groups. Traditionally, Tutsi songs praised excellence

MUSICAL RWANDA

Ania Dudziec

Waiting at Nyabugogo minibus station, shopping in the market, on the taxi home, at a school 'boom', before lessons every morning and afternoon – the air resonates with tunes, popular, religious or traditional. Music is everywhere.

Two types of music in particular get people up on their feet and dancing. However infectious and irresistible 'zouk' may be, nothing has quite the same effect on a dance-floor crowd as either Congolese *ndombolo* or traditional/modern Rwandan music.

The phenomenon of *ndombolo* (literally 'crazy') has spread from its home in the dance halls of Kinshasa to most of East and Central Africa. I love hearing the first few notes of a Koffi Olomide song and watching everyone jump up from their seats. The philosophy behind *ndombolo* is to do the most outrageous dance steps, and this usually ends up with all the boys and men trying to outdo each other with the craziest and most complex moves.

The yang to *ndombolo*'s crazy and wild yin are the controlled and elegant rhythms of Rwanda. The best kind of music is made by individuals, needing no props or instruments. Although much traditional music does include instruments (such as the guitar-like *inanga*), a lot of the time 'real' Rwandan music requires only hands and feet for rhythm and voices for melody. It's amazing how, whether the occasion is a friend's birthday celebration at a nightclub or a wedding party out in the countryside, traditional Rwandan music crosses all barriers of age, class, tribe or country. However dull a party is or however reserved the guests, it's Rwandan music that instantly gets people moving and dancing '*gushyayaya*', otherwise known as the 'cow dance', which is what the elegant, rhythmic stomping and outstretched arms mimic.

Rwanda, as a country in Africa, is also awash with both African and Caribbean zouk, old-style French chansons, American hip-hop, 'slows' and 'funky', and Jamaican and African reggae. But it's impossible, perhaps unnecessary, to write too much about music. The best thing is just to keep your ears open, hear something you like, find out the name, buy it and enjoy it.

and valour; Hutu songs were lighter, sometimes humorous and linked to social occasions; Twa songs related more directly to aspects of their original occupation, hunting. During the time of the monarchy, the court was dominated musically by the royal drummers, and drumming is still of great artistic importance.

A full drum ensemble typically consists of either seven or nine drums. The smallest of these, sometimes called the soprano, which is often (but not invariably) played by the director of the orchestra, sets the rhythm for each tune and is backed up by some or all of the following drums: a tenor, a harmonist alto, two baritones, two bass and two double bass. The other widely used musical instrument is the *lulunga*, an eight-stringed instrument somewhat resembling a harp. It is most often played solo, perhaps as the background to singing or dancing, but may also be used to provide a melodic interlude and/or as a counterpoint to drums.

Dance

Dance is as instinctive as music in Rwanda and its roots stretch back through the centuries. As with music, there are variations of style and subject among the three groups. Best known today are the **Intore dancers**, based in Nyanza and Butare, who perform both nationally and internationally. At the time of the monarchy and for centuries before the arrival of the Europeans, the Intore dancers at the royal court were selected young men who had received a privileged education and choreographic training in order to entertain their masters and to perform at special functions. The name *intore* means 'best', signifying that only the best of them were chosen for this honour.

Traditionally their performances consisted mainly of warlike dances, such as the *ikuma* (lance), *umeheto* (bow) and *ingabo* (shield), in which they carried authentic weapons. In the 20th century dummy weapons were substituted, the dances were given more peaceful names and rhythm and movement (rather than warfare) became their main feature. The Intore dancers were divided into two groups. The first group, the *indashyikirwa* or 'unsurpassables', were all Tutsi. The second, the *ishyaka* or 'those who challenge by effort', were Twa led by a Tutsi. A description nearly three-quarters of a century old leads us through a performance:

> In the opening movement, the group of Twa advances with measured step. The musicians also are Twa. The dancers form a square or line up in double file. They perform the opening sequence and then a dance representing 'safety'. Next they stand at ease, chanting the exploits of real or imaginary Rwandan heroes. Then come movements representing 'tattooing', 'stability', 'the incomparable' and 'the most difficult case'. At this point the Tutsi dancers leap into the arena, armed, to mingle with the Twa and demonstrate that they deserve the name of 'unsurpassables'. The names of some of their dances translate into English as 'that which puts an end to all discussion', 'the crested crane', 'the exit dance' and 'thanks'.

The costume worn by the Tutsi dancers consists of either a short
floral skirt or a leopard skin wound around their legs. Crossed straps
decorated with coloured beads are generally worn across the chest.
On their heads they wear a fringe of white colobus monkey fur.
Depending on the theme of the dance and the region they may carry
a bow, a spear or a stick decorated with a long tail of raffia. Around
their ankles they wear bells, the sound of which adds to the rhythm of
the dance.

The Intore dancers perform regularly today and it's a dramatic spectacle. You
may come across them in Kigali, Nyanza, Butare – or abroad, on one of their
tours. Ask at the tourist office in Kigali for details of any scheduled
performances. See also the photo opposite page 148.

Handicrafts
As in other countries, most genuinely traditional handicrafts have a practical
use or are decorated forms of everyday objects. An object which gives purely
visual pleasure and is unrelated to any function has probably evolved for the
tourist market – although it is none the worse for that. In Rwanda the weaving
(of bowls, mats, baskets, storage containers, etc) from various natural fibres is
particularly fine. The quality of wood-carving is variable, but at best it's
excellent. Pottery made by the Twa community is plain but strong and its
uncluttered style is attractive. See *Chapter 6* (pages 109–10) for details of where
to find handicrafts on sale.

PEOPLE
To quote from the website of the Rwandan Embassy in Washington DC:

> Inhabitants of Rwanda are called 'Banyarwanda'. They speak the same
> language, have the same culture, live on the same hills and, for
> centuries, have intermarried. The three 'ethnic' groups are the
> Bahutu, the Batutsi and the Batwa, referred to in the West as Hutus,
> Tutsis and Twas. The current population of Rwanda is about eight
> million.
>
> www.rwandemb.org

In fact, matters may not be quite so clear-cut and the insistence on 'same-ness'
should not be carried to the extent of concealing historical individuality. But
there's no doubt that the people of Rwanda in general are committed to
overcoming any awkward differences. It's worth repeating a story, also
mentioned in *Chapter 8*, from the genocide, about schoolgirls who were told
by the killers to divide up into Hutus and Tutsis (with the implication that the
Hutus would be spared). The girls refused, saying that they were all
Rwandans. So all of them died. In a different context, a genocide survivor
wrote: 'Before the genocide, Hutus and Tutsis lived together. I remember we
used to play with Hutu children and share everything. There were even
intermarriages. The only time when we felt discriminated against was when a

A FEW HUMAN STATISTICS...

Taken from the report Rwanda Development Indicators, *published by the Ministry of Finance and Economic Planning in July 2000*

Population 4,831,527 in 1978; estimated 8.1 million in 1999; women 54% of population and 60% of workforce, particularly in agriculture

Life expectancy Men 48 years; women 50 years (Kenya 47/48; UK 74.4/79.7)

Major cause of death in children under five years Malaria

Access to health services 87%, but seriously under-utilised

Ratio of doctors One physician per 52,000 people (in 1998 66,666)

Budgetary allocation to the health sector 0.6% of GDP

HIV infection in adults aged 15 to 49 13.7% (Sub-Saharan Africa average: 7.3%)

Adult literacy 48.3%

Budgetary allocation to education 2.7% of GDP

Primary school enrolment gross 89%, net 65% (only 45% of teachers were qualified)

Secondary school enrolment only 7% in 1998, now rising

GNP average per person US$260 (and secondary schooling can cost US$250...)

Budgetary allocation to the social sector 4.6% of GDP

Households headed by women (mainly widows) 32% (1996 figure)

Access to safe drinking water 44%

Families still needing housing 305,086 (they live in damaged houses or tents, or are occupying houses illegally)

Population living below the poverty threshold 65.4% (compared with 71.1% in 1996)

Main export crops Coffee and tea, earned around US$49 million in 1999

Tourism 1,695 visitors to National Parks in 1999 (53% from Europe, 7% North America)

Private cars 7,241 in 1990 and 10,795 in 1999

Minibus-taxis 985 in 1990, 3,607 in 1999

Television ownership 2% (1999)

place at school, or a job, was given to a Hutu, even if there was a Tutsi more qualified for it. But this was no reason for hatred between the two groups.' However, of course individual attitudes cannot accurately be extrapolated to the whole country.

The following section generally describes what people – just *people*, without any other label – are doing in and about Rwanda today. The exception is the Twa, who do have a problem specific to their origins and are therefore named.

The Batwa

Elaine Gardner

The indigenous Twa or 'pygmy' people of Rwanda are a particularly vulnerable and disadvantaged group, and among the poorest of an already impoverished population. Of Rwanda's three groups – Tutsi, Hutu and Twa – the Twa are predominantly specialised as potters and hunter-gatherers, and are famous for their songs and dances. Formerly the Batwa musicians and dancers performed for the king. Much of their music and dance has now been adopted by other Rwandans and today forms a major part of Rwanda's renowned national performance art. The Twa are also respected for their skills in traditional medicine. But as an indigenous people and former forest dwellers, the Twa have long been stereotyped by the rest of society as morally, physically and intellectually deficient. Always a marginalised minority group, during the genocide the Twa suffered disproportionately – with an estimated 30% of the Twa population killed or missing compared with less than 14% of the population overall. The Rwandan Twa are now estimated at around 22,000 (the total population of Twa in the whole Great Lakes region is estimated at 70–86,000), in a Rwandan population which has topped eight million overall. Amongst the most vulnerable categories now emerging in Rwandan society are female-headed households, and this is particularly the case among the Twa, where many of the surviving communities are populated only by widows and orphans.

The Twa's rights to their original forest lands were never recognised, with the result that, as Rwanda's forests were cleared for Hutu and Tutsi farms and pastures, the Twa were dispossessed, and are now facing a severe land crisis. Surveys carried out in 1993 showed that only 2% of Twa had sufficient land for their needs. Over 70% of Twa survive from begging, casual day labour and working on other people's fields in return for food. Survival of the Twa people is actually at risk, with their numbers so seriously diminished and their health and opportunity now in such reduced straits.

A problem in respect of education is that several Twa children a year are completing their final primary school exams with good results, but then cannot afford the cost of secondary schooling so are blocked and unable to fulfil their potential. Sponsorships of less than US$250 annually (equivalent to the cost of just one visit to the gorillas) would help them to continue. Prospective sponsors should ask for more details from CAURWA (below).

CAURWA

As a result particularly of sustained efforts by the organisation CAURWA (Communauté des Autochtones Rwandais), which is an NGO working for the Twa people, their dire situation is beginning to be recognised by the Rwandan authorities. In April 2000 the newly established National Unity and Reconciliation Commission (see page 78) acknowledged: 'the marginalisation of the Twa people is a dark side of our society… they have been systematically forgotten as if they do not exist… They have genuine concerns.' The Commission has recommended affirmative action for the Twa in terms of free education and health services.

CAURWA's aims are to increase the incomes of rural Twa households, foster their sense of pride in themselves and encourage recognition of the unique contribution of Twa people to Rwandan culture, thereby bringing the Twa in from the margins of social and economic exclusion. In its work to help strengthen communities, and in addition to advocacy and schooling, CAURWA is also involved in supporting income-generating projects, whether directly or indirectly.

CAURWA's pottery project

Pottery production is a traditional Twa activity, a skill worthy of pride and an opportunity to generate a sustainable income. But potters are amongst the poorest people in Rwanda and, without access to training in current business skills and modern market knowledge, Twa potters are vulnerable to making losses, thus accelerating their descent into poverty.

CAURWA's pottery project is examining the viability of Twa pottery as a business enterprise and source of income. Its intention is not only to provide the potters with a (rare) opportunity to learn business, technical and marketing skills, but also to create among them the capacity and opportunity to adapt to change, to make informed decisions about their own future, and to meet the commercial challenge of the times, thereby raising their income level and esteem. The pottery project respects and promotes the principles of Fair Trade:

- fair wages in the local context
- participation in decision making
- safe working conditions and practice
- positive/improving situation for young women
- protection of children and young workers
- protection of the natural environment

Rwandan pottery is known for its attractiveness and distinction. The traditional pots are usually a natural terracotta, sometimes with darkly iridescent glints from the fire, or often coloured totally black – matt and sleek. The CAURWA potters produce traditional pots and in addition are learning new designs, so that they can offer products that suit both traditional and contemporary taste. The objectives of the pottery project are:

- to produce products that are appropriate to market demands, in terms of design, quantity, punctual delivery, price and quality, and that provide a positive return for producers
- to develop the CAURWA sales outlet in Kigali as a focal point from which to penetrate the local market further, first in Kigali and later elsewhere
- to identify and access other and wider market opportunities.

Batwa dance

All potters' groups continue to celebrate and enjoy their distinctive dances. Several of the groups come together to rehearse regularly, often on a weekly basis – and often trained by a member of the community whose knowledge and interpretation of the dance are particularly skilful. Any visitor who is in the right place at the right time is welcome to join in, whether as just a spectator or as a dancing participant to the drum-beat and song.

Note Tourists who would like to visit a Twa pottery workshop, to see a session of traditional dance (a donation to the dancers is always welcome) or to find out more about CAURWA's activities in Rwanda should contact (in French) the CAURWA office in Kigali: tel/fax: 77640; BP 3809 Kigali; email: CAURWA@Rwandatel1.Rwanda1.com. Also see further details of CAURWA and the Forest Peoples' Project on pages 88–9.

Rwandan women – determined to contribute to national recovery
Angelina Konkobwa Muganza

Currently Rwanda's population is approximately eight million people of whom an estimated 54% are female. As a result of the 1994 genocide there are many female-headed households; it claimed over one million lives within just 100 days, and now over 120,000 people (mostly men) are in prison on genocide charges. All of these women, regardless of how they became heads of households, face the challenge of rebuilding Rwanda's shattered society. Caring for the remaining children and for the elderly is a difficult task.

Many Rwandan women are illiterate. This, among other things, means that they are not employable in the public or private sectors. Most of them are subsistence farmers and some do petty trade to earn a living. Rwandan women have not been part of the decision-making process of their country because of illiteracy and the highly patriarchal nature of Rwandan society. It is no wonder that almost all of them regret the acts of violence and the genocide that have left them with the present challenges.

The education of girls and women is now a priority for the government of Rwanda. The government is working to achieve education for all despite the financial constraint that it is facing, especially while rebuilding the shattered economy. Schools opened immediately after the genocide; those that were destroyed have been repaired and new ones have been built though donor funding. There is a need for more schools and teachers. The British charity, VSO, has sent over 50 teachers to Rwanda to assist in the field of higher education.

Women have not stood idle in the promotion of education for young Rwandans. For example, the Forum for African Women Educationalists (FAWE), a Rwandan chapter of a Pan-African women's NGO, was established in 1997 (mostly by women returning to Rwanda from exile in other countries) to promote girls' education. These are women who grew up as refugee girls and managed to get education through grants or sponsorship, mostly from Europe or the UNHCR. They believe that, with the help of some sponsorship towards education, even very poor women can make a success of their lives. FAWE encourages parents to send all their children to school without

NATIONAL UNITY AND RECONCILIATION COMMISSION

This was established by parliamentary law in 1999. Its functions are listed as:

- Organising and overseeing national public debates aimed at promoting national unity and reconciliation of the Rwandan people.
- Using all possible means to sensitise Rwandans towards unity and to place this on a firm foundation.
- Conceiving and disseminating ideas and initiatives aimed at promoting peace among Rwandans, and encouraging a culture of unity and reconciliation.
- Denouncing any written or declared ideas and materials seeking to disunite Rwandan people.
- Preparing and co-ordinating Rwanda's programmes of promoting unity and reconciliation.
- Educating Rwandans on their rights, and assisting in building a culture of tolerance and respect of other people's rights.
- Giving advice to institutions charged with drafting laws aimed at fostering unity and reconciliation.
- Monitoring closely whether government organs respect and observe policies of national unity and reconciliation.
- Monitoring whether political parties, leaders and the population respect and observe policies of national unity and reconciliation practices.

A **National Summit** is held once a year, chaired by the President of Rwanda and attended by community leaders from all the country's communities. Its function is to review progress and accomplishments in respect of unity and reconciliation.

The **Commission's Council** is supervised by a nominated president and consists of 12 members, including a president, vice president and executive secretary. The council meets monthly and reviews the programmes of the Permanent Secretariat; it actively mentors the Permanent Secretariat to ensure that its programmes are proving effective.

The **Permanent Secretariat** is managed by the executive secretary and has the following functions: overseeing the day-to-day running of the commission; administering and managing the commission's human and financial resources; linking the commission to the Government and other institutions in unity-building efforts; consulting the national leadership extensively; consulting extensively with civic society, eg: community-based organisations and churches; mobilising international agencies in similar endeavours; seeking national and international support for Rwandan reconciliation efforts.

discrimination. Teachers too are a target so that they work towards equality in education. FAWE also looks for bursaries for poor girls who would otherwise not attend school due to lack of school fees. So far FAWE has received funding for about 60 girls to attend secondary schools within Rwanda.

Rwanda has a government ministry responsible for the empowerment of women and for gender mainstreaming. It has been in existence since 1994 and faces the challenge of reversing a situation in which women have been left behind as regards education, participation in decision-making processes and property ownership. Women are helped to run income-generating projects so that they can send their children to school and take care of their families. Also there is a programme of organising women in female councils at all administrative levels, regardless of their differences and history, to enable them to have a voice and to participate. This programme is proving to be a stepping stone for national reconciliation, since women from different backgrounds come together to analyse common problems and to make plans for their well-being. The participation of women in decision-making is progressing well, and their contribution is being recognised by the national leadership at all levels.

The political will in Rwanda is strongly in favour of women's empowerment. Of course national resources are limited, but where there is a will, there is a way.

For more details of FAWE and how to contribute to its work, contact Ms Anne Gahongayire, FAWE Rwanda Chapter, PO Box 622 Kigali; tel: 82514; email: fawerwa@rwanda1.com. Another organisation that is doing useful work with and for women is the Rwandan Women's Network, founded in 1997, which sponsors several activities such as shelter construction and rehabilitation, micro-credit projects, and the Polyclinic of Hope, a medical and social centre for women victims of rape and violence. Several international agencies have recognised and contributed to its work but additional donations are needed and welcomed. Contact Mary Balikongeri, BP 3157 Kigali; or Peter, tel (mobile): 08511050; email rwawnet@rwandatel1.com.

Rwanda's street children
Juliana Kantengwa

Some 3,000 to 5,000 children in Rwanda live on the streets of the major towns like Kigali, Butare and Gisenyi. Their ages range anywhere between four and 16 years. Most Rwandans believe that the number of children on the streets of Kigali was never as high as this before the genocide. The phenomenon has a lot to do with some of the sequels of 1994's tragic events.

There are many reasons why children prefer street life to a family environment. The children on the Rwandan streets fall into two main categories: those who spend only their days on the street but retire at night to some 'home' or even a family, and those who live day in and day out entirely on the street. Asked why they prefer living on the streets, some children give the reason that they are destitute orphans with no known adult to care for them; others cite family poverty, domestic violence of one form or another, or desire to exercise freedom in an environment where there are no dos and

AFTER THE GENOCIDE...

A report produced in July 2000 by the Statistics Department of Rwanda's Ministry of Finance and Economic Planning concludes that the horrors of the 1994 genocide have left large segments of the population with severe mental health problems that cannot in fact be expressed in statistics. Many people have lost family members, and/or have witnessed, experienced (or participated in) massacres or rapes. A National Trauma Survey by UNICEF in 1995, quoted in the same report, estimated the percentages of children affected by the genocide as follows:

- 99.9% witnessed violence
- 79.6% experienced death in the family
- 69.5% witnessed someone being killed or injured
- 61.5% were threatened with death
- 90.6% believed they would die
- 57.7% witnessed killings or injuries with machete
- 31.4% witnessed rape or sexual assault
- 87.5% saw dead bodies or parts of bodies

Does it make you look at the street kids in Kigali and Butare a little differently...?

don'ts; yet others claim feelings of alienation at home. The last category fall into a group of children who suffered some period of separation from their families as a result of the 1994 events and, once they were reunited, home no longer felt like home to them. To this group of children home was no longer home because what used to be dear to them was no longer there. Many have touching stories to tell and, when asked about their individual experiences, some talk animatedly but close attention reveals the unspoken pain behind their eyes. 'Yes, they have fled from home because home is no longer home.'

Maybe the beloved mother is no longer at home and going back to the same house awakens memories of her last cries as she was beaten to death in front of the child. Maybe the father got remarried to someone whom the child can't accept, whose presence reminds the child of those who came to carry mum away. Maybe the child has been reunited with a caring aunt or uncle, but who lives on the hill where all his former playmates were buried alive.

The memories are too real to tolerate. Maybe his dad is in prison accused of genocide; the youngster actually saw him doing it and no longer wants to live as a member of that family; maybe his friends got killed by his very own parents and the young child hopes to cleanse that guilt by not living with that family. Maybe the surviving parent has remarried and the step-parent just does not match the late mum/dad of the affected child.

Maybe mum brings men home since dad died and the child does not want to put up with it. Or maybe both mum and dad fight every night, and other street children enticed him/her to join them on the street where there are no domestic quarrels. Maybe the child escaped from home poverty in the hope of earning good money on the streets as advised by peers.

Whatever reasons forced the children to leave home, the fate that awaits them on the unfriendly streets is usually the same. Hunger, cold nights, disease, harassment, loneliness, crime, pickpocketing, eating off garbage pits, sleeping in doorways or on pavements and braving the coldness of the night, sniffing solvents or smoking marijuana and cigarettes, begging from unwilling donors, and the emptiness of street life – these and many more are elements in the life of a street child.

For street girls, the story is even more precarious, braving all that the boys go through plus having to live with daily sexual harassment and sexual violence from fellow *mayibobos* (the local slang for street children) as well as street vendors and other adults, men from the real world.

Most of the girls talked to in a girls' drop-in centre in the country did acknowledge some form of sexual engagement with strangers who picked them from the street for an evening meal or a drink. While the life of all street children in Rwanda can be said to be in a sorry state and in need of attention, the girls need even more urgent rescue measures from whoever has a human heart because of the threat of HIV/AIDS and other inherent female risks.

I would like to make a special appeal to Rwandan adults to take in an extra kid so that there are fewer on the streets, and to be more responsive to the needs of children. They need a listening ear and yearn to be understood.

Adults can still do a lot, even for the children already on the streets. Children need to be understood by adults, they too have ideas and opinions; they are still humans and need to be loved. Above all, they are still children and therefore still in need of adult care. Street children are not just vagabonds; they are victims of our own irresponsibility as adults in charge of the society they live in, or as parents who force them out of homes. We owe them education, clothing, food, shelter and healthcare.

A charity on the outskirts of Kigali that does a good job for street kids is the Centre Presbytérien d'Amour de Jeunes, PO Box 56 Kigali; tel/fax: 76929.

Association pour la Promotion de l'Education et de la Culture (APEC)

This is an example, of which there are many others in Rwanda, of what is being achieved privately by groups of concerned, dedicated people working together. Back in 1988, a small group of parents and educators in Tumba, a village near Butare, set up the *Association pour la Promotion de l'Education à Tumba (APET)*, with the aim of promoting education in and around their home village. They established the Ikibondo pre-school, whose object – in tune with that of the association – was for children not only to receive good education but also to learn good behaviour.

After the genocide, those members who had survived reassembled, together with new recruits, to continue their project. In 1996 they theoretically extended its horizons beyond Tumba, renaming it the *Association pour la*

Promotion de l'Education et de la Culture (APEC), although in practice it has not moved physically.

In 2000 the two pre-school classes were continuing, with 27 pupils in each; with the addition of the first three classes of primary school, attended by 34, 18 and 12 pupils respectively. Of these 118 children three are orphans, 36 have no fathers and three have no mothers. There are five salaried teachers, following the national curriculum. The children are bright, confident, lively and (at least on the occasion of this observer's visit!) very well behaved. They learn French and English, and have access to extra-curricular activities (ballet, evening courses, etc).

Further achievements are blocked by lack of funds and the members of the Association are desperately seeking ways to make the school self-financing. Even now, they have hardly any equipment. With proper funding, they have the ability and organisation to make worthwhile progress. Some grants are provided by the Belgian charity *Aid to Displaced Persons* – see page 88.

This association – and many others like it all around Rwanda – is an example of the grass-roots energy and determination that are fuelling the country's recovery.

–o–o–o–o–o–

MC TELLS HER STORY

It was on the night of April 6 1994 that the president of Rwanda died when his plane was attacked. We were at home and didn't know anything had happened – but then at about five o'clock the next morning I heard a lot of people in the area around our house. I quickly ran downstairs to see what was happening and I saw they were armed, with both military and traditional weapons. They were our friends and neighbours, teenage boys and girls like me as well as older men and women, so I thought they must be going to deal with some disturbance in the neighbourhood. I wanted to support them so I went back indoors and told the others someone was in trouble, and that we should join in with the group who were going to help. Back in my bedroom, I didn't understand why I felt a sudden stab of fear.

My older sister told me to pray before I left the house but I said we should hurry in case the others were in danger. We were five girls: my sister and I, and three cousins who were visiting us. Papa was in another house. As we started to pray, the people outside began forcing the door, and some of them climbed on the roof and tried to break through it, and then they poured petrol on the roof so as to burn us inside our house. When we'd finished praying I was the first to go out, and to my horror I saw Papa lying dead in the courtyard. The whole hill was covered in smoke and I heard a lot of noise. We got out of the house but then two of my cousins were killed directly in front of the door. I, my sister and our other cousin ran to hide in the toilet behind the house, just as the mob were entering to loot our possessions. We stayed there all day, hearing the sound of our house burning, and that night we fled into the nearby forest.

On the second day they came to look for the people hiding in the forest, there were so many of them and they came with dogs and with fire. They set fire to the forest and we had to come out, together with others who had been hiding there. They took us to their killing-ground, their *abattoir* [slaughterhouse]; they had also brought my uncle's children and killed them one by one with inexplicable cruelty, torturing them. Girls were raped. They left me, saying that I was there to watch and that I would be killed last of all, because I was the youngest of the family, and that first I'd have to tell them the whereabouts of my brothers who hadn't been in the house. The killing went on for four days – one day they might cut off the feet, the next day the arms, then other parts of the body except for the heart, so that the victim would stay alive as long as possible. My job was to dig the ditch where the bodies were to be thrown, and to bury them, making sure that nothing was left behind to make the place dirty. Last of all they killed my older sister, and I buried her. Then I managed to get away – I ran into Lake Muhazi, saying to myself that it was better to die cleanly in the water than to be killed like the others. After three days in and beside the lake, on the night of the fourth day I managed to get to the church of Rukara, where the people of that parish had gathered for safety.

At that time the war was so fierce, they were killing people as if they were felling trees. When I got to the church I went into a room where other people were sheltering – but 30 minutes later the *interahamwe* arrived. The doors were solid so they broke the glass of the windows with stones, grenades and bombs. Finally they forced open the doors and came in, killing the people inside with machetes, spears and wooden clubs studded with nails. When they thought everyone was dead they poured petrol on the bodies and on the roof and set it alight. I was sitting in a corner, I was so exhausted that I slept despite what was happening around me, but then I was awakened by the heat and by the cries of the people who were still alive. I stayed in my corner wishing that death would come quickly. Because of the heat I took off all my clothes. I stayed like that all night, naked, waiting for death. At about 2pm the next day I felt so hot and thirsty that it seemed better to be killed by men than by fire but it was difficult to know how to get out of the burnt building. When with God's help I managed it and emerged, naked as the day I was born, I saw the *interahamwe* killing the people who were outside so I hid among the dead bodies, and no-one knew that I was still alive. I was among the bodies for two days and then on the third day I said to myself, 'Why are you hiding?' I stood up and shouted, 'Will someone put me out of my misery, I'm so tired and I just want to die!' Then I saw soldiers coming towards me and I asked them to kill me, but they said they were there to save, not to kill. They were the soldiers of the advancing FPR and we were saved. They tried to pick out the living from among the dead; some were still breathing but had no limbs, others still had their limbs but no eyes. It was unimaginable.

They took the survivors to the hospital at Gahini. We camped there in the hospital. I was with my niece and two little cousins – we had nothing and no-one, no family to comfort us. My niece was only four years old and because of the time she'd spent outside with the wild animals she had begun to behave and sound like an animal; when I approached her with food or drink she fled or tried to bite me. And she had been badly injured. It was too much for me – I began to despair, to wish I hadn't survived. All my life I'd been the youngest in the family, with adults to look after me, and suddenly life had become so terrible.

But as time passed, things changed. The war ended, my brothers returned and we tried to look after the children. Their health improved, so did their morale, and they became more hopeful. The same happened to me. God be praised for it. But because of grief I spent eight months without speaking. It was a way of rebelling against God who had left me alone in this impossible position.

One day in the ninth month I shut myself in my room and cried until evening. Then I said to myself: 'This isn't very intelligent! Who do you think is going to come and comfort you? Don't you know that there are little children who depend on you now? Do you think that crying all day is going to produce the answers to your problems? It's up to you now – you've got to cope with your own life and the lives of the children who need you.'

I felt guilty for my past weakness and I asked God to forgive me and to help me. Next morning I was the first person up. I was staying with my aunt and I went to her room and asked her forgiveness. She was astonished and very happy, we told the news to everyone who knew me and a Mass of thanks was held. It was the cause for great celebration in my aunt's house. Later I went back to secondary school and completed my studies.

Since that day I've felt strengthened, determined to live. I'm engaged as a real combatant in my own life and the lives of others in need. You're hearing this today from a young woman who is very optimistic about life. My optimism is based on this principle: 'Work to earn your own living and help those who are suffering. Put the past behind you, concentrate on the present, and then the future will be good.'

Today I have dreams and aspirations to achieve so that my own future and those of my friends and family will be manageable, comfortable and happy. I wish this also for all Rwandans, particularly those who feel their lives are miserable and that they cannot cope. I'm not rich and I'm not strong, but with the little that I have, and with encouragement and help from others, I hope for success, peace in my country and a good future for all Rwandans. I'll do everything I can to promote the rehabilitation of my country and the reconciliation of its people.

I would be ungrateful if I didn't thank all those who have worked to achieve peace for Rwanda, all those who have played their part so that Rwandans may survive. My personal thanks go to Janice Booth for her efforts to discover whether any member of her friend's family was still alive. He was my brother. My thanks too to all those who are collaborating to produce this guidebook to Rwanda – so important for a country emerging from a war which has damaged tourism. I speak for other Rwandans when I say that we will do our best to help and encourage you in every way possible.

BECOMING INVOLVED

You may leave Rwanda without a backward glance, or you may find that it has affected you more than you realised. As Dorette Boshoff and David Hartley said on page 53, it's an amazing country. If you do want to become further involved with its people and its culture, a few suggestions are given below, to

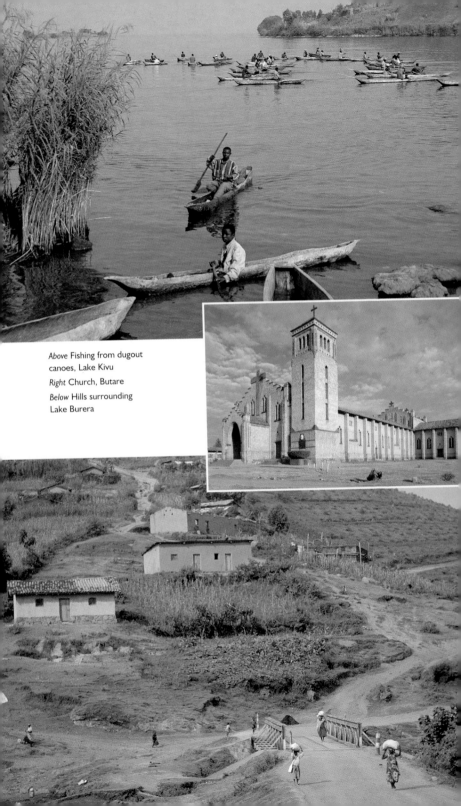

Above Fishing from dugout
canoes, Lake Kivu

Right Church, Butare

Below Hills surrounding
Lake Burera

add to those mentioned in the previous section, and you can certainly track down others for yourselves.

Rwanda United Kingdom Goodwill Organisation (RUGO)
Mike Hughes

The genocide in 1994 brought Rwanda to the world's attention through the horror that filled our TV screens and made headlines in the press. In the period from April 1994 to July 1994 up to one million people were killed. Rugo was formally launched on July 4 1997, on the third anniversary of the end of Rwanda's genocide. The aim of the organisation is to provide a channel whereby the people of the UK can support the people of Rwanda as they rebuild their lives and their country.

RUGO was granted charity status in February 1999 with the Baroness Chalker of Wallasey as its patron; it is registered UK charity number 1074088. RUGO's stated mission is:

> The advancement of education and training of the people of Rwanda
> and the relief of poverty, sickness and distress, through the provision
> and support of community based projects, designed to improve the
> conditions of life for those in necessitous circumstances.

Since its launch RUGO has:

* issued newsletters to provide information about the situation in Rwanda and to recruit support for RUGO.
* received donations of computers and books, which have been sent the National University of Rwanda in Butare.
* organised social events to raise funds, promote Rwandan culture, and encourage support from people in the UK.
* worked with the University of Dundee to help facilitate a scholarship for a Rwandan student in that university.
* organised memorial services on the anniversary of the genocide in Rwanda in remembrance of the victims.
* supported a scheme in Nottingham, which collects donations for orphanages in Rwanda.

The main project that RUGO is supporting is a vocational school to train technicians for the development of Rwanda. The school will be built at Nyamata, about 30km south of the capital Kigali, in an area where some of the worst massacres in the 1994 genocide took place.

RUGO is managed by a committee, elected at the annual general meeting, which considers applications for help and the running of RUGO projects and events. Its income derives from members' subscriptions, donations from well-wishers and fundraising activities.

The organisation employs no-one, is administered by volunteers, and thus almost every penny contributed goes towards RUGO's objectives.

By joining RUGO, members support genuinely good causes, are kept in touch with events in Rwanda, and are invited to attend open meetings and social events which refresh old friendships and create new ones. The annual subscription (December 2000) stands at £20 for an individual, £30 for a family and £100 for corporate bodies.

More details of RUGO can be found on its website: www.rugo.org. If you would like further information, you are welcome to contact either Mike Hughes (Chairman) on 01252 861059, or Ernest Sagaga (Secretary) on 0208 4273186. Or write to: Ernest Sagaga, RUGO Secretary, 158A Harrow View, Harrow, Middlesex HA1 4TL, UK.

Nyamata Vocational School Project

Seven years on from on the darkest time in its history, Rwanda is in the process of rebuilding itself. This is demonstrated by the many different projects being run by either the Rwandan government or NGOs across the whole of Rwanda.

One of the consequences of the genocide is that most of Rwanda's artisans have been lost, and the Nyamata Vocational School is one of the projects instigated by the government to help rebuild this skill base.

Artisans are the backbone of most industrial developments as they make up the majority of the technical workforce. On a personal level, artisans can support themselves by using their skills to produce and sell goods that are relevant to the needs of the society around them. Therefore, to a country such as Rwanda, the training of artisans is necessary for its development economically, as these people will form the lion's share of the labour force that will support industry, the agricultural sector, and small-scale production at every level of Rwandan life.

Nyamata is about 30km south of the capital Kigali and is an area where some of the worst massacres of the genocide took place. Construction of the school at Nyamata is well under way with the initial six classroom blocks now at roof level. This is being funded by the Rwandan government. They approached RUGO for help with supporting the school, as vocational training is high among RUGO's objectives.

RUGO's initial support is limited to raising the funds needed to equip priority departments of the school when it enrols its first students at the end of 2001. These departments include:

* masonry and construction
* carpentry
* plumbing/appropriate technology
* information technology
* tailoring.

The cost of this is estimated at approximately £120,000. The Rwandan Government will carry out the physical construction of the school as well as its actual operation and staffing. The funds RUGO has secured to date amount to over £40,000, which includes a grant of £25,000 from the Tudor Trust. Donations have also been received from many companies and individuals.

Future courses to be included within the curriculum include:

- motor vehicle repair
- welding and fabrication
- electrical installation
- fitting and turning
- home economics
- refrigeration and air conditioning
- electronics for TV and radio repair.

Support is welcomed from individuals and companies in many forms such as:

- donation of equipment – not necessarily new – to suit any of the above courses
- short-term secondment of suitable personnel to help with the project
- cash donations
- storage and transport facilities.

If you are able to help, please contact: Mike Hughes, RUGO Chairman, 28 Hardy Avenue, Yateley, Hampshire, GU46 6XU, UK; tel: 01252 861059.

Kigali public library

The Rotary Club of Kigali-Virunga, in partnership with the local Rwandan community and with support from friends and well-wishers overseas, is committed to providing Rwanda with its first public library. The aim is to raise US$800,000 in order to build and equip the library and provide initial staff training. Already over a quarter of this amount has been raised, donated or pledged. Fundraising so far has included activities as diverse as the sale of promotional T-shirts and a successful secondhand-book sale in Kigali. Main supporters include the Rwandan tea company SORWATHE and the Atlanta-based Dian Fossey Gorilla Fund (DFGFI). In the library, the conservation/gorilla section will be named after Dr Dian Fossey in recognition of the DFGFI's support.

A competition was held to choose the best design from those submitted by architects and building contractors worldwide. The winner was Balkan (Rwanda) in partnership with NPD-Contraco (Rwanda) and Masinoprojekt Kopring (Yugoslavia). The winning design is a modern building reflecting the elegance of Rwandan art and culture, which will be a landmark for many years to come.

This is an exciting project and everyone can help! If you're in Kigali, drop off any unwanted books (or make donations) at the American Embassy in Boulevard de la Révolution, c/o Beth Payne. It's right in the centre of town. In the US or Canada, post books to Beth Payne, American Embassy Kigali, 2210 Kigali Place, Washington DC, 20521-2210. For information about mailing from other countries and/or transferring donations, email: kigalilibrary@aol.com.

The need of the moment is for children's books and French novels, but don't feel restricted by that – if a book isn't suitable to put into the library it can be sold to raise funds. As one of the fundraising leaflets comments, 'Books can be the people we never get to meet.'

Aid to Displaced Persons

This Belgian-based organisation, created by Dominique Pire (Nobel Peace Prizewinner in 1958), has since its inception been helping refugees in Europe and currently aids asylum-seekers in Belgium.

Elsewhere, its programme of **World Sponsorships** helps to provide normal schooling for displaced and refugee children, for example in various countries of Latin America, Slovenia, Kosovo, Lebanon, Burundi – and Rwanda, where in 1995 it launched a programme of sponsorships to provide schooling for teenagers who are either orphaned or live away from their families. The families looking after them receive no other help and often face great difficulty in paying the cost of their education. In every school year, over 200 young people are able to continue their studies thanks to the help and moral support of a sponsor. Several dozen students have already managed to complete their secondary schooling; some are now working while others have moved on to higher education. A sponsorship of this kind costs around US$250 (£160) a year and correspondence between sponsor and student is sometimes possible.

World Sponsorships also provides help to projects which have been set up through local initiative. In Nyanza, the *Ecole Sécondaire des Parents de Nyanza* provides courses in nursing, law/administration and accountancy/commerce. It has 700 pupils, of whom over 300 are orphans. Since 1995, World Sponsorships have been paying the salary of a part-time nursing instructor. At the Ikibondo School in Tumba (see pages 81–2), World Sponsorships helped with post-genocide reconstruction in 1996 and 1997 and now pays the salary of one of the teachers. Soon, as the school grows, it will be necessary to finance more classrooms.

Back in the 1970s and 1980s, World Sponsorships provided help for Rwandan refugee students exiled in Uganda, many of whom returned home after the genocide and are now actively involved in rebuilding their country, so the sponsorships had a visible and successful result. Some of the former students, now in their 30s and 40s, are still in touch with their sponsors.

New supporters are always welcome, whether as sponsors or as donors.

For more details contact: Aid to Displaced Persons (World Sponsorships), 35 Rue du Marché, 4500 HUY, Belgium; tel: 085 213481; fax: 085 230147; email: aidepersdepl.huy@proximedia.be. For the benefit of UK donors/sponsors, there's also a bank account in Britain so the transfer of funds is easy.

The Forest Peoples' Project

This is the UK-based support partner of CAURWA (see pages 75–7), and is the charitable wing of the Forest Peoples' Programme which was established in 1990 to promote a people-centred approach to resolving the crisis facing the world's forests.

The Forest Peoples' Project works to:

• promote the environmental and human rights of forest peoples
• educate policy makers, practitioners and civil society about forest peoples' aspirations

- support forest peoples in the conservation of their lands, sustainable management of their resources and sustainable development.

It achieves these aims by means of support activities and capacity building with grassroots organisations; networking with NGOs, indigenous support organisations and agencies; research and analysis; and outreach. Donations to CAURWA (above) can also be made to the Forest Peoples' Project.

For further information contact Dorothy Jackson, Africa Programme Co-ordinator (email: info@fppwrm.gn.apc.org) or Elaine Gardner, Rwanda Fair Trade/Business Development consultant (email: egardner@ukgateway.net) at Forest Peoples' Project, 1c Fosseway Centre, Stratford Road, Moreton-in-Marsh, GL56 9NQ, UK.

Voluntary Service Overseas (VSO)

Many Rwandan schools were destroyed in the genocide and large numbers of Rwandan teachers were killed. Education is a crucial factor in the country's reconstruction, and in 1997 Rwanda's education minister invited VSO to implement a programme in Rwanda with a strong emphasis on education. After an initial investigation by VSO, a programme office was established in Kigali and the first 15 volunteer teachers started work early in 1999. Now there are over 50, of a variety of backgrounds, specialities and ages.

Conditions for the first recruits weren't easy. Some had to adapt to rigid teaching environments, where staff were reluctant to depart from traditional ways, and others found themselves teaching students still traumatised by their experiences. Currently, over half the students in the volunteers' classes were orphaned in the genocide and almost all lived through it. Trauma, poverty and displacement have stolen part of their childhood and disrupted their schooling. The VSO volunteers are as much friends and social workers as they are teachers to these children, spending time with them after school, getting to know them and becoming involved with their academic and personal welfare.

Volunteers take a crash course in basic Kinyarwanda before starting work. While students who lived through the genocide in Rwanda mainly speak French as a second language, those who have returned home from Uganda, Tanzania or Kenya have studied in English. And Rwanda's education policy is now tri-lingual.

Rwanda is still desperately short of qualified teachers and the volunteers are proving invaluable. VSO is fundraising hard to finance – and if possible to extend – its Rwanda programme, and all donations are welcome.

Check out the website www.vso.org.uk for more details. VSO, 317 Putney Bridge Road, London SW15 2PN; tel: 0208 780 7200.

The Centre for the Formation of Art

This centre, located in Kigali city, is currently Rwanda's only art school. It started in 1999 with only a handful of students; now there are 45, most of them orphans or widows. In addition to painting and sculpture, they can learn English, French, maths and accounting.

The paintings done by the students are for sale; many of them express their feelings about reconciliation and peace. If you want to buy really unusual souvenirs, why not consider a visit to the school? You'll be contributing to a thoroughly good cause, with nothing syphoned off by a middleman. Donations are also welcome, as the school is running on a shoestring .

For more information or to arrange a visit, contact the Reverend Dennis Mungabo; his mobile phone number is 08533697.

Dian Fossey Gorilla Fund International (DFGFI)

After the humans, Rwanda's mountain gorillas in the Volcanoes National Park are the country's most important residents! The DFGFI's Karisoke Research Centre in the Virungas, established by Dr Fossey in 1967, has a number of programmes under way to monitor and protect them, including tracking and anti-poaching patrols. The anti-poaching guards are dedicated spokesmen for mountain-gorilla conservation, and the Karisoke Centre is engaged in ongoing study of the gorillas and their habitat in the Volcanoes Park. Based in Atlanta, USA, the DFGFI is committed on a worldwide scale to gorilla protection, science, field research, education and awareness, and economic development.

The Fund shares its knowledge and experience in order to promote the use of common gorilla-monitoring protocols and practices; collects demographic, behavioural and environmental data, often in collaboration with major universities in Africa; and funds small-scale development activities in communities near the gorilla habitat, in support of the local people. Additionally, it trains rangers and trackers, promotes public awarenesss of gorilla conservation via the media and other communication projects, and conducts conservation action and outreach programmes in other parts of the region.

Supporters who become members will receive a newsletter, information and news of special events. It is also possible to 'adopt' a gorilla (from a distance!) and to receive a photo and information about the adopted animal. Finally, donations of any size are warmly welcomed.

For details contact: Dian Fossey Gorilla Fund International, 800 Cherokee Avenue, SE, Atlanta, Georgia 30315, USA; tel: 1 800 851 0203; email: 2help@gorillafund.org; web: www.gorillafund.org.

INVESTING IN RWANDA

What better way to become actively involved in Rwanda's future? In many senses this is a 'new' country with numerous investment possibilities opening up. In June 2000, the government established the **Rwandan Investment Promotion Agency (RIPA)**. This agency operates a 'one-stop centre' to assist either new investors or else those intending to rehabilitate, expand, renovate or restructure existing enterprises. RIPA registers new investment projects, and helps registered enterprises to obtain the necessary agreements, certificates, work permits and land. Investors can benefit from a number of fiscal and practical incentives; see www.rwanda1.com/economy/

investment_incentives.htm. Bureaucracy is kept to a minimum and procedures are streamlined as far as possible. Rwanda Investment Promotion Agency, BP 6239 Kigali; tel: (250) 510248/510249.

In 1997 the government of Rwanda's **National Tender Board** was set up and has steadily expanded its role. Initially its brief was to issue and manage regulations, guidelines and policies for procurement, but it currently serves as the procurement agency for most government purchases, including those made by international donors. A website is under construction at the time of writing – locate it via www.rwanda1.com. Rwandan National Tender Board; tel: (250) 71682; fax: 71107; email: ntb@rwandatel1.rwanda1.com.

Recognising the importance of the private sector to economic growth in Africa and elsewhere, Rwanda has put in place an ambitious privatisation programme of its state-owned enterprises. The **Privatisation Secretariat** is charged with the day-to-day management and co-ordination of the Technical Privatisation Commission in its implementation of the privatisation programme. A number of enterprises have already been privatised, and at the time of writing two are being advertised for tender: the Sonafruit (production and marketing of fruit juices) company in Cyangugu and the Kiyovu Hotel in Kigali. Other possible acquisitions include several hotels, rice mills, tea factories, coffee factories, a fish farm, dairies, a sawmill, banks and an airline – so the range is wide. Privatisation Secretariat, BP 158 Kigali; tel: (250) 75383/70989/70991/70992; fax: 75384; email pvs@rwandatel1.rwanda1.com

Rwanda's location midway between East and Central Africa gives it access to both of these markets, and it has direct air links to Europe, South Africa and the Tanzanian coast. Given the post-genocide problems that it still faces, its economy is performing well; after declining by a half in 1994 it has been picking up steadily since 1995, and has earned approval from international funding agencies and business partners. Since 1998, inflation has stayed below 5%. Technologically, the country is well advanced, and now has one of the most modern telephone networks in Africa. French and English are both official languages, alongside Kinyarwanda. Finally, Rwanda's potential for tourism – and tourism related investment – is huge, and set to develop rapidly, providing both scope and consumers for additional goods and services.

ORTPN
Office Rwandais du Tourisme et des Parcs Nationaux
(Rwanda Tourist Board)

THE ONE-STOP SHOP FOR
National Park permits and gorilla-trek bookings
Maps; leaflets; brochures; guidebooks; souvenirs

ASK US FOR DETAILS OF
Accommodation; airlines; car-hire agents; climate;
cultural events; entertainments; handicrafts;
itineraries; markets; museums; parks; public
transport; restaurants; tourist sites; tour operators;
water sports, wildlife… and more

French and English spoken

Head office: *Avenue de l'Armée, BP 905 Kigali*
tel: (250) 76514/5, 73396; fax: (250) 76512
email: ortpn@rwanda1.com
Branch office: *Arrivals hall, Kigali airport*

Part Two

The Guide

Kigali

Rwanda's attractive capital, Kigali, straggles over several hills, with the city centre on one and the government/administrative quarter on another. When Ruanda-Urundi (the capital of which was Usumbura – today Bujumbura) split into Rwanda and Burundi at the time of independence in 1962, the strongest contender to become Rwanda's new capital seemed to be Butare, which had been used by the Belgians as Ruanda's administrative capital during colonisation.

However, Kigali's central position and good road links to the rest of the country won out, and it was officially named as Rwanda's capital on June 26 1965. As a result it has grown dramatically, its population rising over ten-fold since 1970, while Butare has avoided capital-city brashness and remains relatively calm.

The centre of Kigali is bustling, colourful and noisy, but (for an African city) surprisingly clean and safe. Its occupants, from smart-suited businesspersons to scruffy kids hawking newspapers or pirated cassettes, go purposefully about their activities, only lessening tempo briefly in the middle of the day. Occasional traffic lights, roundabouts and a cacophony of car horns manage (more or less) to regulate the traffic, although it's heavy and congested at peak times. Peaceful, tree-lined residential streets stretch outwards and generally downwards from the city's heart, and give visitors ample scope for strolling.

The government and administrative area, in Kacyiru quarter on a neighbouring hill, is newer and quieter, with wide streets and some modern architecture. Kigali was the centre of much fighting during the genocide and offices were ransacked; when workers returned after the end of the war they had virtually no usable typewriters, phones, stationery or furniture and had to start again from scratch. Also files, archives and other documentation had been destroyed.

There aren't many tourist attractions in Kigali itself and you're unlikely to want to spend many full days there, but there are some good hotels, the services (shops, banks etc) are plentiful and the ambience is pleasant, making it an excellent base for exploring the rest of Rwanda, all parts of which are easily accessible by road in less than a day.

GETTING THERE AND AWAY
By air
See pages 25–6 for details of flights to and from Rwanda – which means to and from Kigali, since that's where the international airport is situated, about 10km from the centre of town. In the arrivals hall of the airport you'll find exchange and telephone facilities, various shops and a branch of ORTPN (*Office Rwandais du Tourisme et des Parcs Nationaux*) which is Rwanda's tourist office, where you can get a preliminary stock of maps, guides and so forth. (But the main ORTPN office is in Kigali town centre.)

To get into Kigali town you've three options. (Or four, if you're prepared to beg a lift from some fellow traveller who has a vehicle.) If your hotel does airport pickups, you'll have arranged this at the time of booking; give them a ring if no-one has turned up to collect you. If you've very little luggage and some small change in Rwandan francs, you can pick up a minibus-taxi in the road outside the airport and it'll take you to Kigali's central bus station. Otherwise take a *taxi-voiture* (a normal taxi, as opposed to a minibus-taxi). It's worth checking inside the airport what the cost should be; in any case you should agree a price with the driver in advance. At the time of writing I wouldn't go above about US$20, but rates do legitimately rise over time. (If, for any reason, the exchange bureau in the airport is closed, taxi-drivers sometimes accept US dollars.) The same procedure applies in reverse when you're leaving.

Whatever airline you've used, you *must* confirm your return flight at least three days in advance – airline offices or travel agents in Kigali will deal with this for you.

By road
Kigali is a well-connected little city – literally. There are good roads and bus services linking it to all the main border crossings with neighbouring countries.

GETTING AROUND
The centre of Kigali – for shopping, banks, airline offices, tour operators etc – is tiny, so once you're there, you'll never be far from what you're looking for. It's based around two streets, Boulevard de la Révolution and Avenue de la Paix, and the various roads branching off them. However, if you ask directions you'll soon become aware that people don't go much on street names, rather on well-known landmarks. Remember that a lot of people working in Kigali don't actually *know* Kigali all that well – they'd never been there until they returned from some other country after the genocide.

Maps covering the whole of Kigali (as opposed to just the centre) are available from ORTPN, as well as from some tour operators and hotels. There's a network of urban **minibuses** (minibus-taxis) serving all areas, and plenty of **taxis** – they park (among other places) in Boulevard de la Révolution and at the top of Place de la Constitution, also cruising the streets waiting to be flagged down. The **central minibus-taxi station** in Kigali is at the junction of Avenue de Commerce and Rue Mont Kabuye – you'll recognise it by the gaggle of beat-up white minibuses (with no indication of their destinations) and general air of chaos, but in fact there's an underlying level of sanity and, if you ask someone, you'll be pointed to the bus that you need. This is where you pick up minibus-taxis to take you down to the Nyabugogo minibus-taxi station (see page 113) from which transport to other parts of Rwanda leaves.

If you don't mind the hills, Kigali is an easy place for sightseeing (not that there are actually many sights, but it's still a pleasant place for people-watching) on foot. There are plenty of snack-bars and kiosks with drinks if you get weary. See suggested strolls on page 111.

WHERE TO STAY
Luxury
Two hotels fall into this bracket: the Hotel des Mille Collines in the centre of Kigali and the Windsor Umubano Hotel in the administrative quarter. Both have swimming pools; both can arrange airport pick-ups; both are extremely comfortable, have the facilities you'd expect for the price and offer a relaxing stay. Both have good restaurants/bars, tennis courts, conference and business facilities including internet access, and various boutiques. The **Hotel des Mille Collines** (BP 1322 Kigali; tel: 76530/3; fax: 76541; email: millecollines@hotmail.com; web: www.sabenahotels.com/millecollines) has 113 rooms and suites from US$145 to 340; a standard double room on the city side (there's sometimes some traffic noise at night) costs around US$160 including tax, on the pool side US$176. Deduct 10% for single occupancy. Rates are negotiable for groups or long stays. The hotel has a pleasant garden where you can engage in a spot of urban birdwatching. (I have it on good authority that the massive tree next to the swimming pool, which looks as if it has been there since time began, is only 30–40 years old.) Credit cards are accepted here, but the transactions pass via Belgian francs, so if they're strong against your own currency then you'll get a poor rate.

The **Windsor Umubano Hotel** (BP 874 Kigali; tel: 82176/7/8; fax: 82957; email: umubano1.@rwanda1.com) is more quietly situated (in the administrative quarter, between Kigali and the airport) and there's plenty of transport, whether minibus-taxis or *taxi-voitures,* to and from the centre. It's very popular with local people for functions and the staff are friendly; an efficient but relaxed place. It has 100 rooms including 15 suites: comfortable standard doubles are around US$125–135, including tax. Credit cards are accepted. There's a post office nearby and banking facilities in the hotel. Maxim's Nightclub, located here, is popular with Kigali's smart set – entry US$5.

Upper/middle range
Top in this category is the little **Motel le Garni du Centre** (BP 548 Kigali; tel/fax 72654, 71275; email: garni@rwanda1.com), with a small swimming pool. It's tucked away down a side street close to the centre of town, is only four years old, and has 11 quiet, comfortable en-suite rooms (TV, phone, fridge) for around US$90 single, US$110 double, including tax and continental breakfast. There's no restaurant for main meals, but the hotel is

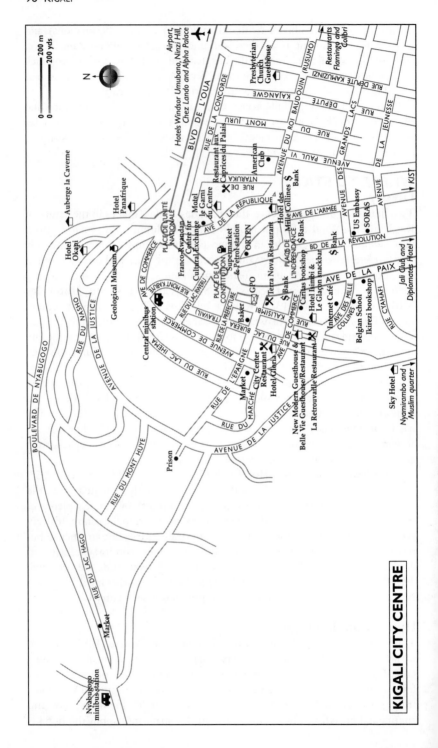

KIGALI CITY CENTRE

only a few minutes away from a good range of eateries at the Hotel Mille Collines or (slightly further away) in the town centre. Mobile phones are available for rent here at around US$4 per day

In Boulevard de la Révolution, the formerly state-owned **Hotel des Diplomates** is due to be privatised, so details aren't available at the time of writing. An attraction is its position, just a shady, tree-lined, 15-minute stroll from the centre of town.

Out in Remera suburb, but an easy taxi or minibus-taxi ride from town, **Hotel Chez Lando** (BP 1519 Kigali; tel: 82050, 84328, 84394; fax: 84380; email: lando@rwandatel1.rwanda1.com; web: www.hotelchezlando.com) is a comfortable, well-established place, popular with locals and tourists alike. Accommodation is in attractive villas set in a quiet garden: 32 rooms with TV and phone, US$75 double, reductions possible for groups or long stays. Staff are friendly and helpful, the restaurant (French and African cuisine) is good and barbecues are often held. Internet facilities are available. The Zoom nightclub/disco is popular at weekends.

Middle range

The modern **Hotel Okapi** (BP 1775 Kigali; tel: 76765; fax: 74413; email: okapi@rwandatel1.rwanda1.com) in central Kigali offers a good range of services – there's an efficient travel agency next door which can handle all your travel needs (including trips to tourist sites in Rwanda and visits to neighbouring countries) and a daily minibus (the *Okapicar*) runs daily to Goma in the DRC and back. (At present, visa-free day visits across the DRC border are possible.) The hotel itself, only two years old, has a good restaurant with a range of cuisines, rooms with balconies and TV, and a terrace with a panoramic view across the Kigali landscape. Unfortunately it's in a side street, between Boulevard de Nyabugogo and Avenue de la Justice, which at present is unsurfaced and a bit tatty – guests might not feel safe walking back there at night. But the area is being reconstructed, so this may improve. Standard doubles cost US$50 upwards.

The **Alpha Palace Hotel** (BP 2632 Kigali; tel: 82981; fax: 84134; email: alphapalace@inbox.rw), on Boulevard de l'OUA, about 1km from the airport, is a new hotel, with swimming pool, on the (quite noisy) road to the airport, which gets good reports from locals. It can arrange airport pick-ups, also car hire. There's a 24-hour restaurant with French, African and oriental cuisine, also a snackbar for grills etc, and a popular nightclub open four nights a week. Its 38 double rooms and suites have colour TV and phone; single US$50, double US$60, suite US$80, all including continental breakfast.

The **Ninzi Hill Hotel** (tel: 87712; fax: 87716), in the administrative quarter not far from the Windsor Umubano, is a quiet, comfortable place well away from city bustle. Rooms at the back look out over gardens and greenery and it has a pleasantly laid-back feel to it. There are 15 en-suite rooms with phone and TV at US$45 single/$60 double upwards and that includes 'tropical' breakfast – ie: continental plus fruit! Reductions are possible for groups or long stays. If you want a change from eating in the hotel restaurant (although it's good), there's a Chinese restaurant nearby.

The **Hotel Isimbi** (BP 1163 Kigali; tel: 72578/81; fax: 75109; email: isimbi@isimbihotel.com) is right in the centre of town (Rue Kalisimbi), just a few minutes' walk from the market, post office and shops – which does mean that guests are a target for street vendors. But it's a plain, efficient, clean, city-centre hotel, with 26 simple, en-suite rooms (the back ones are quiet), hot water, an all-day snackbar (non-smoking), a restaurant for main meals, and room service. Single US$40, double US$45.

The **Sky Hotel** (BP 206 Kigali; tel: 516692/3, tel/fax: 516690) in Avenue de la Justice opened while I was checking out the hotels and hadn't had time to settle down, but looks promising – 28 en-suite double rooms, some with small sitting rooms, hot water, lovely view over the valley from the back, US$30 per room upwards.

The **Hotel Baobab** (BP 1406 Kigali; tel: 75633, 516616; fax; 71048) is a great place, full of character but some distance from the city centre, down in the southwest of outer Kigali near Mount Kigali and the Islamic Cultural Centre. If you have your own transport (or don't mind taking taxis), do consider it. The area is peaceful, with widespread views across the valley. The Baobab has nine en-suite rooms with hot water, phone and TV, for US$25 single and US$33 double, including continental breakfast (those prices almost put it in the 'budget' range below), and is very clean. The restaurant (eating outside at individual tables under thatched roofs) has an excellent reputation among local people, particularly for the barbecues, so probably gets busy at weekends.

The **Iris Guesthouse** in Avenue Député Kamuzinzi, very near the Presbyterian Church guesthouse, only opened in January 2001; 17 doubles at US$45 and two apartments at US$1,700 per month; BP 228 Kigali; tel/fax: 501181.

Budget

High on my list for central Kigali is the **Auberge la Caverne** (tel: 74549), a pleasant, clean, new place (it opened in May 2000) with 12 simple en-suite rooms (hot water) set away from the traffic around a central courtyard in Boulevard de Nyabugogo. Back windows have a good view out over the valley. US$13 single, US$20–$25 double depending on size. The restaurant menu looked good but I wasn't there at a mealtime. It's a steepish walk up into town.

The **Hotel Panafrique** (tel: 75056) is an older and well-established place, just off the top end of Boulevard de Nyabugogo, with a popular rooftop restaurant (the food's good) and nightclub. It badly needs a face-lift now but was full when I visited so can't be too bad. Eight en-suite doubles (hot water) at US$13 per room.

Very central is the **Gloria Hotel** (tel: 71957), in the commercial area near to the market, at the traffic-light junction in Rue du Lac Burera (aka Bulera, aka Rue du Travail) just downhill from the Caritas bookshop. It's basic, safe, clean, functional and friendly. There's no restaurant, not even for breakfast, but there are lots of eateries in the area. They'll take phone calls for you at reception but you can't phone out – however there's a phone kiosk next door.

En-suite rooms (cold water in the taps, but they'll bring you a bucket of hot on request) cost US$15 single (some are quite small) and US$20 double.

Two cheaper places opposite each other near the Gloria (in a small, unnamed road on the right as you go uphill from the Gloria towards the Caritas bookshop) are the **Belle Vie Restaurant/Logement** (BP 2755 Kigali; tel: 70158) and the **New Modern Guest House** (BP 1459 Kigali; tel: 74708). The Belle Vie is friendly and quite good value: four plain rooms with washbasins sharing a separate (clean) shower/WC; hot water. The restaurant is cheerful, serving good, simple meat/vegetable mixes. Rooms US$10 single, US$13 double. The New Modern is the same price – 11 rooms, shared facilities – but seedier, worth considering only if the Belle Vie is full.

Further from the centre, a ten-minute walk downhill from the Hotel des Mille Collines, is the **Guesthouse of the Presbyterian Church** (Rue Député Kamuzinzi; tel: 78915; fax: 78919) – a clean, peaceful place with en-suite rooms and a good-value dining room. It can get busy with church guests. US$25 single, US$30 double – sometimes reduced rates for charities, aid workers etc. Another church guesthouse is that of the **Episcopal Church** (Avenue Paul VI; tel: 73219) in Biryogo (aka Bilyogo) district, a considerable distance southwest of the centre – it's clean and friendly, and you can park there safely. US$20 en-suite single, US$30 double, cheaper dormitory accommodation.

I was told of a cheap and friendly place out in the administrative (Kacyiru) district, if you want to be away from the centre: **Ituze Guesthouse** (tel: 86330), 36 rooms, US$13 single, US$15 double, shared facilities, bar/restaurant. Further out from the centre, in Remera suburb near the Hotel Chez Lando, the **Auberge Beau Séjour** (BP 3655 Kigali; tel: 82625/6/7; fax: 82601) has a good reputation locally: 11 rooms at US$25.

Finally, a handful of little places down in Nyamirambo district are worth mentioning, because the area is so appealing. This is a lively, characterful quarter, near the mosque and Islamic Centre, which in fact was one of the first parts of Kigali to be settled. A friendly place there is the **Kigali Hotel** (BP 697 Kigali; tel/fax: 71384) on Avenue de la Justice, with 18 small en-suite rooms with hot water, phone and TV, US$18 single and US$25 double; it's recommended by travellers who've stayed there. Minibus-taxis from central Kigali stop nearby – ask for 'Chez Mayaka' or the Mosque. Nearby down a turning off Avenue de la Justice is the **Hotel La Vedette** (BP 850 Kigali; tel: 73575), really no more than a guesthouse; three singles at US$10 and three doubles at US$15 with shared (clean) facilities. Guests 'live as family' there, the welcoming owner told me. Further on there's the **Auberge de Nyamirambo** (tel: 72879), near the Bahai Centre – six doubles with showers, US$13 single and US$20 double; also the **Hotel la Mise** (tel: 78369), which is clean and pleasant with a good restaurant, but the en-suite rooms seem a touch expensive at US$40 double, despite having phone and TV.

Apartments

The **Prima 2000 Apartment Building** (BP 924 Kigali; tel/fax: 510260) is on Boulevard de l'Umuganda opposite Telecom House, near the Windsor

Umubano Hotel. It has 36 self-contained apartments, with from one to four bedrooms, ranging from US$1,000 to US$3,000 per month according to size. The Iris Guesthouse (above) also has two apartments.

WHERE TO EAT AND DRINK

The best way to explore Kigali's restaurants is to ask local people to recommend their favourites; every time I asked for advice I was told something different. In fact I didn't have a bad meal anywhere – food is generally taken seriously, whether it's basic local cuisine or international. The list below is far from exhaustive; experiment for yourself too.

Upper range

The **Mille Collines** and **Windsor Umubano Hotels** both have excellent restaurants (see *Where to stay* listing above); Several of the other 'smart' places in Kigali are in the Kiyovu district, downhill from the Mille Collines. As you go southwards down Avenue du Roi Baudouin (also known as Avenue de Rusumo), the smart **Aux Caprices du Palais** (tel: 75573) is in Rue de Ntaruka on your left. It's open Tuesday to Sunday, 12.00–14.00 and 18.00–22.30. Check out its (tempting!) French and African specialities on website www.aw7.com/caprices – main dishes go up to about US$15 but with extras you'll pay much more. Just beyond it is the **American Club**, good for a relaxed evening out. Further down, at 14 Avenue de Kiyovu, is the very popular **Flamingo** Chinese restaurant (tel: 511506) – a relaxed, gracious atmosphere and good food with all the trimmings, so not cheap – and you'd be wise to book in advance. It's open 12.00–15.00 and 18.00–23.00, closed Monday. Close to the Flamingo is the cheaper **Colibri Pizzeria** (tel: 75128); open Monday 19.00–23.00, closed Wednesday, other days 12.00–14.00 and 19.00–23.00. Now head east as if going to the administrative quarter (Kacyiro) and you're near the **Hellenic Greek restaurant** – nothing outstanding, but tasty Greek food. Well away from the centre and in a different direction (southwest) is the **Baobab Hotel/Restaurant** (tel: 75633) (see *Where to stay*, above) which has a great atmosphere and food and is praised by locals; phone in advance and try to go when they've got a barbecue on.

In Kigali centre, and rather surprisingly located down in the fairly scruffy market area, the **City Center Restaurant** (tel: 71278), which looks unprepossessing outside, does good French cuisine at US$10 or so per main dish. Go up the rather bleak staircase and it's a pleasant little place – but the area can get a bit scary for walking late in the evening. It's small, so, if you're a large party, make a reservation. The **Jali Club** in Boulevard de la Révolution has a pleasantly relaxed atmosphere and staff are attentive. It's not far from the centre of town but set in spacious grounds. The restaurant offers a predictable but good menu.

Medium range

In the centre of Kigali, you've the **Palmier** and the **Sierra** in Boulevard de la Révolution; sitting out in the garden of the Palmier is pleasant and it serves a standard range of meals and snacks. The Sierra's timing is complicated: breakfast on the terrace 07.00–11.30, lunch buffet in restaurant 12.00–2.30, dinner 19.00–22.00; closed Sundays. Most hotels with restaurants will rustle up something passable; for example the main restaurant of the **Isimbi Hotel** (as opposed to its cafeteria) is a handy town-centre place for lunch.

Budget

Wherever you stroll in Kigali, you're never far from a snack or a drink. The market area is full of cheap and interesting places; try **La Retrouvaille** just off Avenue Mille Collines where a generous plateful of rice, meat, vegetables, sauce and salad costs under US$2. **Le Glaçon** near the Isimbi Hotel is quick and uncomplicated; chicken with rice or chips, curries, omelettes, samosas etc. Its imaginatively spelt menu offers 'chaps' but neither of the authors felt inclined to experiment. The **Caiman Restaurant**, opposite the Banque Commerciale du Rwanda in Boulevard de la Révolution, has a set lunch menu each day for about US$5 and a good range of snacks at other times. Its breakfast croissants are wonderfully fresh but sometimes sell out quite fast. Closed Sundays. Extremely popular with local people are the buffet lunches at the **Terra Nova Restaurant** near the main post office: a tasty mélange of rice, meat/fish and various vegetables/salad costs around US$3. It was one of the first restaurants in Kigali to serve buffet lunches (see page 56). **The Oasis** in Avenue de la Paix is popular with locals and always busy – serving snacks, drinks, coffee etc.

NIGHTLIFE

This is an expanding scene and certainly new places will have opened by the time you go, so ask around. The nightclub currently very popular with Kigali's smart set is **Maxim's** at the Windsor Umubano Hotel – entry costs around US$5. The one at Hotel **Chez Lando** is similar. Scruffier but also popular and half the price is the one at the **Panafrique Hotel**. **Tananarivo** in Remera suburb is smartish and recommended – US$4 entry fee. A new one at the **Cercle Sportif** is apparently good ($2.50), and the place everyone recommends when you ask about nightclubs is the **Cadillac** Restaurant/Club in the same area as the Hellenic Restaurant. We'll give Dorette Bosham and David Hartley the last word: 'For a real treat go to the **Turtle Café** on Rue du Travail, right next to the traffic lights with Avenue de la Justice. Friday and Saturday nights are live music nights, some vibey African and Western stuff, and a very popular hangout all week long for both expats and locals.'

PRACTICAL INFORMATION
Money

The three most accessible **banks** in central Kigali are the Banque Commerciale du Rwanda (BCR) and the Banque Continentale Africaine Rwanda (BACAR) in Boulevard de la Révolution and the Banque de Kigali in Avenue de la Paix. All three will change cash and travellers' cheques; the Banque de Kigali (and possibly the others too by the time you visit) will

KIST

The Kigali Institute of Science, Technology and Management (KIST), created in 1997, is the first Rwandan public institute to provide such high-level technological training. The land it stands on, in Avenue de l'Armée, was originally earmarked for a military academy for high-ranking officers, but was then given by the Ministry of Defence to the Ministry of Education as the location for an appropriate technology centre.

The institute, which at the time of writing had 1,200 full-time and 400 part-time students, provides bilingual (French/English) courses from five faculties and centres:

- the Faculty of Technology, which includes departments of ICT (information and communications technologies) engineering, electro-mechanical engineering, and food sciences and technology;
- the Faculty of Management, covering finance, marketing and human resources;
- the Faculty of Sciences, which offers basic training in maths, physics and chemistry;
- the Language School, providing courses in English, French and African languages;
- the Centre for Further Education, with part-time or evening courses leading to diplomas in management, languages, practical technologies (repair of TVs and radios, electrical installation, welding, plumbing, carpentry) and ICT.

In addition, KIST has a second campus in the suburb of Remera, where basic courses in maths, physics and chemistry are held to prepare students for higher education. A new five-storey building was completed there in 2000 and houses classrooms, a library and offices for the teaching staff.

advance cash on credit cards. Queues are slow but orderly and there's generally no hassle. The BACAR has a Moneygram service and the BCR a Western Union service via which funds can be transferred quickly from abroad. In the BCR the counters for foreign exchange and Western Union are round a corner to the right – generally numbers 16 to 20.

In addition, there are various **foreign exchange (forex) bureaux** around the city; conspicuous ones are opposite the BCR in Boulevard de la République and in Avenue de la Paix midway between its junctions with Avenue des Mille Collines and Avenue de Commerce.

Money changers hang out around the main post office in Avenue de la Paix and down Rue de l'Epargne, and may well crop up elsewhere too. They seem not to be illegal – or at any rate to be tolerated – and in general they offer better rates than either banks or forex bureaux, but be vigilant, and decide in advance the lowest rate you're willing to accept.

See also *Chapter 4*, pages 50–1.

KIST has an efficient cyber-café in Avenue de l'Armée, open to the public, where one hour online costs around US$1.20. Its Virtual African University, financed by the World Bank in support of distance learning, has organised numerous seminars in (for example) accountancy, management and languages, and can provide course material in both English and French. The Institute is well advanced in ICT and aims to make Rwanda a leader in this field.

In contrast to its high-tech specialities, KIST also offers practical training in various rural crafts so that young people in the countryside can develop their skills and earn a living. Subjects include the making and marketing of soap, chalk, school equipment, cooking oil, candles, fruit juice, sweets, toys and various metal objects. Training courses for trainers are also planned. Finally, KIST is involved in developing appropriate technologies including solar heaters, efficient cooking stoves, bio-gas and bio-mass technologies, and means of retaining rainwater and increasing fuelwood sources. It produces and sells the relevant items to various agencies by request.

KIST is contributing very actively to Rwanda's reconstruction. Compulsory language studies are a part of all its courses and students must pass a language exam when graduating, so they acquire a working knowledge of English or French (or both). Standards are high. Increasing numbers of young people are applying for entry – but many cannot afford the fees of around US$500 per year, as well as living costs. External help is needed to provide study grants, to enable KIST to train more teachers, to buy more laboratory equipment and to maintain its present programmes effectively.

Kigali Institute of Science, Technology & Management; Avenue de l'Armée, BP 3900 Kigali; tel: 74696; fax: 71924/5; email: info@kist.ac.rw; web: www.kist.ac.rw.

Communications

The main **post office** in Avenue de la Paix has a counter for international phone calls and an efficient fax office outside; faxes to Europe cost US$4 per page, to the US US$4.50. If you want someone to send a fax to you there, the number is (250) 76574. This is where you can collect post restante (see page 65). There's also a philatelic counter.

On no account post your mail in the red box out in the entrance hallway – it's for suggestions! The letter box is inside.

Cyber cafés are springing up fast; there's one in the upper level of shops opposite the Belgian School in Avenue des Mille Collines (one hour online costs US$1.50) which also offers scanning services, typing and photocopying and has another branch at the Hotel des Diplomates. Others in central Kigali are at the Hotel des Mille Collines and the Kigali Institute of Science and Technology – and probably elsewhere too, by the time you read this.

Public telephones are in to be found in shops and kiosks all over the centre of Kigali – they are metered, so you pay when you've finished and don't need handfuls of small change. Calls to mobile phones are more expensive than those to normal phones. Rwanda is now said to have one of the most modern telephone systems in East Africa. You can get a 'starter pack' to convert most imported mobiles for use in Rwanda; these cost around US$25 and are available (among other places) at the airport on arrival and at Video Dreams, which is above Changa Travel in Avenue des Mille Collines, opposite the Belgian School.

Shopping

Apart from the market area (see page 110), the shops you're likely to use are in the 'square' formed by Boulevard de la Révolution, Avenue de Commerce, Avenue des Mille Collines and Rue de l'Epargne. Outside this area there's a good supermarket on the eastern side of Place de la Constitution, next to the petrol station that is opposite the ORTPN office; and the very good Ikirezi bookshop is on Avenue de la Paix but just westward of the 'square'.

In **Boulevard de la Révolution**, the large Banque Commerciale du Rwanda is on the eastern side, almost on Place de l'Indépendance (where the fountain is). Looking across the road from the bank and starting from the left, you have, among other small shops/offices: the Caiman Restaurant, a small supermarket, the Palmier Restaurant, a forex bureau, Gama Travel, Phaurwa pharmacy (open 24 hours), Alliance Express, archway leading to Top Travel & Tours, La Sierra Restaurant, the Banque Continentale Africaine Rwanda, and a petrol station.

Turn right at the petrol station into Avenue des Mille Collines, then right again into **Avenue de la Paix**. On the opposite side of Avenue de la Paix before it reaches Avenue de Commerce you have (not necessarily in order) a dry cleaners, various clothing and stationery shops (including one with a public phone), the small Primavera supermarket, a photographic shop, the Oasis café/restaurant, Nord-Sud International Travel Agency, a Forex bureau, Swift Tours & Travel and Kenya Airways.

At Kenya Airways turn left into **Avenue de Commerce** (the Banque de Kigali is on the opposite corner); on the left a little way down is the Caritas bookshop. Take the first left turn after it, into **Rue Kalisimbi** – on your right (opposite the Isimbi Hotel) is a good photographic shop (Fotolab; BP 155 Kigali; tel: 76508; web: www.aw7.com/fotolab), with a small dairy/milkbar just before it. (If you had continued downhill past the Kalisimbi turning, the next left would have taken you to the Belle Vie and New Modern Guesthouses, and the little restaurant La Retrouvaille.)

Continue along Rue Kalisimbi passing the Isimbi Hotel and then the Glaçon snackbar on your left: as you come to the T-junction with **Avenue des Mille Collines** there's a supermarket opposite which sells goods from various co-operatives. (They sometimes have good local honey.) Turn left up Mille Collines; the Belgian School is on your right with Changa Travel, Video Dreams (mobile phone shop) and an internet café opposite it on your left.

To complete your city-centre tour: go back to the junction of Avenue de la Paix and Avenue de Commerce, where you turned left at Kenya Airways.

Go downhill but, instead of turning left into Rue Kalisimbi, turn right (also into Kalisimbi). On your right you'll come to the ASAR craft shop (see page 109). The next junction is with **Rue de l'Epargne**; if you turn left (downhill) there's an excellent bakery on your right. If you turn right (uphill) you get back to Avenue de la Paix, with the post office on your left at the top and the Terra Nova Restaurant (see page 103) on your right. Opposite the post office is a kiosk with a public phone; just beyond the kiosk is a craft shop.

Further information

If there's anything else you want to know, try ORTPN. They should have – or be able to get – most information you may need.

WHAT TO SEE AND DO IN KIGALI

Your first stop in Kigali should be at the office of ORTPN (Office Rwandais du Tourisme et des Parcs Nationaux) which is the **Rwanda Tourist Office** (BP 905 Kigali; tel: 76514/5, 73396; fax: 76512; email: ortpn@ rwandatel1.rwanda1.com). It's in Avenue de l'Armée by the junction with Boulevard de la Révolution. They should have information about all current events and can advise you. They also have street maps of Kigali and information about transport – minibus-taxis, car hire and so forth.

The ORTPN office is where you buy permits to visit the national parks – you *must* do this before setting off for the park (or at the very least check with ORTPN whether you can do it on arrival at the park), otherwise you risk being refused entry. Also see ORTPN entries on pages 49 and 92.

In terms of buildings, museums and historical/cultural sites, Kigali offers little – but it is a pleasant place for strolling and people-watching. There is one small museum, the **Geological Museum** in the Ministry of Mines and Energy on Avenue de la Justice, but you need to give two to three days' notice if you'd like to visit, and you should ask beforehand if you want explanations in English. Opening times are Monday to Friday during office hours. At the time of writing, a large **genocide memorial** is being constructed in the Gisozi district of the city; this will be completed some time in 2001 and powerfully conveys the scale of the tragedy.

Arts and entertainments

Performances of traditional dancing and music take place from time to time in Kigali's stadium and other venues around the city – ORTPN will have an up-to-date list. These events are also publicised in the local newspapers. The Centre Culturel d'Echanges Franco-Rwandaises (tel: 76223), not far from the Hotel des Mille Collines, has a small theatre, reopened in late 2000 after damage during the genocide, and presents a variety of shows – theatre, films, music, dance and so on. Call in to ask them for their current monthly programme or else check with ORTPN. The Centre Culturel can be a useful source of other information too, as they have a comprehensive library (see below).

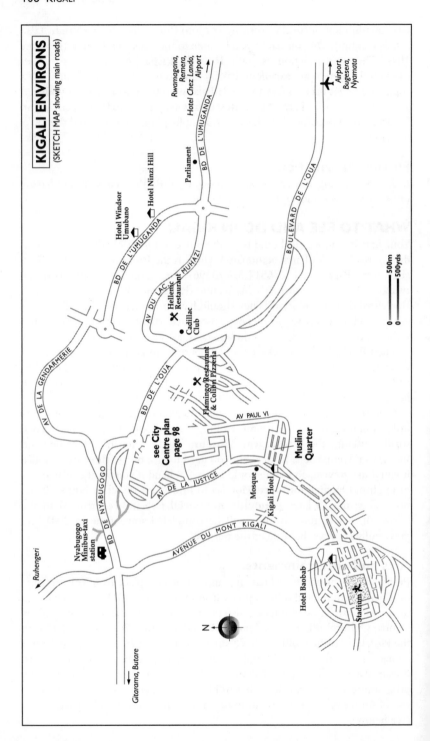

Libraries and bookshops

Depending on how soon you visit, Kigali may have its own, brand-new, specially designed **public library**, built with funds raised both nationally and internationally. It's still on the drawing-board at the time of writing but should be a striking construction. See page 87 for more details and ask at ORTPN for its exact location. In connection with fundraising for the library, secondhand book sales are held regularly in Kigali.

The **Centre Culturel d'Echanges Franco-Rwandaises** (see above) has three lending libraries: for adults, for children and for scientific research. The latter is used by (for example) civil servants and students, as well as visiting researchers. Material is largely in French, although more in English will probably be acquired. There's also a reading room.

Two good bookshops in Kigali, both of them stocking a wide range of books on the history and culture of Rwanda, the background to the genocide and an assortment of other relevant themes, are the **Librairie Caritas** (BP 1078 Kigali; tel: 76503) in Avenue de Commerce just downhill from the junction with Avenue de la Paix, and the **Librairie Ikirezi** (BP 443 Kigali; tel: 70298, tel/fax: 71314; email: ikirezi@rwandatel1.rwanda1.com) in Avenue de la Paix. The Ikirezi, which sometimes holds book-signings and other events, is open 09.00–12.30 and 14.00–18.00 (09.00–13.00 on Saturday) as well as 10.30–13.00 on Sunday.

Handicrafts

A wide range of handicrafts is sold in Kigali and there's great scope for browsing.

If **pottery** interests you, you can visit a Twa pottery workshop and watch the pots being made – arrange this through CAURWA (see page 76). A container selling Twa pottery is also set among the woodcarving stands on Avenue de l'Armée (below). Also a selection of their pots, some with plants inside, are laid out on the pavement near the bottom of Avenue du Roi Baudouin – keep walking downhill from the Hotel des Mille Collines. (Taxis generally cruise this area if you don't want to walk back up the steepish hill.)

For **woodcarvings** of all sorts, stroll along Avenue de l'Armée between ORTPN and the traffic lights at the junction with Avenue du Roi Baudouin; a treasure-trove of items is laid out on the pavement. The quality is variable – at best, very good indeed, but some is substandard – so check the workmanship carefully and be prepared to bargain. (But if something has been beautifully made, consider the value of such artistry and expertise.) Here you'll see traditional carvings – adaptations or originals of genuine household objects – alongside items of no former or current practical value which have probably evolved for the tourist market. There are some traditional **musical instruments** on sale here too.

Weaving is one of the specialities of Rwanda – baskets, mats, hangings and pots appear in a variety of shapes and sizes, with carefully interwoven traditional patterns. They are sold by some street vendors; and there's a good selection (including woven hammocks) in the craft shop called **ASAR**

(Association des Artistes Rwandais) (BP 939 Kigali; tel: 71139) in Rue Kalisimbi. This is an excellent little shop, combining the work of several craft-making co-ops; some items are very touristy but others are traditional and all make good gifts. As well as the weaving there are carvings, musical instruments, pottery, beadwork, palm-leaf crafts (including decorated notepaper and cards) and even stuffed toys.

You'll find **street vendors** selling most kinds of small handicrafts – carvings, jewellery, woven baskets, masks, musical instruments, notepaper and postcards decorated with palm fibres – and so on. One who works the area between approximately the post office and the Isimbi Hotel sometimes has interesting items – carvings, masks, instruments, jewellery, paintings – that he has brought over from the DRC and western Rwanda; but bargain hard.

Finally, if you'd like to see (and perhaps buy) some painting and sculpture done by Rwandan art students, an interesting project to visit is the little **Centre for the Formation of Art** – see pages 89–90 for details of how to make contact beforehand.

Handicrafts outlets are expanding and becoming more organised, so ask at ORTPN for details of any good new sources, or workshops that can be visited by tourists.

Markets

In all market areas, *take care* – crowds are popular with pickpockets and opportunistic thieves, and there have been instances of crime. Also be tactful about taking photos; for every dozen people who don't object to being in a picture, there'll be someone who does. Respect their privacy.

The main market area, off and around the Avenue de Commerce, is a cramped, busy area of trestles, stalls and small shops. Just about everything you could want is on sale there, from shiny, plastic household gadgets to chunks of fresh honeycomb. There are stacks of mattresses in floral cotton covers; roughly made wooden furniture; ancient, dented kitchen utensils being recycled; clothing imported from far-off countries; cassettes blaring out of ghetto-blasters; eggs teetering precariously on shaky tables; rows of multicoloured vegetables with their damp, earthy smell; footwear; shiny watches; creamy candles made of local beeswax; chunky farm cheeses; tools, cushions, mirrors…. and that's only a beginning.

In Avenue de Commerce near the central bus station (turn left as you leave the bus station) there's a good pavement market on Sundays: a wide assortment of goods laid out along the pavement so that shoppers have to step over and among them as they select. (If you're in this area – but not at weekends – look out for the men with elderly, battered typewriters who sit at tables on the pavement at the western side of Place de la Constitution, ready to type letters to order. They make a refreshing change from cyber cafés!)

Probably the most frenetic market is the one across the road from the Nyabugogo minibus-taxi stand, at the bottom of Rue du Lac Hago. It's like a human kaleidoscope, a changing, shifting mass of colours and noise. A few minutes being jostled by these brisk crowds, determinedly going about their own business, may be enough for you, but it's a typical and non-touristy experience which it would be a pity to miss completely. See also the walk to Nyabugogo below.

Strolling round Kigali
If you don't mind the unavoidable hills, Kigali offers some good strolls. There are plenty of places where you can stop for a snack or a drink if you need to cool off. Two walks which could each fill up a morning, depending on how often you stop en route, are given below, but just look at a map of the whole city and you'll see that there are plenty more.

To the mosque and Nyamirambo district
One way of getting to the big mosque in the Muslim quarter is to walk southwards along Avenue de la Justice, with views out across the valley to your right; the mosque is at the junction where Rue de la Sécurité joins from the left. Continue for a few minutes and you're in a lively, busy district (Nyamirambo) of small streets and colourful little local shops. The atmosphere has a touch of London's Soho about it. This is said to be the part of the present-day city where people first settled, long ago. There's a lot of small-scale activity going on here, and small bars and cafés where you can stop for a drink.

To return to the centre, you can either catch a minibus-taxi (they serve Avenue de la Justice; look out for the yellow signs indicating bus stops) or flag down a taxi. Or else retrace your steps towards the mosque and look out for Avenue Paul VI on your right – follow this upwards and it'll bring you on to the area covered by the map on page 98. Or be adventurous and find your own variations!

To Nyabugogo market
This takes you through an area of many small shops and market stalls, finishing at the busy market opposite Nyabugogo minibus-taxi stand. If you enjoy crowds and people-watching, try it.

Walk down Rue de l'Epargne or along Avenue de la Justice until you come to the prison. As you face it from the road, the first road beside it to your right, turning off at a sharpish angle, is Rue du Mont Huye, an unsurfaced road running downhill. Take this and follow it – you'll pass homes, small shops, an enclosed market area off it to your right, and then you arrive at the bottom – and the chaos of Nyabugogo market. Just look at the variety of people here: you'll see so many different bone structures, shades of colour, styles of clothing...

If you cross over into the minibus-taxi station (which is a 'market area' all of its own, with vendors offering everything from leather shoes and hi-fi equipment to – improbably – plastic hair curlers and freshly baked bread) you can get a minibus-taxi back to the central minibus station or else take a normal taxi; they park just inside the main gate. Or turn right up the main road as you leave the market; this upward hill is Boulevard de Nyabugogo and will take you back to Place de l'Unité Nationale and the centre of town.

EXCURSIONS FROM KIGALI
Via tour operators

All the tour operators in town can organise excursions for you and/or arrange vehicle hire. There are so many that it's repetitive to list them all: the ones selected below (all of which have some English-speaking staff) give you an idea of what is on offer. They'll all book accommodation for you, collect you from the airport, arrange permits for gorilla-viewing and so forth. For an up-to-date list, check with ORTPN when you arrive or look on the Rwanda website: www.rwanda1.com/government/tourism/htm. It is claimed that there are over 230 sites of historic or cultural interest in Rwanda (no-one has yet listed them all to me!) so you shouldn't be stuck for choice. If you're phoning from abroad, remember that the international code for Rwanda is 250. There are no regional codes in Rwanda.

Some tour operators in Kigali

In the SORAS building, on the left-hand side of Boulevard de la Révolution as you walk along it from the town centre, you'll find two agencies: International Tours & Travel and Concord Rwanda. **International Tours & Travel** (BP 924 Kigali; tel: 74057, 78831/2; fax: 75582; email: itt@rwandatel1.rwanda1.com) can fix trips to any of the national parks, with car hire, hotel reservations and English-speaking personnel. They can also organise complete tailor-made packages for you in advance, including international air transfers. **Concord Rwanda** (BP 4152 Kigali; tel: 75566, 75988; fax: 74452; email: concord@rwandatel1.rwanda1.com) can also organise excursions and packages, and is a good place to get up-to-date information on trekking in the Virunga mountains. If it's safe to go, they'll arrange this for you and provide a knowledgeable guide.

Swift Tours & Travel (BP 1003 Kigali; tel: 77472, 77074; fax: 77070; email: sfint@rwanda1.com) at 10 Avenue de la Paix can also organise tailor-made packages in advance, including international flights, and take you to all of Rwanda's attractions. They take groups regularly to view gorillas in the Volcanoes National Park and currently organise short (one-day or weekend) tours to historic sites – the one-day tour includes examples of traditional buildings, the reconstructed King's Palace in Nyanza (see page 119), the National Museum in Butare (page 128), a display of *Intore* dancing (pages 72–3) and Kabgayi cathedral and museum (page 117). If you find yourself with some hours to spend in Entebbe (Uganda) while awaiting a connecting flight to/from Kigali, Swift can arrange a trip to visit the chimp colony on Ngamba Island in Lake Victoria (but currently you'll need a Ugandan visa).

Top Travel Tours (BP 10 Kigali; tel: 78646, 72552; fax: 73853; email: bernaku63@hotmail.com) at 10 Boulevard de la Révolution (it's set back from the road in a small courtyard near the Alliance Express office) can also organise full tailor-made packages in advance, whether for individuals or for groups, with international flights included. They can arrange cultural events in Kigali, Butare, Gisenyi and Kibuye, and currently run a five-day tour which includes a tour of Kigali, a gorilla trek, visits to Gisenyi, Kibuye and Cyangugu, Nyungwe Forest, the National Museum in Butare, and Nyanza

Among other tour, travel and car-hire agencies that you'll see as you walk in the centre of town are the **Changa Travel Agency** (opposite the Belgian School in Avenue des Mille Collines; tel: 77564, 77103; fax: 77669; email: changatravel@hotmail.com), **Gama Travel & Tours** (Boulevard de la Révolution; BP 2520 Kigali; tel/fax: 78215; email: jpgat@hotmail.com), **Nord Sud International Tours & Travel** (Avenue de la Paix; tel: 75310; fax: 75349), **Satguru Travel & Tours** (tel: 73079; fax: 72231), **Travel Agency Services** (BP 3859 Kigali; tel: 74990; fax: 71138; email: moniquemutesi@hotmail.com) and **Travel & Tours Services** (near the Gloria Hotel; BP 4778 Kigali; tel/fax: 71278).

For details of the **Okapi Travel & Tours Agency** see the Okapi Hotel on page 99. This agency can arrange car hire and trips throughout Rwanda, and put together tailor-made packages in advance. It runs a daily minibus, the *Okapicar*, across the western border to Goma in DRC, which you can currently visit on a day-trip without a visa.

Independent visits
Minibus-taxis

Most places in Rwanda are easily accessible by public minibus-taxi, leaving from the **Nyabugogo minibus-taxi station** (*Gare routière Nyabugogo*) about 2km from the centre of Kigali. It's a huge place and they are lined up in ranks – some signposted with destinations and others not – but just ask someone and you'll be shown the right place to wait. The minibuses leave as soon as they've a full complement of passengers – and that does mean *full* as in can-of-sardines full – but everyone gets a seat. There's a no-smoking policy on board. Fares are collected just before you alight rather than when you board; you'll see other passengers getting their money ready as their destinations approach. If you're not sure of the fare (it's helpful to offer the correct money) ask anyone what you should be paying. If you're carrying luggage, either keep it on your lap (if it's small enough) or else ask for it to be stuffed in at the back or put on the roof. If you have anything fragile, keep it with you.

If you're returning to Kigali the same day, don't leave it too late as there's no set schedule; it's sensible to ask the driver for an estimate of the time of the last bus, and to be there well before it's due to depart.

While you're waiting for your minibus to leave, vendors of all sorts will be trying to catch your eye and sell you something – including bottled drinks and fruit, as well as fresh bread and cakes, which are handy if you've a long journey ahead. You can even buy hard-boiled eggs, and season them from the salt and pepper pots conveniently provided!

Minibus-taxis to the Nyabugogo station leave from the central minibus station (see page 96) at the junction of Avenue de Commerce and Rue Mont Kabuye. Or take a *taxi-voiture*.

Minibus-taxis leave Kigali at 09.00 daily for Bujumbura in Burundi (arriving there at 15.00) from the Titanic Express office next to the central bus station in Rue Mont Kabuye, and a private minibus runs daily to Goma in the DRC from the Okapi Hotel (see page 99).

National parks
Akagera Park (see *Chapter 9*) can be visited from Kigali in a day but you'll need your own transport. The mountain gorillas in the **Volcanoes Park** can also be visited as a day trip, but again you'll need your own transport in order to get to the park entrance in time for the trek, otherwise you should spend the previous night in either Ruhengeri (and arrange transport from there) or in Kinigi. See *Chapter 8*. The **Nyungwe Forest** is too far for a day trip, but minibus-taxis running between Butare and Cyangugu can drop you off nearby (see *Chapter 7*).

Butare
Butare and the National Museum (see *Chapter 7*) are an easy day trip from Kigali. Apart from public minibus-taxis leaving from Nyabugogo, there are private companies (eg: Taxi Ponctuel, Volcano Taxi Express) with several minibuses a day leaving from near the central minibus-taxi station. Going into Butare by public minibus-taxi, you can ask to be dropped at either the museum or the centre of town; to return to Kigali, you must start from the minibus-taxi station on the northern edge of town (see map on page 124). The private companies stop and start in the centre of Butare.

Genocide memorials
There are two memorials to the south of Kigali, both accessible as a day trip. The church at **Nyamata**, about 30km from Kigali, was the scene of a horrific massacre. The interior has been cleared and left empty. There are still some bloodstains on the walls, and, in the courtyard outside an underground chamber has been dug in which are stored – and displayed – the skulls and bones of many hundred victims. Visitors can see them and be reminded of the enormity of the crime. A guide will take you round and explain the background – and ask you to sign the visitors' book, in which you may spot some internationally known names.

Ntarama church, about 5km down a right-hand fork which branches off the Nyamata road roughly 20km outside Kigali, has been left empty and just as it was after the bodies had been removed – there are scraps of cloth and personal items still on the floor. Beside it is another building where more people, seeking safety, were slaughtered. It's a silent place, surrounded by trees: very evocative, very poignant. The guide (French-speaking) recounts the events precisely and powerfully. A sign outside the gate records that around 5,000 victims died there.

Both memorials are grim, Nyamata more so than Ntarama because of the bones and skulls, and both convey the appalling scale of the tragedy. There's no charge for entry to the sites and the guides do their job with dignity – a tip is expected and deserved.

Southwest Rwanda

The mountainous southwest of Rwanda boasts a variety of different tourist attractions, none of which has much in common with the others except for the consistently memorable montane scenery that surrounds them – and the arbitrary fact of being linked by the same surfaced road.

Coming from the capital, the first regional highlight is Butare, the country's second city, and its cultural and intellectual heart. Butare is the site of the National University, as well as the fine National Museum – rated by many to house the best ethnographic collection in East Africa – and within easy day-tripping distance of the well-maintained traditional Royal Palace at Nyanza.

To the west of Butare lies the recently gazetted Nyungwe National Park, a 970km² expanse of Afro-montane rainforest which sprawls magnificently across the mountains that stretch towards the Burundi border. A magnet for botanists and ornithologists alike, Nyungwe is best known for the volume and variety of its primates – 13 species in all, including chimpanzee, l'Hoest's monkey and troops of 400-plus Ruwenzori colobus. Nyungwe is the most accessible of Rwanda's reserves, easily reached on public transport, while facilities include a comfortable resthouse and campsite, and an excellent network of day trails.

Other attractions in this part of Rwanda include the attractive Lake Kivu ports of Cyangugu and Kibuye, both with a good selection of hotels, and the more remote Bugarama Hot Springs and Cyamudongo Forest.

Main roads through this part of Rwanda are surfaced and covered by plenty of minibus-taxis, and in some cases buses. A good selection of mid-range and budget accommodation is available in all main centres. Altitudes range from 1,500m on the shore of Lake Kivu to a peak of 2,950m in Nyungwe; the climate is comfortably warm by day, but can be chilly at night, so take enough warm clothing.

THE ROAD FROM KIGALI TO BUTARE
Gitarama

This small and scattered town 51km from Kigali, where the road forks south to Butare and continues westward towards Lake Kivu, has often been involved in Rwanda's recent history. It is famous as the location of the historic gathering

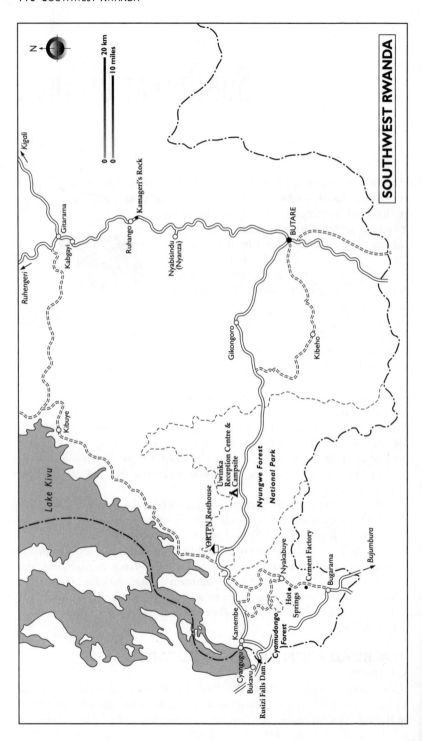

Above Topi in Akagera
National Park

Left Ankole bull

Below Red-chested alethe,
Nyungwe Forest Reserve

Above Nyanza Royal Palace
Below left Girl in homestead, Nyanza
Below right House with traditional
cow-dung decorations

on January 28 1961 at which the people first declared Rwanda a republic (see page 14), and is also remembered as the birthplace of Grégoire Kayibanda, Rwanda's first president. Earlier, in November 1959, it was probably the starting point for the violence that led to the imposition of martial law under Colonel Guy Logiest (see page 14).

Opposite the taxi-minibus stand in the centre of Gitarama is the Banque de Kigali (which can change travellers' cheques), a handful of small shops, and the bar/restaurants Tranquillité and Le Palmier. The post office is about 1km away: turn right as you leave the minibus stand and keep straight on; you'll come to it on the left just after the Rwanda Revenue Authority. There are motorbike-taxis at the minibus stand – but you won't be given a helmet, so be sure that your insurance includes this form of transport. Really there's little to see here, except people, going about their daily lives, which can be a change from more intensive tourism.

Minibus-taxis pass through Gitarama en route from Kigali to either Kibuye or Butare and, if you want to break your journey, simple accommodation is available. Just outside the town and signposted on the left as you come from Kigali is the newish **Minihotel Tourisme**: eight clean rooms with hot water, US$15 single and US$18 double. It's a pleasant, peaceful place and serves evening meals by request. In the centre of Gitarama there are three options, all small, simple and friendly: **Le Palmier** (tel: 62183), across the road from the minibus stand, has two en-suite rooms (US$13) and four with shared facilities (US$8–10). Turn right as you leave the bus station and you'll come (on your right) to the **Gloria** (tel: 62234) and **Papyrus Hotels**, both offering some en-suite rooms and others with shared facilities at around US$7–10.

Kabgayi

The massive cathedral of Kabgayi, 3km from Gitarama along the Butare road, is the oldest in the country, dating from 1925; missionaries were already installed in Kabgayi by 1906 and it became the seat of the first Catholic bishop. The cathedral, with its huge and tranquil interior, is worth a visit, and there's a small museum nearby. Children may spot you and come to sell handicrafts. During colonisation various training schools were set up in Kabgayi – for midwives, artisans, printers, carpenters and blacksmiths, among others.

Kabgayi Church Museum
With thanks to Gaston Gatare of Swift Tours & Travel

The little museum beside the cathedral opens Monday to Friday 08.00 to 17.00. Saturday and Sunday visits are also possible if booked in advance. Entry costs RFr1,000 ($2.50 approximately) for non-nationals and RFr500 for Rwandans. Within the very small interior are many historically and culturally interesting items such as:

- ancient hand tools and weapons: knives, hoes, spears, arrows, etc
- tools and implements connected with the iron industry
- ancient examples of clothing: bark cloth etc

- musical instruments
- methods of transportation used for chiefs, high-born women and the sick
- clay pots and pipes
- baskets – ornamental and for domestic use
- the prestigious Milk Bar and jugs from the palace of the last queen mother (1961)
- old indoor games such as Igisoro which is still popular in Rwanda and neighbouring countries
- ancient military officers' costumes and pips
- a national drum captured from Ijwi Island (Kivu) in 1875, thereby effectively annexing it to Rwanda
- information about traditional medicines, and tokens (kwe) formerly used as currency
- modern clothing and historical photographs

In the complex of associated buildings behind the cathedral in Kabgayi there's the large **Centre St André** (tel: 62450), with 82 guestrooms of various categories – single, double, triple, en suite, shared facilities and so on. The most you'll pay is about US$9 per person, but it can fill up if there's a religious convocation, so book in advance. It's very new (opened in May 2000) and very clean.

Ruhango

This small town is of interest primarily for *Uratare rwa Kamageri* (Kamageri's Rock), signposted along the roadside a ten-minute walk south of the town centre. An odd legend lies behind the name of this otherwise unremarkable chunk of stone. When a local chief asked his advisers to think up a punishment for an adulterer, one of them, Kamageri, came up with the brainwave of heating a flat rock to oven temperature, then throwing the offender on it. The chief was so appalled at the severity of this punishment that he decided it befitted the person who dreamed it up, and Kamageri was duly roasted alive on the rock which today bears his name.

More mundanely, Ruhango also boasts one of the largest markets in the country, which takes place on Friday mornings and contains an astonishing range of merchandise, from livestock and vegetables to hi-fi equipment and household goods. Vendors trek in from far afield, carrying their wares. You could consider spending a Thursday night here and then watching activities unfold. Ruhango has a few restaurants and supermarkets, as well as the comfortable and sensibly priced **Hotel Umuco**. Centrally located, and arranged around a pleasant courtyard, this hotel offers singles for US$7 and doubles with en-suite showers for US$12, as well as inexpensive meals and drinks.

Nyanza

The turning to Nyanza is on the right as you travel southwards. *Nyanza* is the ancient name, although it's still used; on the signpost you will see the town's modern name, Nyabisindu.

Some minibus-taxis go into the town centre while others will drop you at the junction. This little town with its wide, dusty streets has almost a Wild West feeling to it. It's a good place to stop for lunch and explore a little if you're driving between Butare and Kigali; the **Umubano Restaurant** is a friendly, family place serving good Rwandan food, where a filling *mélange* (meat, chips, rice, beans, cabbage, plantain etc) costs around US$1, and their groundnut sauce is not to be missed! Other restaurants offer similar fare. The 'Nyanza brochette' is said to be thicker and juicier than any elsewhere. Only very, very basic accommodation is available here so far (**Chez Mr Seneza**, off Avenue Principale near the Pharmacie l'Unité), although plans for a tourist hotel outside the town are rumoured to be in the air.

The King's Palace

This is the top touristic reason for visiting Nyanza. It's several kilometres from the centre, and signposted. The traditional ancient palace of the Mwami has been reconstructed, together with some other buildings, 3–4km away from its original site, beside the newer *mwami's* palace (built for the Mwami Rudahigwa Mutara III in 1932) which is now the part-time home of Rwanda's National Ballet (the *Intore* dancers, see pages 72–3). In olden times, Nyanza was the heart of Rwanda and seat of its monarchy, background to the oral tradition of battles and conquests, power struggles and royal intrigues. It is where the German colonisers came, at the end of the 19th century, to visit the *mwami* – and contemporary reports tell of the great pomp and ceremony these visits occasioned, as well as the impressive size of the *mwami's* court.

> The capital of the kingdom was composed of a group of huts, an ephemeral town of some 2,000 inhabitants, well organised as far as the administration of the country and the comfort of the nobility were concerned... At his court the Mwami maintained the following retinue: the 'Ntore', adolescent sons of chiefs and notables, who formed the corps de ballet; the 'Bakoma', soothsayers, magicians and historians; the 'Abashashi', keepers of the arsenal, the wardrobe and the furniture; the 'Abasisi' and 'Abacurabgenge', mimes, musicians and cooks; the 'Abanyabyumba', palanquin bearers and night watchmen; the 'Nitalindwa', huntsmen and runners; the 'Intumwa', artisans working for the Mwami; and finally the hangmen, attentive servants of jurists, ever ready to respond to the brief order to fetch and kill.

> *Traveller's Guide to the Belgian Congo and Ruanda-Urundi,*
> Tourist Bureau for the Belgian Congo and Ruanda-Urundi, Brussels, 1951

The traditional palace has been carefully reconstructed and maintained, and contains various items including the king's extensive bed – an animal skin stretched tightly on a frame. When I visited, there seemed to be no means of lighting the interior and a torch would have been an asset; also no-one

WORKING IN NYANZA

Ania Dudziec

Last summer, the chorus of one of the songs played on the radio, and at every dance, went like this:

> Kuya kwetu
> Kinshasa, Kampala na Buja…

And that's what has happened. Rwandan people from all over have come home and settled back in the land of their grandparents. I came here at about the same time and, in a different way, I feel I've come home to Rwanda as well, although I've never had any links with it before.

Nyanza, where I live and work, is known for two things: first, for being the former residence of the Rwandan kings, and secondly for being the home of Ikivuguto, the National Dairy. Its wide, dusty roads and numerous 'saloons' (as in hairdressing salon) make it look more like a set for a cowboy film than a small town in central Africa.

My favourite time of day is just before sunset, walking home from some quick shopping in the market after a day at school, with the sun setting behind the volcanoes in a pink sky. Yes, I know it's a cliché, but that doesn't make it any less beautiful. One of the words heard most often by an outsider is 'umuzungu' ('white foreigner'), and it was one of the hardest things that I had to get used to – constantly being made aware of my skin colour and difference. Now, on my walks home in the early orange evening, together with workers returning home after a day of selling mats or bananas in the market, I don't hear that word: the much-repeated 'umuzungu' is replaced by my name, a smile and acceptance. People will glance at me once, say hello, stop for a chat or walk on without a second thought; and I know that I'm almost home, passing by the house of an elderly neighbour who sits outside it all day in his wicker chair greeting everyone with a huge grin. At times like this I know why I'm happy here in Rwanda.

Obviously, Rwanda is now primarily known to the world because of what

spoke anything but Kinyarwanda, until a couple of local students came by and helped in French. But it is an impressive construction and there are plans to make it more tourist-friendly. At the time of writing, you'll gain most if you go on a guided trip (see pages 112–13 for tour operators who offer these).

The newer palace is empty and badly needs a face-lift now, but must have been beautiful once. A 1951 report states: 'In certain circumstances, and with the permission of the local authorities, he [the Mwami] may be visited at his palace which is built on modern lines, furnished in good taste and richly decorated with trophies in an oriental manner.' Now the walls of the gracious rooms are stained, footsteps echo in the emptiness, and the only decorations are a few painstakingly collected old black-and-white photos and happened in 1994. It's impossible to write anything about life here without returning to that past. Looking around, it would be easy never to suspect what lies beneath the surface – life goes on, women dig in the fields with their babies on their backs, primary school kids in blue uniforms play football with their homemade plastic-bag-and-string balls, and old ladies walk their goats. It's only later that you might wonder why it's mainly women who work in the fields, why people are fearful of walking anywhere at night and why there's a strange, sombre silence countrywide at the beginning of each April. Although it may not be immediately evident, the past does touch very strongly upon the life of every person here and will continue to do so.

As in the majority of developing countries, it's often difficult at first to have close contact with women. Many of my colleagues are male and, for that reason, most visitors during my first few months in Nyanza were men. It has taken a while, but now it seems that I have more contact with women than before, partly because most of my students are girls. Perhaps as a result of the war or perhaps owing to more established tradition, women in Rwanda seem to have a very strong sense of a shared sisterhood. Whilst men sit in bars drinking home-brewed banana beer and sorghum wine, women work together in the fields, on building sites and at home. And in the cool evenings after work, it is groups of women who gather to talk, sing, dance and pray together.

Inevitably, I had certain expectations and apprehensions before coming to Rwanda. Although many things have become apparent through just being here, I know that much remains hidden. Rwandan people are, in general, very reserved and perhaps difficult to form close friendships with initially. Before I came to Rwanda, I spoke with someone who had been here for a while. She said that the true Rwandan character is deep and multi-layered. Like an onion, as each layer is peeled away, something new is revealed. This is true also of everyday life – nothing is quite what it seems. Each day really does bring something new and different – which is why I love it here.

Ania Dudziec is a teacher from London working with Voluntary Service Overseas

newspaper cuttings, mostly about the Intore dancers, who sometimes come there to rehearse and give performances. For its history and for its peaceful, attractive location, it is still worth seeing, especially if you go with a knowledgeable guide.

En route to the palaces you'll pass the **Ikivuguto National Dairy**, started during Belgian colonisation and still going strong. In theory you can just turn up and ask for a free tour, but in practice it would be courteous to ask about this on your way out to the palaces and then have your tour (if convenient) on the way back. Also out in the direction of the palaces is Nyanza's **stadium**, not only the home of enthusiastic local football matches on Sundays during the dry season but also, in 1999, the venue of Rwanda's national celebration of culture.

BUTARE

This pleasant, businesslike town is the site of Rwanda's university and is often called the country's 'intellectual centre'. Named Astrida by the Belgians (after Queen Astrid), it reverted to its original, local name of Butare in 1962. At the time of independence it seemed possible that it might become Rwanda's capital; during colonisation, although the capital of the joint territory of Ruanda-Urundi had been Bujumbura, Butare was the administrative capital of Ruanda. However, in the end Kigali was chosen, largely because of its more central location. So Kigali has mushroomed, while Butare remains peaceful and compact.

During term-time Butare has probably the country's greatest concentration of students, in relation to its size – not only at the university but also at other technical and training schools and colleges. In fact the first secondary school in the country opened here in 1928. It's something of a religious centre, too, with its massive cathedral and other churches. The proportion of Protestants to Roman Catholics is said to be higher in the Butare area than in most parts of Rwanda.

The genocide

The intellectual and cultural spirit of Butare was so strong that initially it seemed that it could remain intact and resist the madness of slaughter. For decades Hutus and Tutsis had lived and studied peacefully together there. When the killing started, people flocked to Butare from outlying areas believing that they would find safety – as indeed they did, for a while. The prefect of Butare at the time of the genocide was the only Tutsi prefect in Rwanda; he took charge, welcoming the refugees, reassuring parishioners, and demonstrating such authority that, for two weeks while the killing raged elsewhere, relative calm (although there were isolated instances of violence) prevailed in his prefecture. But it couldn't last. Because of his defiance he was sacked from his post and subsequently murdered, to be replaced by a hard-line military officer, Colonel Tharcisse Muvunyi, and an equally hard-line civilian administrator. Under their orchestration, the killing started immediately – and the massacres in Butare prefecture proved to be some of the worst of the genocide. Tharcisse Muvunyi later fled to Britain, where he was tracked down and arrested in Lewisham (London) in February 2000.

Getting there and away

Butare is 136km (a two-hour drive) from Kigali, along good tarred roads. Public minibus-taxis to Butare start from Kigali's Nyabugogo bus station; the fare is about US$4. There are also direct minibuses from Cyangugu and Gitarama. In Butare, you can be dropped either at the minibus station on the northern edge of town or opposite the market in the centre. However, for returning to Kigali (or continuing to Cyangugu) you must start from the bus station as there are no central pick-ups.

Alternatively there are private minibuses, the *Taxi Ponctuel* ('Punctual Taxi') and Volcano Express Taxi, starting from near the Avenue de Commerce bus station in central Kigali, which go direct to Butare, with buses leaving at 07.00,

RICH VERSUS POOR

In Butare, I chatted to a young man who worked in a hotel there. He told me that he had fled to Burundi when the genocide began, and when he returned (he made the familiar cut-throat gesture) his family had 'gone'. He was alone. He married in 1996 and now has two daughters. He said wryly, 'So I'm building myself a new family.' In his spare time he makes delicate, decorated greetings cards and tries to sell them, to earn extra income. I asked whether he was optimistic about Rwanda's future. 'Yes, as a whole it will be OK. No more trouble. But, the poor are *very* poor. Big gap between them and the rich.' I asked, 'Is it worse for the poor now than it was before the genocide?' 'No no. Always bad. No difference now. But now they expect more.' In a mixture of French and English he went on to explain how the perceptions and aspirations are changing. New, fast roads make the passing traffic more visible and more accessible. Villagers can travel further to market, where flashier and more desirable goods are now on sale. They see 'development' and 'progress' happening to others and they feel overlooked.

I was reminded of a Rwandan friend who has been working on government surveys nationwide, travelling from village to village in search of statistics on rural life, poverty, health, income and so on. She said that when the survey team arrives in a village the response isn't necessarily co-operative. Villagers ask, 'What are you going to do for us? Are you going to solve our difficulties? If not, don't bother to ask us your questions.'

A huge amount has been achieved since 1995. Many problems have been tackled. Probably the young man is right when he says, 'As a whole it will be OK. No more trouble.' But development is – has always been – an agonisingly slow process.

10.00, 13.00 and either 16.00 or 17.00 depending on the company. (There may well be more by now.) They return from Butare at more or less the same times and the fare is roughly the same as that of the minibus-taxis.

Plenty of traffic uses this road, so hitching should be easy too.

Getting around

The National Museum and the University are no more than about 5km apart, so theoretically everything is manageable on foot. If you should get weary or want to go further afield, however, a few beat-up taxis wait by the turning from the main street leading to the market. The prices asked seem to be standard, but, if you feel you're being overcharged, either bargain or ask to see the official tariff. In any case, agree on a price in advance. Rates may well have increased by the time you read this, but at the time of writing it costs about US$2.50 from the town centre to the museum, US$20 to Nyanza and US$25 to Kibeho (see below). Waiting time costs extra, currently US$7.50 per hour.

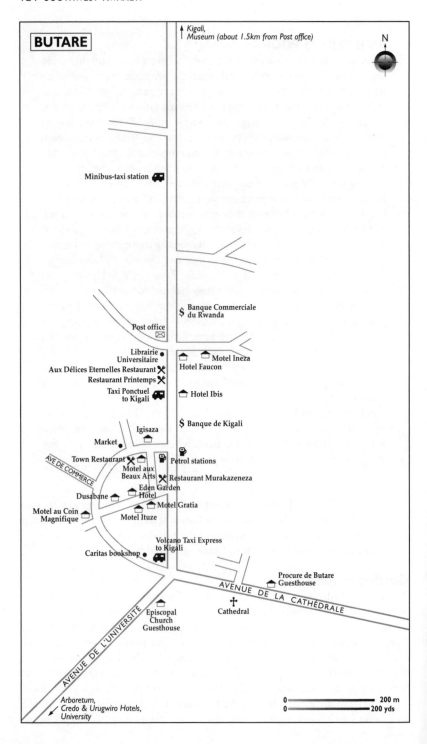

BUTARE

Kigali,
Museum (about 1.5km from Post office)

N

Minibus-taxi station

Banque Commerciale
du Rwanda

Post office

Librairie
Universitaire
Aux Délices Eternelles Restaurant
Restaurant Printemps

Motel Ineza
Hotel Faucon

Taxi Ponctuel
to Kigali

Hotel Ibis

Banque de Kigali

Igisaza

Market

AVE DE COMMERCE

Town Restaurant

Petrol stations

Motel aux
Beaux Arts

Restaurant Murakazeneza

Eden Garden
Hotel

Dusabane

Motel Gratia

Motel au Coin
Magnifique

Motel Ituze

Volcano Taxi Express
to Kigali

Caritas bookshop

Procure de Butare
Guesthouse

AVENUE DE LA CATHÉDRALE

AVENUE DE L'UNIVERSITÉ

Episcopal
Church
Guesthouse

Cathedral

Arboretum,
Credo & Urugwiro Hotels,
University

0 — 200 m
0 — 200 yds

Where to stay

Starting at rock bottom, the cheapest (but also the least appealing) accommodation is at the **Episcopal Church Guesthouse**, by the crossroads en route to the university, where the friendly welcome doesn't compensate for cell-like double rooms ($6 per room) opening off a long dark passage, and the shared facilities are far from fragrant. Far better is the **Procure de Butare Guesthouse** (BP 224 Butare; tel: 30993) opposite the cathedral, where the shared facilities are clean, and bright rooms (with wash-basins) cost US$6.50 single, US$10 double. All meals are available here (breakfast US$1.50, lunch and supper US$2.50) and there's secure parking.

In the market area there are several passable small hotels all in the range of US$5–10 per person – the cheapest is the **Eden Garden Hotel**, newly opened in August 2000, which has plain, clean rooms set around a central courtyard for US$5 per person whether single or double, with shared facilities. The **Igisaza** (tel: 32082) has four good twin en-suite rooms (cold water) and is quiet. At **Motel au Coin Magnifique** (tel: 32095) the eight en-suite rooms (cold water) are darkish but clean. The **Dusabane** (12 rooms) looks unprepossessing but the shared facilities are clean and the restaurant does a generous mixed plateful of rice, vegetables and meat/fish. The **Motel Ituze** has rooms with wash-basins and shared shower/WC, set around a patch of grass and with deckchairs outside – it's clean and quiet.

Still in the market area, going up a bit in price but still very good value is the two-storeyed **Motel aux Beaux Arts** (tel: 30584). All its ten rooms have washbasin, shower and WC, and the restaurant offers a good range of meals and snacks; rooms cost US$10–18 depending on facilities. The **Motel Gratia** (tel: 30278) is also a comfortable place, with a restaurant and 14 rooms set round a small, well-watered courtyard garden: US$10–$15. Some rooms have a small sitting-room.

Down a side-road opposite the post office on the north side of town, the **Motel Ineza** (BP 170 Butare; tel: 32060/30987) has 12 tiny, en-suite rooms (cold water, but they'll give you a bucket of hot) set around a secluded garden, where you can sit out and eat, write or just enjoy the peace and quiet. The bar/restaurant has a good range of food and snacks (the *mélanges* are tasty) and the whole place is good value. It's popular, so you'd do well to book in advance. Rooms are about US$8 single, US$12 double.

Two mid-range hotels in the main street which have been there for several decades are the Ibis and the Faucon. The **Ibis** (BP 103 Butare; tel/fax: 30335) has 14 en-suite rooms at a variety of prices depending on facilities – suites, single, double, twin etc. They're comfortable, with TV and phone, and the bedside lights are a welcome touch. Prices from US$30/$42 single/double upwards; payment by Visa can be arranged on request. The main restaurant is good (quite pricey) and there's a convenient bar/snack restaurant on the street. You can buy pay-as-you-go mobile phones here. The **Faucon** (BP 366 Butare; tel/fax 32061) is more laid back – an old building, thick walls, high ceilings – a few colonial echoes here! The façade needs a face-lift, but the eleven comfortable en-suite rooms (some suites) are set round a courtyard, away from the street, and the back windows look out on to a peaceful view of greenery. There's a good (not cheap) main restaurant, also a bar/snack restaurant. Prices (which include continental breakfast) are set to rise in 2001; on the basis of 2000 prices I estimate around US$28/$40 single/double upwards, depending on facilities.

Finally, on the road to the university are the Urugwiro and Credo Hotels. The **Urugwiro** (tel: 530786) is a serviceable budget place, with ten rooms with washbasins and shared facilities for around US$5/$10 single/double. It's very clean, but a bit of a walk from town. The **Credo** (BP 310 Butare; tel: 530855/530505; fax: 530505; mobile 083 02216) has a range of 25 comfortable en-suite rooms – some of them are suites – as well as what it calls a 'home', consisting of two simple family rooms, one with four beds and the other with two beds and a wash-basin, sharing impeccably clean WC and showers, for US$8 per person. Otherwise this is an upmarket, mid-range place, with a swimming pool, restaurant (with a promising menu) and night-club. Rooms vary in size and have TV, telephone and (mostly) balcony, with a lovely view across fields at the back. It's very new (opened in 1999) and very clean. Room prices run from about US$35 upwards for a double and include continental breakfast. With a bit of notice, car-hire can be arranged here for trips to Nyungwe Forest. It's sometimes used by tour groups, so you'd do well to book in advance.

Where to eat

Plenty of small restaurants round the market offer snacks and good-value *mélanges* of rice, vegetables and meat/fish. Try the **Town Restaurant** next to the Beaux Arts and the self-service **Dusabane**. For snacks or drinks in the main street, the **Ibis** and **Faucon** are both convenient and reasonably priced. Also in the main street, **Aux Délices Eternelles** opposite the Hotel Faucon has an unspectacular menu of cheapish snacks and main meals but is quiet and friendly; the next-door **Restaurant Printemps** does a reasonable lunch-time buffet for about US$3 upwards – and I can vouch for the freshness of the chicken on the day I was there because I'd seen it carried in earlier, squawking. **The Motel Ineza** is a pleasant and economical place for lunch or dinner (or a drink) even if you're not staying there – one traveller reports having had 'a whopping dinner there – US$9.00 for a meal and some drinks for two people'. Considerably pricier but good if you feel like a treat are the main restaurants at the **Ibis** and **Faucon**. For a filling and beautifully presented local mixture (the manager/cook will tell you what's available and you can choose) try the little **Restaurant Murakazeneza** in the main street. We had a generous two-person mixed platter with separate salad for less than US$5.

Nightlife

There's not a huge amount, but the **M16** nightclub near the Hotel Faucon is quite lively in the evenings, often with dancing later. Also ask around for the latest 'dives' used by college students.

Practicalities

The **post office** is at the northern end of the main street. Of the **banks**, the Banque Commerciale du Rwanda opposite the post office can change cash but not travellers' cheques; the Banque de Kigali midway down the main street changes both cash and travellers' cheques. There are two **bookshops**: the Librairie Universitaire at the northern end of the main street has a fair range of books and student stationery, as well as some dusty but original handicrafts. Librairie Caritas at the other end of the main street has a few more touristy books and items of stationery, as well as some international magazines and games. I felt a surge of homesickness at the sight of a set of Travel Scrabble. For **handicrafts**, there's an excellent shop opposite the Ibis Hotel, selling products made by the *Co-opérative des Producteurs Artisanaux de Butare* (COPABU). The items are priced, but a little gentle bargaining will do no harm, particularly if you're buying more than one. The co-op was set up in 1997 with 47 members, working in banana-leaf products, wood-carving and reed baskets. Three years later it had 954 members (99 individuals and 35 associations) of which 66% are women. Handicrafts in the Butare area have been well organised and you can even check them out on the COPABU website: www.peoplelink.org/copabu.

Security

For all its laid-back atmosphere, Butare is a busy town with a mixed population, so take normal precautions such as not carrying conspicuous wealth. The larger street kids can be a bit pushy, but treat them understandingly and they're manageable. In the evenings some may gather to sniff solvents around the petrol stations. See box *After the genocide* on page 80. If you go out to eat at night it's wise to take a torch/flashlight. Yes, the streets are well lit, but if there's a power cut (rare, but it happens) they become very black indeed, and finding your way back to your hotel might not be easy.

What to see

Although not really a tourist 'sight', the National University of Rwanda (BP 56 Butare; tel: 530122; fax: 530121; email: nurcc@nur.ac.rw; web: www.nur.ac.rw) is by far Butare's most important institution. Created in 1963, and with only 51 students and 16 lecturers when it opened, it now has some 4,540 students and 275 lecturers. The university lost many of its students and personnel during the genocide and suffered considerable damage, but managed to reopen in 1995. It is now a vibrant and forward-looking institution, comprising faculties of agronomy, law, arts and human sciences, medicine, science and technology, economics, social sciences and management, and education, as well as schools of journalism and communication and of modern languages. You may run across visiting professors in any of Butare's hotels and guesthouses.

Out by the university is the **Ruhande Arboretum**, started in 1934. Its objective at the outset was to study the behaviour of imported and indigenous species, to determine what silvicultural methods were most suitable, to evaluate the trees' productivity and timber quality, and to develop the best of them. Now, it is of interest for the range and variety of its species – and it's a peaceful, shady place.

The huge, red-brick, Roman Catholic **cathedral**, built in memory of Belgium's Princess Astrid in the 1930s, is the largest in the country and worth a visit. Its interior is fairly basic, but the atmosphere is tranquil and the size impressive. A service there can be a moving experience.

There is some attractive **architecture** and the tranquil, tree-lined residential streets away from the centre are good territory for strolling. It's possible to take a turning to the right a short distance east of the Motel Ineza and then to cross twisty tracks through the green and cultivated valley until you reach the cathedral, but ask for directions and advice. A clear heritage of Belgian colonisation (in Belgium even the motorways are lit) is the generous amount of street lighting in Butare.

The **market**, although not extensive, is crowded and atmospheric.

Spectacular displays of **traditional dance** (*Intore*) take place in Butare and can be arranged on request (and for a fee); ask at the museum (below) about this.

The National Museum of Rwanda

If you're in Butare – indeed even if you're in some other part of Rwanda – you should allow time to visit this beautifully presented collection of exhibits on Rwandan history and culture.

The museum is exceptional. Opened in 1988, and presented to Rwanda as a gift from Belgium's King Baudouin I, its seven spacious rooms illustrate the country and its people from earliest times until the present day.

Room 1 (the entrance hall) has space for temporary displays as well as numerous shelves of traditional handicrafts for sale. **Room 2** presents a comprehensive view of Rwanda's geological and geographical background and the development of its terrain and population. In **Room 3** the occupations of its early inhabitants (hunter-gathering, farming and stock-raising) are illustrated, together with the later development of tools and methods of transport. The social importance of cattle is explained and there are even detailed instructions for the brewing of traditional banana beer. **Room 4** displays a variety of handicrafts and the making of traditional household items: pottery, mats, baskets, leatherwork and the wooden shields of the *Intore* dancers. **Room 5** illustrates traditional styles and methods of architecture – and a full-scale royal hut has been reconstructed. In **Room 6** traditional games and sports are displayed and more space is given to the costumes and equipment of the *Intore* dancers. Finally, **Room 7** contains exhibits relating to traditional customs and beliefs, history, culture, poetry, oral tradition and the supernatural.

At the reception desk, various pamphlets and books are on sale. At present no descriptions or background material are available in English, only in French and Kinyarwanda; but, at the time of writing, some translations are being prepared.

The museum is open 09.00–12.00 and 14.00–17.00; the entrance fee is US$2.50. Tel: 530586; fax: 530211; email: museum@nur.ac.rw; web:

THE PREPARATION OF BANANA BEER

(Free translation)

When the bunches of fruit are ready, cut them.

Cover the bunches with banana leaves and leave them in the courtyard to ripen for two to three days.

Clean out the pit in which the fruit ripened.

Lay banana branches across the top of the pit.

Place the bananas on top of the branches.

Wrap the bananas in fresh banana leaves and then scatter a layer of earth on top.

Put leaves in the ditch under the bananas and set the leaves alight.

Leave for three days.

Peel the fruit, then crush it, then mix a little water into the pulp.

Press the pulp and filter the juice.

Grind up a small amount of sorghum.

Pour the juice into a large jar and add the sorghum to it.

The beer is ready to drink.

www.nur.ac.rw/rwanda4.htm. If you get caught out by the lunch-time closing and want to go somewhere for a drink and snack, a short walk Butare-wards along the main road brings you to the Bar-Restaurant Loiret, a new and pleasant place dating from 1999 which is open 07.00–23.00. (It also has rooms to let, but at present these are reserved for university and museum personnel.)

If you don't fancy the walk from Butare (about 1.5km from the centre), then a taxi to the museum will cost about US$2.50, or more if you ask it to wait. If you're coming by minibus-taxi from Kigali you can ask to be dropped off there; and, if you want to go straight back to Kigali afterwards, you could try flagging down a minibus that has come from Butare – if it has spare seats inside, it will probably stop. Or to be sure of getting one you can walk to the minibus-taxi stand, which is less than 1km away.

BUTARE TO NYUNGWE FOREST
Gikongoro

There's not a lot to see around here except for a few shops and some beautiful, dramatically hilly landscapes; if the area appeals to you and you feel like some steepish strolling, there's simple, good-value accommodation available in Gikongoro at the Gikongoro Guesthouse near to the Prefecture office, where clean rooms cost around US$10. An alternative is the Hibiscus Guesthouse, close to the petrol station.

The genocide memorial at Murambi, close to Gikongoro, is one of Rwanda's starkest: over 1,800 bodies, of the 27,000-odd exhumed from mass graves here, have been placed on display to the public in the old technical school. They people the bare rooms, mingling horror with poignancy, as a mute but chillingly eloquent reminder that such events must never, ever, be allowed to recur. During the genocide, under orders from the prefect and with the support of the church authorities, between 40,000 and 60,000 inhabitants were assembled together in and around the school on Murambi hill, supposedly for protection; there were 64 rooms crammed full with people. Then the *interahamwe* attacked, throwing grenades through the windows. Within four days, most of those on the premises had been slaughtered. Later, French soldiers were installed on the site as part of *Opération Turquoise,* and a volley ball pitch was built over one of the mass graves.

Kibeho

This small town can be reached either via a turning to the left a few kilometres after Gikongoro or else more directly from Butare. You may already have heard the name. Before the genocide, Kibeho hit the headlines because of the visions of the Virgin Mary allegedly seen there by young girls from 1981 onwards, starting with that of teenager Alphonsine Mumureke in November 1981. The phenomena were reported both nationally and internationally, and the small, remote community became a centre of pilgrimage and faith, as believers travelled from all over Rwanda and further afield to witness the miracles.

During the genocide Kibeho suffered appallingly: hospital, primary school, college and church were all attacked. The church was badly burned while still sheltering survivors. At the time of writing it has not been rebuilt and a genocide memorial site is beside it.

Kibeho sadly made world news again after the genocide, in April 1995, with the massacre of (most reports agree) up to 4,000 people – 'internally displaced persons' or IDPs – crammed into a refugee camp there. In this case it seems that the generally disciplined RPA was responsible; the chain of command is still unclear. A great deal of reconstruction, both mental and physical, remains necessary for this wounded community.

NYUNGWE FOREST NATIONAL PARK

If the mountain gorillas in the Volcanoes National Park form the single best reason to visit Rwanda, then the less-publicised Nyungwe Forest (soon to be designated a national park) is probably the best reason to prolong your stay. Extending for 970km² over the mountainous southwest of Rwanda, Nyungwe protects the largest single tract of montane forest remaining anywhere in East or Central Africa. As such, it is a remarkably rich centre of biodiversity, harbouring (among other things) 75 mammal species, 275 birds, 120 butterflies, and more than 100 varieties of orchid.

Nyungwe is magnificent. The forest takes on a liberatingly primal presence even before you enter it. One moment the road is winding through the characteristic rural Rwandan landscape of rolling tea plantations and artificially terraced hills, the next a dense tangle of trees rises imperiously from the fringing cultivation. For a full 50km the road clings improbably to steep forested slopes, offering grandstand views over densely swathed hills which tumble like monstrous green waves towards the distant Burundi border. One normally thinks of rainforest as the most intimate and confining of environments. Nyungwe is that, but, as viewed from the main road, it is also gloriously expansive.

Vast though it may be, Nyungwe today is but a fragment of what was once an uninterrupted forest belt covering the length of the Albertine Rift (the stretch of the western Rift valley running from the Ruwenzoris south to Burundi). The fragmentation of this forest started some 2,000 years ago, at the dawn of the Iron Age, when the first patches were cut down to make way for agriculture – it is thought, for instance, that the isolation of Uganda's Bwindi Forest from similar habitats on the Virunga Mountains occurred about 500 years ago.

It is over the past 100 years that the forests of the Albertine Rift have suffered most heavily. Nyungwe, protected as a forest reserve since 1933, has fared relatively well, decreasing in extent by roughly 20% prior to the implementation of a co-ordinated forest protection plan in 1984. But it is the only substantial tract of forest left in Rwanda: the Gishwati Forest, which in the 1930s covered an area comparable to that of Nyungwe, had by 1989 been reduced to two separate blocks covering a combined 280km². Recent reports – not to mention our own tragi-comic attempt to locate it – suggest that all that remains of Gishwati are a few isolated trees dotted on the freshly cultivated hills surrounding a large refugee resettlement camp.

The main attraction of Nyungwe Forest is its primates. Chimp tracking can be arranged at short notice and relatively minor expense. Several other monkeys are readily seen, including the acrobatic Ruwenzori colobus in troops of up to 400 strong (the largest arboreal primate troops in Africa) and the beautiful and highly localised l'Hoest's monkey. Nyungwe is also highly alluring to birders, botanists and keen walkers. One of the joys of Nyungwe is its accessibility. Not only is the forest bisected by the surfaced trunk road between Butare and Cyangugu, but it is serviced by an excellent and inexpensive resthouse and campsite, and easily explored along a well-maintained network of walking trails.

Natural history

Nyungwe is a true rainforest, typically receiving in excess of 2,000mm of precipitation annually. It is also one of the oldest forests in Africa, which is one reason why it boasts such a high level of biodiversity. Scientific opinion is that Nyungwe, along with the other forests of the Albertine Rift, was largely unaffected by the drying up of lowland areas during the last ice age, and thus became a refuge for forest plants and animals which have subsequently re-colonised areas such as the Congo Basin. Nyungwe's faunal and floral diversity is not a function only of its antiquity, but also of the wide variation in elevation (between 1,600m and 2,950m above sea level), since many forest plants and animals live within very specific altitudinal bands.

NYUNGWE'S MONKEYS

The 13 primate species which occur in Nyungwe represent something like 20–25% of the total number in Africa, a phenomenal figure which in East Africa is comparable only to Uganda's Kibale Forest. Furthermore, several of these primates are listed as vulnerable or endangered on the IUCN red list, and Nyungwe is almost certainly the main stronghold for at least two of them.

Disregarding the chimpanzee (see box on pages 136–7), the most celebrated of Nyungwe's primates is the **Ruwenzori colobus** (*Colobus angolensis ruwenzori*), a race of the more widespread Angola colobus which is restricted to the Albertine Rift. The Ruwenzori colobus is a highly arboreal and acrobatic leaf-eater, easily distinguished from any other primate found in Nyungwe by its contrasting black overall colour and snow-white whiskers, shoulders and tail tip. Although all colobus monkeys are very sociable, the ones in Nyungwe are unique insofar as they typically move in troops of several hundred animals. A semi-habituated troop of 400, resident in the forest around the campsite, is thought to be the largest troop of arboreal primates anywhere in Africa – elsewhere in the world, only the Chinese golden monkey moves in groups of a comparable number.

Most of the other monkeys in Nyungwe are guenons, the collective name for the taxonomically confusing *Cercopithecus* genus. Most guenons are arboreal forest-dwelling omnivores, noted for their colourful coats and the male's bright red or blue genitals. The most striking of Nyungwe's guenons is **l'Hoest's monkey** (*C. l'hoesti*), a large and unusually terrestrial monkey, whose cryptic grey and red coat is offset by a bold white 'beard'

Ruwenzori colobus

which renders it unmistakable. As with the Ruwenzori colobus, l'Hoest's monkey is more or less confined to the Albertine Rift, and is very scarce elsewhere in its restricted range. In Nyungwe, it is the most frequently encountered monkey, with troops of 5–15 animals often seen along the roadside, within the forest, and even in the campsite.

Two distinct races of blue monkey – the most widespread of African forest primates – occur in Nyungwe. Likely to be encountered along the road and around the campsite, the **silver monkey** (*C. mitis doggetti*) is similar in build and general appearance to l'Hoest's monkey, but lacks the diagnostic white beard. The silver monkey typically lives in small family parties, though solitary males are also often encountered in Nyungwe. The beautiful **golden monkey** (*C. mitis kandti*) is an endangered race of blue monkey restricted to high elevation forest in the Albertine Rift; it is most common in the Virungas, where the population is estimated at around 1,000, but small numbers are known to survive in Nyungwe, in the remote bamboo forests close to the Burundi border.

Sharing the golden monkey's remote bamboo habitat is the rare and secretive **owl-faced monkey** (*C. hamlyni*), another Albertine Rift endemic whose modern range is restricted to a handful of montane forests. This thickset, plain grey, pug-faced monkey was first recorded in Nyungwe as recently as 1989, and it remains the least-known of the monkeys in the reserve – researchers monitoring the population close to the Burundi border reckon they encounter the monkeys at most twice a week.

continued overleaf

L'Hoest's monkey

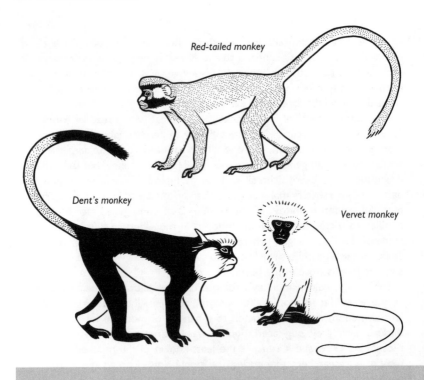

Red-tailed monkey

Dent's monkey

Vervet monkey

Another guenon whose status within Nyungwe is uncertain is the **red-tailed monkey** (*C. ascanius*), a small and highly active arboreal monkey most easily distinguished by its bright white nose. Generally associated with low elevation forest, the red-faced monkey now faces extinction within Nyungwe owing to much of its habitat having been cleared for cultivation over recent decades. The solitary individual that hangs out with a colobus troop on the tea estate is presumably unlikely ever to find a breeding partner, though we have been told that a small but viable population of red-tailed monkeys survives on the fringes of the forest reserve near Banda.

Dent's mona monkey (*C. mona denti*) is widespread within Nyungwe, and occurs at all elevations, but it is infrequently seen by tourists. Another typical forest guenon, Dent's mona is distinguished from other monkeys in the forest by its contrasting black back and white belly, blue-white forehead, and yellowish ear tufts. It often moves with other guenons, and is mostly likely to be seen around Uwinka and the disused campsite at Karamba, not far from the ORTPN Resthouse. Some sources incorrectly list the **crowned monkey** (*C. pogonias*) for Nyungwe, but this is a West African lowland species, regarded by some to be a race of mona monkey. Unlikely to be seen within the forest proper, the **vervet monkey** (*C. aethiops*) is a grizzled grey guenon of savannah and open woodland, with a distinctive black face mask. Probably the most numerous monkey in the

Baboon

Grey-cheeked
mangabey

world, the vervet is occasionally encountered on the forest verge and around the ORTPN Resthouse, where it is often quite tame and regularly raids crops.

Another savannah monkey occasionally seen along the road through Nyungwe is the **olive baboon** (*Papio anubis*), a predominantly terrestrial primate which lives in large troops. After the chimpanzee, this is by far the largest and most stocky of the forest's primates, with a uniform dark olive coat and the canine snout and large teeth characteristic of all baboons. The olive baboon is very aggressive and, like the vervet monkey, it frequently raids crops.

Intermediate in size between the olive baboon and the various guenons, the **grey-cheeked mangabey** (*Cercocebus albigena*) is an arboreal monkey of the forest interior. Rather more spindly than any guenon, the grey-cheeked mangabey has a uniform dark-brown coat and grey-brown cape, and is renowned for its loud gobbling call. It lives in small troops, typically around ten animals, and is localised in Nyungwe due to its preference for lower altitudes.

In addition to chimpanzees and monkeys, Nyungwe harbours four types of prosimian, small nocturnal primates more closely related to the lemurs of Madagascar than to any other primates of the African mainland. These are three species of bushbaby or galago (a group of tiny, hyperactive wide-eyed insectivores) and the sloth-like potto. All are very unlikely to be encountered by tourists.

CHIMPANZEES

Chimpanzees are distinctive black-coated apes, more closely related to humans than to any other living creatures. Two species are recognised, the common or robust chimpanzee *Pan troglodytes* and the 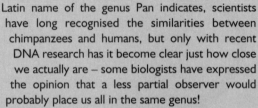 bonobo or gracile chimpanzee *Pan paniscus*. As the Latin name of the genus Pan indicates, scientists have long recognised the similarities between chimpanzees and humans, but only with recent DNA research has it become clear just how close we actually are – some biologists have expressed the opinion that a less partial observer would probably place us all in the same genus!

While the bonobo is relatively scarce and confined to a small area of lowland forest in the DRC, the common chimpanzee is the most numerous of the great apes. An estimated wild population of 180,000 ranges across 20 countries, from western Uganda and Tanzania through to the Senegambia. About half of the wild population – including the estimated 500–1,000 which are resident in Nyungwe – belong to the eastern race *P. t. schweinfurthii*. This has been genetically isolated from other races for about a million years, and may yet be classified as a discrete species.

Chimps live in loosely bonded troops of between ten and 120 animals, normally based around a core of related males with an internal hierarchy topped by an alpha male. Females are generally less strongly bonded to their core group than are males; emigration between communities is not

Flora

The forest comprises at least 200 tree species. The upper canopy in some areas reaches 50–60m in height, dominated by slow-growing hardwoods such as *Entandrophragma excelsum* (African mahogany), *Syzygium parvifolium* (waterberry), *Podocarpus milanjianus* (Mulanje cedar), *Newtonia buchananii* (forest newtonia) and *Albizia gummifera* (smooth-barked albizia). A much larger variety of trees makes up the mid-storey canopy, of which one of the most conspicuous is *Dichaetanthera corymbosa*, whose bright purple blooms break up the rich green textures of the forest.

Of the smaller trees, one of the most striking is the giant tree-fern *Cyathea mannania*, which grows to 5m tall, and is seen in large numbers along the ravines of the Waterfall Trail. Also very distinctive are the 2–3m tall giant lobelias, more normally associated with montane moorland than forest, but common in Nyungwe, particularly along the roadside. Bamboo plants, a large type of grass, are dominant at higher altitudes in the rather inaccessible southeast of the forest, where their shoots are favoured by golden and owl-faced monkeys. Nyungwe also harbours a huge variety of small flowering plants, including more than 100 varieties of orchid and the wild begonia.

unusual. Mother-child bonds are strong. Daughters normally leave their mother only after they reach maturity, at which point relations between them may be severed. Mother-son relations have been known to survive for over 40 years. A troop has a well-defined core territory which is fiercely defended by regular boundary patrols.

Chimpanzees are primarily frugivorous (fruit eating), but they do eat meat on occasion: young baboons, various types of monkey, small antelopes and bushpigs. Most kills are opportunistic, but stalking of prey is not unusual. Cannibalism has also been observed. The first recorded instance of chimps using tools was at Gombe Stream in Tanzania, where they regularly use modified sticks to 'fish' in termite mounds. In West Africa, they have been observed cracking nuts open using a stone and anvil. Chimpanzees are among the most intelligent of animals: in language studies in the USA they have been taught to communicate in American Sign Language, and have demonstrated their understanding, in some instances even creating compound words for new objects (such as rock-berry to describe a nut). Chimpanzee behaviour has been extensively studied in recent decades, most famously by Jane Goodall, whose research programme at Gombe Stream in Tanzania was initiated in 1960 and is still active today. Before heading out to see chimps, it's worth reading one of Jane Goodall's books (see *Further Reading*), which give detailed explanations of chimp behaviour in a highly readable style. Those who prefer their reading in a less academic form are pointed towards William Boyd's superb novel *Brazzaville Beach*, much of which is set in a fictional chimpanzee research centre.

Within Nyungwe lie several swampy areas whose biology is quite distinct from that of the surrounding forest. The largest of these is the 13km² Kamiranzovu Marsh, sweeping views of which are offered along the main road between the campsite and the resthouse. Formerly a favoured haunt of elephants, this open area is also rich in epiphytic orchids and harbours localised animals such as the Congo clawless otter and Grauer's rush warbler. The higher-altitude Uwasenkoko Marsh, bisected by the main road towards Butare, is dominated by the Ethiopian hagenia and protects a community of heather-like plants sharing unexpected affinities with the Nyika Plateau in distant Malawi.

Mammals

The most prominent mammals in Nyungwe are primates, of which 13 species are present, including the common chimpanzee (see box above) and nine types of monkey (see pages 132–5). In total, however, an estimated 75 different mammal species have been recorded in Nyungwe, including several rare forest inhabitants.

Of the so-called 'Big Five', elephant, buffalo and leopard were all common in pre-colonial times. Buffalo are now extinct – the last one was shot in 1976

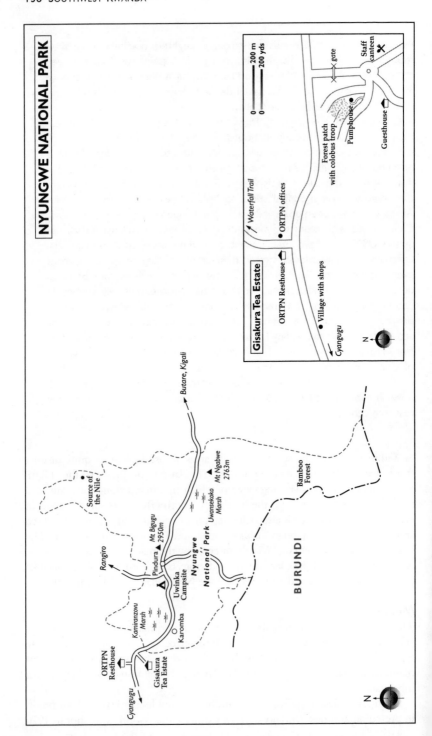

NYUNGWE NATIONAL PARK

Gisakura Tea Estate

Waterfall Trail

ORTPN offices

ORTPN Resthouse

Village with shops

Cyangugu

Forest patch
with colobus troop

Pumphouse

gate

Staff
canteen

Guesthouse

0 ___ 200 m
0 ___ 200 yds

N

Butare, Kigali

Source of
the Nile

Rangiro

Mt Bigugu
2950m

Pindura

Uwasekoko
Marsh

Mt Ngabwe
2763m

Nyungwe
National Park

Bamboo
Forest

Uwinka
Campsite

Kamiranzovu
Marsh

Karomba

BURUNDI

ORTPN
Resthouse

Cyangugu

Gisakura Tea Estate

N

– and elephant may well have gone the same way since 1990, when it was estimated that at least six and perhaps as many as 20 elephant lived in the forest. For several years after the civil war, no elephant were seen in Nyungwe. In mid-1999, elephant spoor was observed during a forest inventory, but in November of that year an elephant corpse was found (cause of death unknown) and no spoor has been seen since then. Leopard, by contrast, are still present in small numbers, and regularly seen by local villagers, but as a tourist you'd be very lucky to encounter one.

A number of smaller predators occur in Nyungwe, including golden cat, wild cat, serval cat, side-striped jackal, three types of mongoose, Congo clawless otter, common and servaline genet, and common and palm civet. Most of these are highly secretive nocturnal creatures which are infrequently observed.

The largest antelope found in Nyungwe is the bushbuck. Three types of duiker also occur in the forest: black-fronted, yellow-backed and an endemic race of Wein's duiker. Formerly common, all the forest's antelope have suffered from intensive poaching as bush meat. Other large mammals include giant forest hog, bushpig, several types of squirrel (including the monkey-sized giant forest squirrel), Derby's anomalure (a large squirrel-like forest animal which has large underarm flaps enabling it to glide between trees) and the tree hyrax (a rarely seen guinea-pig-like animal whose blood-curdling nocturnal screeching is one of the characteristic sounds of the African forest).

Birds

Nyungwe, in my opinion, is the single most important birdwatching destination in Rwanda, with more than 275 bird species recorded, of which the majority are forest specialists and 24 are regional endemics whose range is restricted to a few forests along the Albertine Rift. Birdwatching in Nyungwe can be rather frustrating, since the vegetation is thick and many birds tend to stick to the canopy, but almost everything you do see ranks as a good sighting.

You don't have to be an ardent birdwatcher to appreciate some of Nyungwe's birds. Most people, for instance, will do a double take when they first spot a great blue turaco, a chicken-sized bird with garish blue, green and yellow feathers, often seen gliding between the trees along the main road. Another real gem is the paradise monarch, a long-tailed blue, orange and (sometimes) white bird often seen around the resthouse. Other birds impress with their bizarre appearance – the gigantic forest hornbills, for instance, whose wailing vocalisations are almost as comical as their ungainly bills and heavy-winged flight. And, when tracking through the forest undergrowth, watch out for the red-throated alethe, a very localised bird with a distinctive blue-white eyebrow. The alethe habitually follows colobus troops to eat the insects they disturb, and based on our experience it sees humans as merely another large mammal, often perching within a few inches!

The priorities of more serious birdwatchers will depend to some extent on their experience elsewhere in Africa. It is difficult to imagine, for instance, that a first-time visitor to the continent will get as excited about a drab Chubb's cisticola as they will when they first see a paradise monarch or green pigeon. For somebody coming from southern Africa, at least half of what they see will be new to them, with a total of about 60 relatively widespread East African forest specials headed by the likes of great blue turaco, Ross's turaco, red-breasted sparrowhawk and white-headed wood-hoopoe.

From an East African perspective, however, it is the 24 Albertine Rift endemics that are most alluring. Depending on your level of expertise, you could reasonably hope to tick off half of these over a few days in the forest. The more common regional endemics are handsome francolin, Ruwenzori turaco (a stunner!), stripe-breasted tit, red-collared babbler, red-throated alethe, Archer's ground robin, Kivu ground thrush, Grauer's rush warbler (confined to marshy areas), red-faced woodland warbler, Kungwe apalis, Grauer's warbler, yellow-eyed black flycatcher, Ruwenzori batis, blue-headed sunbird, regal sunbird and strange weaver.

On a more practical note, be warned that the guides at Nyungwe are generally not very knowledgeable (two different guides we used misidentified common monkeys). Guides with specialist knowledge of birds can be arranged a day in advance, but even they cannot be trusted to identify anything correctly. For this reason, you will be highly dependent on a field guide, and without a great amount of advance research you are bound to struggle to identify every bird that you glimpse. Given the above, relic forest patches and the road verge are often more productive than the forest interior, since you'll get clearer views of what you do see.

Small stuff

While monkeys and to a lesser extent birds tend to attract the most attention, Nyungwe's fauna also includes a large number of smaller animals. With only 12 species recorded, snakes are relatively poorly represented, due to the chilly climate – probably good news for most visitors – but colourful lizards are often seen on the rocks, and at least five species of chameleon occur in the forest. Nyungwe also harbours more than 100 different types of colourful butterfly, including 40 regional endemics. Look out, too, for the outsized beetles and bugs that are characteristic of all tropical forests. Equally remarkable, but only to be admired at a distance of a metre or so, are the vast columns of army ants that move across the forest trails – step on one of these columns, and you'll know all about it, as these guys can bite!

Further information

A basic fact sheet about the forest is available from the ORTPN tourist office in Kigali. An excellent 60-page booklet entitled *Nyungwe Forest Reserve* is sold for around US$5 at the ORTPN office next to the resthouse. Mysteriously, the booklet is not for sale at Uwinka. Be warned, too, that it might take some urging to encourage the staff at the ORTPN office to offer you this booklet in preference to their range of faded old postcards, but do persist – a pile of several hundred copies was stashed away in the back room when we visited!

Keen birdwatchers should try to lay their hands on the out-of-print checklist of the forest's birds, which gives Latin, English and French names as well as a good indication of each species' habitat and relative abundance within the reserve.

Getting there and away

Nyungwe Forest Reserve is transected by the main surfaced road between Butare and Cyangugu. The Uwinka Reception Centre and Campsite lies alongside the main road, and is well signposted 90km from Butare and 54km from Cyangugu. The ORTPN Resthouse is also on the main road, 18km closer to Cyangugu, on the right side of the road and about 2km after you exit the western boundary of the forest reserve coming from Butare. The resthouse on the Gisakura Tea Estate is along the dirt road to the tea estate about 500m from the main road; coming from Butare it is signposted to the left about halfway between the western boundary of the forest and the ORTPN Resthouse.

Where to stay and eat

Set in the heart of the forest, yet only a couple of hundred metres from the main road, the **Uwinka Reception Centre and Campsite** is the best option provided that you have a tent and are reasonably self-sufficient. The campsite has a perfect location at an altitude of about 2,300m on a high ridge, with individual sites scattered over a wide area of forest. A semi-habituated troop of l'Hoest's monkey passes through the campsite every morning and most afternoons, as does the occasional troop of silver monkey and a variety of forest birds. The campsite doubles as the trailhead for the Coloured Trails; this makes it the most convenient base, particularly for travellers without a private vehicle, from which to explore the forest and track the 400-strong troop of colobus. The main road adjacent to the campsite is also worth exploring, for the great views and variety of birds. Camping costs US$10 but, since this includes the US$10 forest visitation fee, it is effectively free. Drinks are available at reasonable prices, and firewood can be arranged, but campers must bring all food and should have sufficient warm clothing to offset the chilly night temperatures at high altitude.

The popular option for those unequipped for camping is the **ORTPN Resthouse**, which lies 2km outside the forest close to the Gisakura Tea Estate. The accommodation here is clean and comfortable, and good value at US$7 per person for a single or twin, or US$12 per person for a double room in a large self-contained chalet. The communal showers and toilets are also clean, though the water supply was a problem when we visited. Huge meals can be prepared with a couple of hours' notice for the reasonable charge of US$5 per person. In December 2000, Dorette Boshoff and David Hartley wrote: 'We ended up at the guesthouse just outside the park and found it very good value for money – clean, all in working order and our dinner was an absolute feast, prepared and served with a lot of TLC!' The main drawback to the resthouse – particularly for travellers dependent on public transport – is that it is outside the forest and 18km from Uwinka, the trailhead for most of the trails. The resthouse does, however, offer good access to the Waterfall Trail and the colobus troop on the Gisakura Tea Estate. Vervet monkeys occasionally pass through the resthouse grounds, and a fair variety of birds are present in the small patch of forest in front of the resthouse. A number of nearby relic forest patches offer good birdwatching, as well as a chance of encountering forest monkeys.

A cheaper **guesthouse**, run by the management of the Gisakura Tea Estate, lies about 1km back towards the forest boundary. This is a very friendly set-up, and excellent value, with two four-bed dormitories available at US$3 per person (unless it is full, female travellers or couples will probably be given private use of a room). Meals must be arranged a few hours in advance, but are astonishingly good value at US$2 for a huge spread (whole grilled fish, chips, rice and fruit). There is a communal lounge, and beers and sodas are available at the nearby estate canteen. The guesthouse lies less than 500m from the forest patch where colobus are resident, and the area offers good birding. Other trails can be arranged at the ORTPN office next to the ORTPN Resthouse, a 20-minute walk away. To reach the tea estate's guesthouse, following the dirt road into the tea estate (signposted *Usine à thé Gisakuru*) for about 500m until you reach a large traffic circle, then follow the central road branching from this circle (at roughly two o'clock) for about 200m. You'll see the resthouse to your right, next to a concrete volleyball court.

Fees

Forest entrance fees are not expensive by comparison with those of national park fees in many neighbouring countries, but the system as it stands is somewhat ill conceived and confusing – and worth thinking through should you be on a budget with a few days in the forest.

A daily forest visitation fee of US$10 per person is charged to all visitors, and this allows you to walk guided or unguided along any of the forest trails. This fee is included in the camping charge of US$10 per person at Uwinka, which effectively means that no visitation fee is charged to campers (or, depending on how you choose to look at, that camping at Uwinka is free). This fee excludes specific primate visits, though it doesn't preclude you from stopping to look at any primates you happen to see along the trails.

A fee of US$20 per person is charged for any primate visit – which includes specifically going to look for the Angola colobus troop close to Uwinka, visiting the colobus troop on the Gisakura Tea Estate, or tracking the chimpanzee or grey-cheeked mangabey. This US$20 also includes the daily forest visitation fee (in other words, having paid for a primate visit, you are free to walk along any other forest trails that day), but it excludes a camping fee (so if you camp on the same day that you track chimps, you pay a total of US$30 in fees).

So far as I could ascertain, the fees are all charged per calendar day rather than per 24 hours. This means that for somebody camping a night or two in the forest, it would, on the basis of budget alone, make sense to leave any specific primate visit until the morning of your departure, since all other forest walks on other days would be covered by the camping fee. Another reason why you might want to leave primate visits to the end of your stay is that you are likely to see a good number of them in the course of ordinary forest walks. L'Hoest's and silver monkey often pass through the campsite (and are commonly encountered along the roadside), colobus are regular and chimps occasional along the coloured forest trail, and we saw colobus and silver monkey along the waterfall trail. After a couple of days in the forest you will know what primates you still have left to see and whether you want to pay extra to track them specifically.

Incidentally, I'm not advocating that travellers try to avoid paying fees which seem inherently quite reasonable, merely that they seek clarity regarding ambiguities which might otherwise penalise them for taking 'wrong' decisions about the timing of various activities. The fee structure may be idiosyncratic, but when we spoke to the wardens about it, my firm impression was that this is not an attempt to rip anybody off, merely a system dreamed up in a distant office: the wardens were adamant that no pressure is put on visitors to do specific primate visits, and that any primates encountered during the course of an ordinary walk are there for the seeing!

Walks and excursions

A large selection of walking possibilities and other excursions are available within Nyungwe. Visitors with a vehicle and sufficient interest could easily keep themselves busy for three or four days without significantly retracing their steps. The options for travellers without private transport are more limited, and depend on whether they base themselves at Uwinka Campsite (where the main attraction is the network of coloured trails, a good place for colobus and seasonally for chimps) or at the resthouse (the best base for the Waterfall Trail and for visiting the colobus in Gisakura Tea Estate). In the dry season, you need a private vehicle to go chimp tracking wherever you are based, and at all times of year you need a vehicle to visit the habituated grey-cheeked mangabey troop and to explore the road to Rangiro.

The forest trails are steep and often very slippery. Dress accordingly; jeans, a thick shirt and good walking shoes are the ideal outfit, and a waterproof jacket will be useful during the rainy season.

Uwinka and the Coloured Trails

A network of seven walking trails, each designated by a particular colour, leads downhill from the Uwinka Campsite into the surrounding forested hills. Ranging in length from the 1km Grey Trail to the 10km Red Trail, the footpaths are all well maintained and clearly marked, but don't underestimate the steepness of the slopes or – after rain – the muddy conditions, which can be fairly tough going at this high altitude.

The coloured trails are the most popular walks in Nyungwe, not least because they pass through the territory of a habituated troop of 400 colobus monkeys. It is up to the individual visitor to decide whether to go on an ordinary forest walk and leave the colobus sightings to chance, or pay more to go on a specific primate visit, in which case the guides will search for (and almost certainly find) the colobus. During the rainy season, a troop of chimpanzees often moves into this area as well, and once again it is up to individuals to decide whether to pay extra to track them.

Whatever you decide, you can reasonably expect to see some primates along any of the coloured trails, as well as a good variety of forest birds – though the latter require patience and regular stops where there are open views into the canopy. Unless you opt for a specific primate visit, chance will be the decisive factor in what you see, though the 2.5km Blue Trail is regarded as especially good for primates and birds, while the 10km Red Trail is good for chimpanzees and passes four waterfalls. For those spending a bit of time in the forest, the Kamiranzovu Trail leads to a quite different ecosystem, a marshy area rich in orchids and swamp-associated birds. This used to be the best place to see Nyungwe's elephants, but none has been sighted here in recent years.

Birdwatchers in particular are advised to explore the main road close to the campsite, as they will probably see a wider variety of birds than from within the forest. About 500m east of the campsite, the road offers some stunning views over the forested valleys, and passes a stand of giant lobelias.

The Waterfall Trail

This superb trail starts at the ORTPN Resthouse and takes between three and six hours to cover as a round trip, depending on how often you stop and whether you drive or walk from the resthouse to the car park about 3km from the resthouse. The first part of the trail – in essence following the road to the car park – passes through rolling tea plantations dotted with relic forest patches which are worth scanning closely for monkeys (we saw a troop of silver monkeys en route). These relic forest patches can also be rewarding for birds; keen ornithologists might well want to take them slowly, and could perhaps view this section of the trail as a worthy birdwatching excursion in its own right

The trail then descends into the forest proper, following flat contour paths through a succession of tree-fern covered ravines, and crossing several streams, before a sharp descent to the base of a pretty but small waterfall. Monkeys are often seen along the way (colobus seem to be particularly common) and the steep slopes allow good views into the canopy. I found this trail to be the most rewarding of those we walked for true forest interior birds, with perhaps 20 species identified including Albertine Rift endemics such as Ruwenzori turaco and yellow-eyed black flycatcher.

Gisakura Tea Estate

A relic forest patch in this tea estate, only 20 minutes' walk from the ORTPN Resthouse, and less than five minutes from the tea estate's guesthouse, supports a resident troop of 38 Ruwenzori colobus monkeys. This troop is very habituated, far more so than the larger troop at Uwinka, and the relatively small territory the monkeys occupy makes them very easy to locate and to see clearly. Oddly, a solitary red-tailed monkey moves with the colobus – some of the guides say that it is treated as the leader. A visit to this forest patch is treated as a primate walk by the ORTPN office and thus costs US$20.

Particularly in the early morning, the relic forest patch is also an excellent birdwatching site, since it lies in a ravine and is encircled by a road, making it easy to see deep into the canopy. Most of what you see are forest fringe or woodland species (as opposed to forest interior birds), but numerically this proved to be the most rewarding spot we visited in Nyungwe, with some 40 species identified in an hour, notably black-throated apalis, paradise and white-tailed crested monarch, Chubb's cisticola, African golden oriole, green pigeon, olive-green cameroptera, three types of sunbird, two greenbuls and two crimson-wings.

Further afield

One monkey, the grey-cheeked mangabey, can only be seen by those who make a special excursion, on a trip which requires a private vehicle. A mangabey troop, resident in a patch of forest along the Banda road, has been habituated by researchers, who normally spend every Monday and Friday with it (consequently, these are the best days to visit the monkeys, as they will already have been tracked down when you arrive). The turn off to Banda, 800m from the Uwinka Campsite towards Butare, is signposted *Eclise Episcopa de Rwanda*. The monkeys are usually found between 5km and 10km along the turn-off. Tracking the mangabeys is regarded to be a formal primate visit, and must be done in the company of a guide. L'Hoest's, silver and colobus monkeys are also often seen in this area.

During the rainy season, chimpanzees are often present in the vicinity of the coloured trails, and chimp tracking can be undertaken on foot from the campsite. During the dry season, however, the chimps tend to move to higher elevations, and tracking them normally entails a drive followed by a hike of up to four hours in either direction. The chimps are not fully habituated, but they are reasonably approachable. You'll have to check the current situation with the guides.

There are no habituated mona monkeys in Nyungwe, but a troop is resident in the vicinity of Karamba, the site of former gold-digging and – immediately before the civil war – a campsite which might yet be reopened. Karamba lies between the campsite and resthouse, but the area can only be explored on foot accompanied by a guide. The troop at Karamba is very large, and reportedly sometimes keeps company with red-tailed monkeys.

The dirt road to Rangiro, which leaves the main tar road about 1.5km east of Uwinka, is regarded as the best excursion for birdwatchers. This is because the road takes passes through both high- and low-elevation forest within a relatively short distance, and affords good views into the canopy in several places. A 4x4 vehicle is essential, and a guide recommended. In addition to birdwatching, the Rangiro road offers some stunning views over the mountains, and is a good place to see mangabeys, silver monkeys, and a variety of butterflies.

THE CREATION OF LAKE KIVU
A new variation on an ancient tale

Long, long ago, before the beginning of what we now remember, there was nothing but a dry, grassy plain covering the area where Lake Kivu lies today. It was a hard, hot place, whose people had to work ceaselessly to scrape a living from the land. One of these people was a man whose heart was kind; he helped his older neighbours to till their ground and to gather in their crops. His wife scolded him for this, saying: 'Why do you spend so much time filling their grain-stores when our own lies empty?' But Imana had seen his good deeds and was pleased, and wanted to reward the man, so he gave him a cow whose udders yielded milk, millet, beans and peas. Imana warned the man that he must not speak of his special cow to others, lest they envy him and try to steal it, so the man milked his cow in secret and carried home the produce to his wife who began to scold him a little less.

A day came when the man was called away to work at the Mwami's court. Anxiously, he asked Imana what he should do about his cow. Imana said that his wife might be told, and might milk it in the meantime, but that she must not pass on the secret of the cow to others. With her husband away from home, the woman invited a young man to her house. He dined off the milk and the millet and the beans and the peas, and he wondered how her poor land could produce so much. He searched all round her homestead for an extra storeroom or piece of land but he

THE SOUTHERN LAKE KIVU SHORE
Cyangugu

The most southerly of Rwanda's Lake Kivu ports, Cyangugu (pronounced *Shangugu*) is also the most amorphous, sprawling along a 5km road through the green hills that run down to the lake shore. The upper town, more correctly called Kamembe, is a lively business centre, and the site of the main minibus-taxi stand, hospital, market, banks and supermarkets, as well as a clutch of local guesthouses and restaurants. Aside from the views of the lake, and a couple of flaking colonial-era buildings, Kamembe is all energy and no character – bustling it may be, but in truth you could be in pretty much any small undistinguished African town anywhere on the continent.

Far more intriguing is the lower town – Cyangugu proper – which has an almost cinematic quality, coming across rather like an abandoned film set used years ago to make a movie about some colonial West African trading backwater. Cyangugu is situated on the lake shore, alongside a bridge across the Rusizi river where it flows out of the lake, which is also the main border crossing between southern Rwanda and the DRC. The town consists of little more than one pothole-scored main road, yet within its abrupt confines it does have a decidedly built-up feel, and must once have been rather grand and prosperous. Today, however, many of the old multi-storey found nothing, and the cow looked just like an ordinary cow. Insistently the young man questioned the woman, using all kinds of persuasion to discover her secret, and eventually she weakened. She milked the cow in front of him and he was so amazed that he ran to the neighbours, crying: 'Here is an animal that will feed us all – we need work on the land no more!'

Imana heard this, and he frowned deeply, and that night he prepared a punishment. Before going to bed, the woman went out into her field to empty her bladder as usual, thinking to take only a few moments. But the flow was unstoppable. On and on it went, flooding her house and her fields and the land around about. Deeper and deeper it became, until the woman herself was drowned in it and even the trees were covered. Her household utensils – her wooden bowl and her woven mat and the gourd which held her grain – floated away into the distance, broke into bits and became islands. And as the morning sun rose into the sky it lit the new and shining surface of Lake Kivu as it is today.

When the man returned from working at the Mwami's court he found a lake of sweet water lapping at the edge of his fields. The land had become soft and fertile. Fish swam in the lake, and waterbirds bobbed on the wavelets. Of the cow there was no sign, but she had left behind a big heap of millet and peas and beans which he then planted, and his crop and all those after it grew richly on the irrigated land.

And Imana smiled.

buildings have been reduced to shells – victims of one or other war, perhaps, or just decades of neglect – generating an aura of dilapidation underscored by the anomalous Hotel du Lac Kivu, with its freshly painted modern exterior, and the neatly cropped lawn of the Home St François. The outmoded façades of Cyangugu speak of better times past, and while the town's aura of tropical ennui is less than invigorating, it is also somehow rather moving.

While the prefecture of Kibuye (see page 153) has the sad distinction of being the site of the most extensive extermination of Tutsis during the genocide, the prefecture of Cyangugu comes second. Before the French set up their 'safe zone', it was estimated that 85–90% of Tutsis here had died. Many communities were completely wiped out.

Unless you are thinking of crossing into the DRC – at the time of writing, not an option that attracts many takers – Cyangugu has to be classed as something of a dead end in travel terms. It is, however, the closest town to Nyungwe, with far smarter accommodation than anything in the forest, and might therefore make an attractive alternative base for self-drive visitors to Nyungwe. The lake-shore setting is lovely, too, and this atmospheric old town forms a good base from which to explore more off-the-beaten-track destinations such as the Bugarama Hot Springs and Cyamudongo Forest.

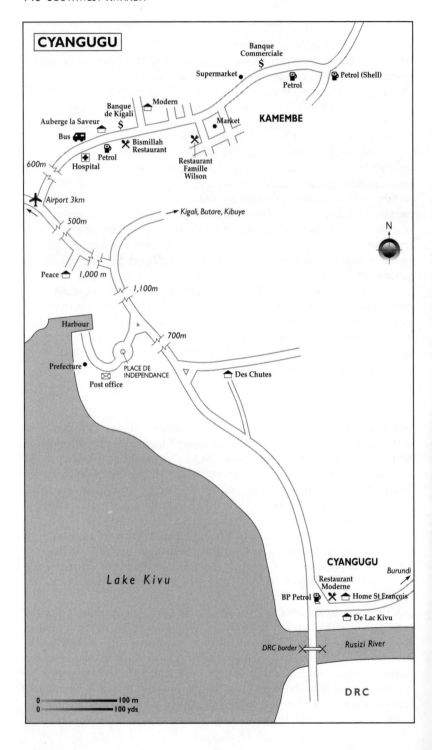

CYANGUGU

Banque Commerciale

Supermarket

Petrol

Petrol (Shell)

KAMEMBE

Modern

Banque de Kigali

Market

Auberge la Saveur

Bus

Bismillah Restaurant

Petrol

Hospital

Restaurant Famille Wilson

600m

Airport 3km

500m

Kigali, Butare, Kibuye

Peace

1,000 m

1,100m

700m

Harbour

Prefecture

PLACE DE INDEPENDANCE

Post office

Des Chutes

N

Lake Kivu

CYANGUGU

Burundi

Restaurant Moderne

BP Petrol

Home St François

De Lac Kivu

DRC border

Rusizi River

DRC

0 ———— 100 m
0 ———— 100 yds

Above Local woman with pipe
Below left Traditional dancer, Butare
Below right Young girl, Cyangugu

Above Boy in dugout canoe
Right Young boy, Cyangugu
Below Children carrying water,
Ruhengeri

Getting there and away
By road

Regular minibus-taxis connect Kigali and Butare to Cyangugu – or more accurately to Kamembe, which is where the main minibus stand for Cyangugu is situated. The fare from Kigali is around US$7, and from Butare around US$4. Direct transport between Kamembe and Kibuye is restricted to one bus daily, leaving at 08.00 in either direction.

A steady stream of minibus-taxis run back and forth between Kamembe and the border post at Cyangugu, at a cost equivalent to US$0.25 for the 5km trip. The Peace Guesthouse and Hotel des Chutes both lie within 50m of the taxi route, as does the main harbour and port.

By air

Rwanda Airlines operates two return flights weekly between Kigali and Cyangugu, on Tuesday and Friday mornings.

By boat

Travelling between Cyangugu and the more northerly ports is a definite possibility, though our hypothetical enquiries around the port left us little wiser than before we asked. We were initially told that a regular passenger boat runs up to Gisenyi, leaving at 10.00 daily, but were then asked a 'fare' of US$100, which suggests either that we had the wrong end of the stick or else that we looked indecently rich and stupid! What is certain is that cargo boats cover this route most days, and will often take passengers informally for a negotiable fare, perhaps US$2–3 to Gisenyi, and half that to Kibuye. There is also some talk of small motor-boats starting up operation. It's one of those situations where interested travellers just have to ask around.

Where to stay
Near the border post

The **Hotel du Lac Kivu** (tel: 085 27709) is about the smartest option in Cyangugu, a beacon of relative prosperity amidst the row of semi-dilapidated buildings that runs along the river immediately south of the border post with the DRC. The hotel has an appealing open bar and restaurant area on the riverfront, and the rooms are very comfortable. Prices range from US$15/20 B&B for an ordinary single/double with en-suite hot shower and balcony, through to US$30–40 B&B for a large suite with television and en-suite hot bath – as well as a big barren volleyball court of a spare room, whose role is difficult to discern. Somewhat irritating was a transparent attempt to make us take a suite (the cheaper rooms were 'full' when we first made enquiries, but suddenly became available as we wandered off).

Opposite the Hotel du Lac Kivu, the church-run **Home St François** (tel: 537097) is easily the best budget option in Cyangugu – in fact as good a deal as you'll find anywhere in Rwanda. Clean, secure rooms using communal toilets and hot showers cost US$3.50/5.50 single/double. Meals are available, cheap but otherwise nothing to shout about, and the atmosphere is very homely if not exactly full of cheer. Be warned that unmarried couples are emphatically not accepted, and married couples shouldn't rely on being given the benefit of whatever doubt might exist in the receptionist's mind (all the rooms were 'full' until we shoved our wedding rings under her nose).

Set on a rise about 500m back from the border post, the **Hotel des Chutes** (tel: 537405) boasts an attractive location overlooking the lake, and the balcony is fun for a drink or snack. The self-contained double rooms, however, are a bit on the sleazy side for the asking price of US$20, and don't stand comparison with their identically priced counterparts at the Hotel du Lac Kivu. On the plus side – at least from the point of view of a beleaguered travel writer – the process of actually getting to see a room is mercifully uncomplicated.

Kamembe and surrounds

About 1km from Kamembe, along the road to Cyangugu proper, the **Peace Guesthouse** (tel/fax: 61423) has a rustic setting on a hill overlooking the lake. Constructed by the Anglican Church in 1998, this is a very spick-and-span set-up, and friendly too, with no restrictions on who stays there. Basic rooms using communal hot showers cost US$7/12, while small rooms with en-suite hot bath cost US$12/17. Also available is a large chalet with a lounge, two bedrooms, nets and hot bath which costs US$35 per double bedroom (or US$70 for the full unit). Meals are available.

Of two basic local guesthouses in Kamembe, the better is the **Auberge la Saveur**, set alongside the minibus-taxi stand. Small but clean twins with en-suite hot shower cost US$12, while rather more grubby singles using communal showers cost US$9. The rooms surround a quiet courtyard, set back a few hundred metres from a lively restaurant and bar. Not significantly cheaper, and a whole lot scruffier, the misleadingly named **Modern Rest Lodge** has to be considered a last gasp option at US$8/12 single/double.

Where to eat and drink

We settled on the **Hotel du Lac Kivu** as our local; the riverfront location makes the open-air bar a pleasant place to down a chilled *Primus*, and the house speciality of spicy barbecued half-chicken with chips is tasty and good value at around US$3.50 for a brimming plate. With a similarly attractive location, the bar at the **Hotel des Chutes** is also good for a drink and snack, although the atmosphere is somewhat more boozy. Both hotels have more expensive restaurant menus.

A dozen local restaurants are scattered around Kamembe: there's not much to choose between them superficially, but the busier places are likely to be the best value. The restaurant at the **Auberge la Saveur** is pretty good, very affordable, and organises barbecues on request.

Foreign exchange

The Banque de Kigali on the main road through Kamembe changes travellers' cheques during normal banking hours, but proof of purchase is required. The Banque Commerciale du Rwanda, also in Kamembe, changes travellers' cheques on Mondays only, and no proof of purchase is required. Both the banks will change US dollars cash, but better rates can be obtained from money changers around the market in Kamembe.

Excursions

Cyangugu forms the obvious base from which to explore the far southwest of Rwanda, a region which sees very few tourists. The southwest boast a couple of points of interest in the form of the Bugarama Hot Springs and Cyamudongo Forest, though you could argue that these landmarks provide a good pretext to explore a remote corner of Rwanda as much as they rank as worthwhile goals in their own right. With access to a private vehicle, this area could be explored as a day trip out of Cyangugu. Using what limited public transport exists, you're definitely in for an adventure: you should probably plan on spending at least one night out of Cyangugu, and should be prepared for long waits at the roadside, or a lot of walking.

Note that several travel guides refer to the **Rusizi Falls** (*Les Chutes des Rusizi*) on the Rusizi river along the border with the DRC. We spent a morning searching in vain for this, following a variety of confusing directions, only to conclude that whatever waterfall may once have existed has long been submerged beneath the waters of a colonial-era dam (which also serves as an obscure border crossing into the DRC) about 10km south of Cyangugu. My best guess as to the cause of the apparent confusion is that, like the Owen Falls Dam in Uganda, this is referred to locally as the Rusizi Falls Dam. If any readers are able to enlighten me further, we'd be grateful to hear from them.

Another possible excursion from Cyangugu is to the town of **Bukavu** across the border in the DRC. Bukavu is currently under Rwandan control, and at the time of writing cross-border day trips are sometimes permitted, with no visa charge attached. This situation is rather fluid, however, so you'll have to check things out at the border post.

Bugarama Hot Springs (Amashyuza ya Bugarama)

Situated slightly less than 60km from Cyangugu by road, the Bugarama Hot Springs lie at the base of a limestone quarry, 5km from the Cimerwa Cement Factory, in a lightly wooded area dotted by large sinkholes. The springs bubble up into a large green pool which, as viewed from the roadward side, is initially somewhat disappointing. You can, however, follow a path around the edge of the pool, past a large sinkhole to your left, then leap over the outlet stream to the base of the cliff. Here you are right next to the main springs, which bubble into the pool like a freshly shaken and opened fizzy drink bottle, and are sizzling hot to the touch.

In a private vehicle the springs can be reached in about 90 minutes from Cyangugu, but they are rather more inaccessible using public transport. The first part of the trip involves following the partially surfaced road that connects Cyangugu to Ruha (a border post with Burundi) for approximately 40km to the junction town of Bugarama. You need to turn left at this junction, along a dirt road that passes through Bugarama and a series of small villages, until after 11km you reach the strip of tar outside the Cimerwa Cement Factory. Here you must turn right, passing the factory gate. After another 5km, immediately past a signpost reading *Secteur Nyamaranko*, you'll see a hillside quarry and three-way fork to your left. Follow the leftmost fork for about 100m, then turn right on to a small dirt track, and after 100m or so you'll see the pool in front of you. If in doubt, ask for directions to the *Amashyuza* (aka *Amahyuza*).

Using public transport, one (very slow) bus and several minibus-taxes cover the Ruha road daily, leaving from Kamembe rather than Cyangugu proper, and taking up to two hours to reach Bugarama town. Bugarama itself isn't much to shout about – a hot, dusty small town ringed by plantations of plantains and pines – but accommodation is available at the **Tripartite Bar**, 50m from the main junction in the direction of the cement factory, where basic single rooms cost US$6 each. There is no regular public transport along the 16km road between the town and the springs, but we noticed quite a few pick-up trucks, so finding a lift – at least as far as the cement factory – shouldn't present a major problem. From there, the 5km walk is along flat terrain, and shouldn't take longer than an hour in either direction.

Cyamudongo Forest

Covering an area of about 6km², this isolated patch of montane forest is bisected by a rough dirt road, making it very accessible in a 4x4 vehicle, and a realistic goal for some off-the-beaten-track hiking. Despite its small size, Cyamudongo harboured populations of chimpanzee and l'Hoest's monkey prior to the civil war, and, while no research has taken place subsequently, the consensus is that these endangered primates are probably still present in small numbers. The forest is also an important ornithological site, as one of the few true high-altitude forests left in Rwanda, and it may well hold a few rare forest species that are no longer found in Nyungwe. Although Cyamudongo is currently afforded no official protection, my impression (based on comparison with old survey maps) is that it has not shrunk significantly in area over the last couple of decades. There is some talk of protecting it as an isolated annexe of the mooted Nyungwe National Park.

The closest town to the forest is Nyakabuye, a sprawl of traditional homesteads and a few tall concrete buildings centred around a bustling marketplace. Nyakabuye lies about 20km from Bugarama town, and 5km past the hot springs, in an area of plantation and bamboo forest. From the town, a steep road leads uphill for 8km, past traditional homesteads (evidently totally unused to tourists), before it winds through the indigenous forest for 2km. The forest ends at a T-junction in front of a large pine plantation, where a left turn along a 15km road, through rolling hills planted with tea, emerges on the surfaced Butare–Cyangugu road at the Shagasha Tea Estate. If you are driving to the forest directly from Cyangugu or the Butare road, it would probably be preferable to approach it via this tea estate, which is signposted from the main road. Either way, there are several forks along the road between the tea estate and the forest, so keep asking directions (bearing in mind that the forest is known locally as Nyirandakunze after a deceased queen).

It isn't easy to reach Cyamudongo Forest without private transport. With patience, it should be possible to catch a lift as far as Nyakabuye on the back of a truck from Bugarama. According to locals, Nyakabuye is also serviced by some sort of public transport direct from Kamembe (Cyangugu) on Wednesdays and Fridays. You'll almost certainly have to walk the 8km from town to the forest boundary, a steep but attractive trail, along which you are bound to attract a lot of friendly attention from curious children (and adults, for that matter). No formal accommodation exists in the area, but it is difficult to imagine that anybody would refuse permission to pitch a tent at one of the homesteads which line the road up to the forest, or that any significant risk would be attached to doing so. But the reality, as with any truly off-the-beaten-track travel, is that this trip should only be attempted by adventurous, flexible travellers who are prepared to deal with a total absence of tourist facilities.

Kibuye

The most conventionally pretty of the lake ports, Kibuye sprawls across a series of hills interwoven with the lagoon-like arms of the lake. Now that the new road from Kigali has been completed (or almost; at the time of writing just a few kilometres remained to be surfaced and work was under way), it is the lakeside town most quickly accessible from the capital, and seems much busier with tourists – both foreign and Rwandan – than Gisenyi or Cyangugu. At weekends you'll find families from elsewhere in Rwanda enjoying the small beaches and the swimming, some of them former exiles who returned after the genocide and are rediscovering their country. Hills planted with pines and eucalyptus give the locale a pristine, almost Alpine appearance, in contrast to the atmosphere of fading tropical languor which to some extent afflicts the other ports. It's a green, peaceful and appealing place, whose sudden views of the lake sparkling amid overhanging trees are true picture-postcard material.

It's hard to believe, amid today's sunlight and tranquillity, that during the genocide the prefecture of Kibuye experienced the most comprehensive slaughter of Tutsis anywhere in Rwanda. Previously there had been around 60,000 in the prefecture, an unusually high proportion of about 20%. When the French troops arrived afterwards they estimated that up to nine out of every ten had been killed. Whole communities were annihilated, leaving no witnesses to the crime. If you alight from your minibus-taxi near the sports stadium you will see just one of the mass graves, with a sign announcing: 'More than 10,000 people were inhumated here. Official ceremony was presided over by H E Pasteur Bizimungu, President of the Republic of Rwanda. April 26th 1995.' Now birds chirp on the surrounding wall and the laughter of children in the nearby primary school echoes across the enclosure. Here and throughout Rwanda, memories of the genocide remain acute but daily life carries on determinedly around them. As does tourism.

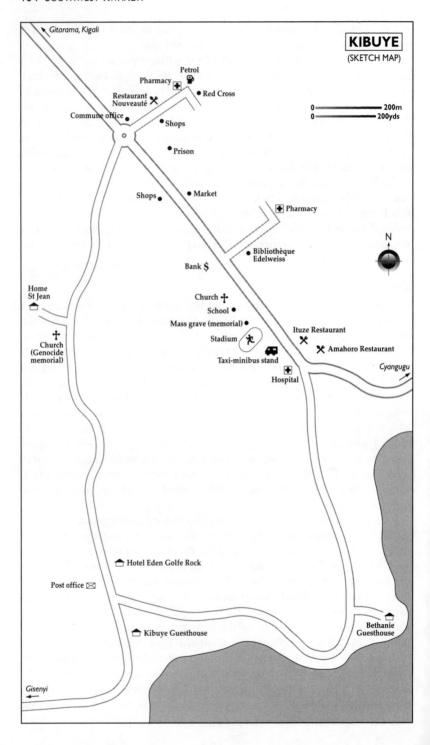

↖ *Gitarama, Kigali*

KIBUYE
(SKETCH MAP)

Petrol
Pharmacy
Red Cross
Restaurant
Nouveauté
Commune office
Shops
Prison

0 ——— 200m
0 ——— 200yds

Shops
Market
Pharmacy

Bibliothèque
Edelweiss

Bank $

N

Home
St Jean

Church
(Genocide
memorial)

Church ✝
School
Mass grave (memorial)
Stadium
Taxi-minibus stand
Hospital

Ituze Restaurant
✗ Amahoro Restaurant

Cyangugu
↗

Hotel Eden Golfe Rock

Post office ✉

Bethanie
Guesthouse

Kibuye Guesthouse

Gisenyi
←

Getting there and away

For transport by boat, see the *Cyangugu* section on page 149. There are a few minibus-taxis daily from Gisenyi, charging a fare of around US$2.50. Apparently no minibus-taxis run regularly between Cyangugu and Kibuye, but there's one bus daily in either direction, leaving at 08.00 and taking up to five hours. The main access is by an excellent road from Kigali via Gitarama, started by the Chinese in 1990. (From the bus windows you can still sometimes spot a labourer or an engineer wearing a traditional Chinese coolie hat.) On some stretches it's a considerable feat of engineering, cutting through hillsides and teetering around steep valleys. The journey from Kigali's Nyabugogo bus station takes around two and a half hours. When you arrive by minibus-taxi, alight at the crossroads at the entry to town if you're going to the Kibuye Guesthouse or the Home St Jean; continue to the final stop by the sports stadium if you want the Bethanie Guesthouse. There are sometimes some bicycle-taxis around if your bags are heavy.

Where to stay

The **Kibuye Guesthouse** (BP 1982 Kigali; tel: 68554/68555; mobile: 0832 3555/0850 1645; fax: 77278), with 18 simply furnished, self-contained rondavel-style rooms at US$25 single/$38 double, isn't cheap. But the beds and bedding are comfortable and good quality, the water is hot, and the location – beside a small beach on the grassy lake shore, with great views and technicoloured sunsets – is idyllic. The restaurant (indoor and outdoor) is excellent, with meals in the US$4–6 range (or more expensive dishes if you feel like a treat), and the place is popular with holidaying Rwandans at weekends. If you had a tough gorilla trek and you don't mind the cost, you could well relax here for a couple of days – swimming is safe and there are boat trips and water-skiing (for a price) on the lake, as well as tennis and ping pong. Plans are afoot to build more rondavels, in traditional style and using local materials.

A cheaper choice is the peaceful **Bethanie Guesthouse** (BP 9 Kibuye; tel: 68235) at the other end of town. More accommodation is being built there at the time of writing so prices may change, but in 2000 self-contained doubles with hot water cost US$15 and simpler rooms US$10. It's a church-run place so there's no alcohol, but meals are available (best to book them beforehand) in the dining room and the welcome is friendly. And the lakeside location is beautiful; it is more wooded than around the Kibuye Guesthouse so there are more birds. Normally there is plenty of space but the rooms can fill up if there's a religious gathering or seminar, so it's safer to book in advance:.

Finally, the cheapest accommodation option is the **Home St Jean** (tel: 68193), tucked away down a lane to the right-hand side of the large church that you'll see on a hill as you enter Kibuye from the east. It is signposted from near the church but rather indistinctly. It took a battering during the genocide but reopened in 1996: ten clean doubles at US$6.50 per person with shared facilities. At the time of writing breakfast wasn't available, so you'd have to walk either into the town or down to the Kibuye Guesthouse.

The **Hotel Eden Golfe Rock** may look promising, but in fact it has just been bought by the Chinese company building the Kigali/Kibuye road and is now used to house Chinese personnel. In an emergency they would take tourists if rooms were vacant: around US$25 per en-suite double.

Where to eat/drink

The restaurant at the **Kibuye Guesthouse** is excellent, either for a full meal or just for a drink sitting out at a lakeside table admiring the view. See details in *Where to stay*, above. The dining room at the **Bethanie** is fine if you're staying there – the set meals are filling and cheap – but not worth a special visit. In town, various small restaurants near the hospital serve traditional *mélanges* of rice, meat and vegetables, as does the fancifully named **Restaurant Nouveauté** (also good for a snack or drink) at the northern end of town. There are plenty of places for a quick beer or fruit juice when you're strolling – I liked the little **Boutique Ituze Chez Maman Colette**, which has a couple of tables outside and is raised up above the street opposite the market. From the tables you've a view across to the surrounding hillsides, with their patchy vegetation and tin-roofed homes. Also on sale there were bottles of Ugandan *Waragi* at US$6.50 and small bottles of banana wine for less than US$1.

Practicalities

The **post office** down near the Kibuye Guesthouse has international telephone and fax facilities and the staff are endlessly helpful. In town, the **Banque Continentale Africaine Rwanda** can change cash – I suspect US dollars may be easier than other currencies. There's a **pharmacy** down a side road to the right of the market as you face it; follow the sign to it and you'll pass the **Bibliothèque Edelweiss**, a tiny lending library with a stock of children's and adults' literature in French. Opposite the market, I checked out a shop with a sign 'International Fax/Telephone Office' – it was actually closed and full of mattresses but an unconnected phone/fax machine sat hopefully on a table.

What to see

Kibuye is such a relaxed, pleasant town that it's enjoyable just strolling and watching life unfold. There's a big **market** on Fridays, in an open area just beyond the hospital, when people come in from outlying villages and across the lake from Idjwi Island. The week-long market in the centre of town hasn't a huge range but is still worth a browse – take care not to wander into the adjacent prison compound by mistake! You'll come across work parties of prisoners here quite often, in their silly pink uniforms and Bermuda shorts – without them, far less reconstruction would have been completed in Kibuye. Walking past a straggle of them and responding politely to all the shouts of *Bonjour, Good morning* and even *Guten Tag* can be quite demanding. They seem to be very casually guarded, with only a couple of officials in evidence, and the atmosphere is good-humoured.

As the sketch map shows, you can do a **circular walk** around Kibuye. This offers some beautiful views across the lake and can be stretched to fill a couple of hours or so, depending on how often you stop to photograph, birdwatch or just enjoy the surroundings. Views are slightly better going clockwise rather than anti-clockwise. Once you've passed the hospital on your way up to the Bethanie there's nowhere to get a drink until you're back down by the Kibuye Guesthouse, so you may want to carry some water.

Motor-boat trips on the lake are possible – the guesthouse can arrange them for you – I was quoted around US$17.50 per boatload of four to five people for a circular trip on the lake, and ten times that amount for a trip to Idjwi Island and back; so it's only really economic for a small group.

The genocide memorial
As you enter Kibuye from the east, you'll see a large church perched on a hill above the town. During the genocide, over 4,000 died there. Lindsey Hilsum describes it with powerful economy of words in *Granta issue 51*:

> The church stands among trees on a promontory above the calm blue
> of Lake Kivu. The Tutsis were sheltering inside when a mob, drunk
> on banana beer, threw grenades through the doors and windows and
> then ran in to club and stab to death the people who remained alive.
> It took about three hours.'

The church is still being repaired and now stands empty as a genocide memorial. A further memorial has been built outside by relatives of those who died there and in the area nearby. The church's interior is full of silence, shadows, and shafts of light breaking in through the windows and stained glass. It is completely peaceful. For me, a memorial of this kind is far more evocative and far more moving than the skulls of Nyamata or the corpses of Murambi. Here there is an echoing beauty, which is no bad accompaniment to thoughts of death. Above the altars, someone has sketched religious scenes in red and white chalk on the bare, unfinished walls: a simple and haunting tribute. Try to find time for a few reflective minutes in this deeply memorable place.

Ndaba Falls
On your way back by minibus-taxi along the road to Gitarama, look out for this waterfall some distance away on your right about 20km out from Kibuye. Passengers will point it out to you if you warn them beforehand – in French it's the *Chutes de Ndaba*. In the rainy season it's an impressive 100m cascade, in the dry season a fairly unimpressive straggle. You can ask for the minibus to drop you at the viewpoint. Going in the other direction it's harder to spot.

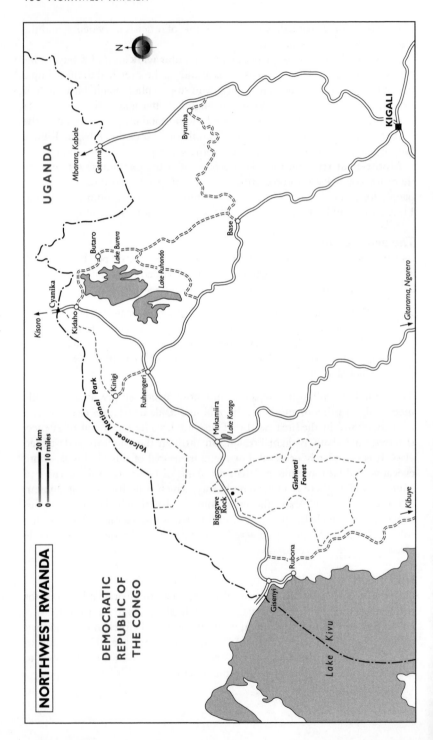

Northwest Rwanda

The far north of Rwanda is the focal point of the country's renascent tourist industry. The main point of interest for most travellers is the Volcanoes National Park (*Parc des Volcans*), which protects the Rwandan section of the Virunga volcanoes, and harbours approximately half of the world's mountain gorillas. The Volcanoes Park is currently the best place anywhere in Africa to go gorilla tracking, while also supporting a number of other localised mammal, bird and plant species.

Only 90 minutes' drive from Kigali, the modestly sized town of Ruhengeri is the most important tourist centre in the north, situated at the base of the Virunga mountains only 15km from the forest inhabited by the mountain gorillas. Ruhengeri has a good range of tourist facilities, mostly catering towards budget travellers, and it also forms an excellent base from which to explore a number of less celebrated attractions, notably the stunningly curvaceous Lakes Burera and Ruhondo.

The other important tourist centre in the region is Gisenyi, an attractively faded resort town and active port on the shore of Lake Kivu, 60km west of Ruhengeri. Better equipped for upmarket tourism than Ruhengeri, Gisenyi forms a good alternative base from which self-drive tourists can visit the gorillas, while also boasting an excellent selection of more affordable amenities, and a seductive tropical ambience that makes it a great place for backpackers to settle into for a few days.

Good roads connect Ruhengeri and Gisenyi to Kigali and southern Uganda, and the region as a whole has an agreeably moderate year-round climate and consistently attractive mountain scenery. Its location close to the Ugandan and the DRC borders made it an unsettled area both before and for some time after the genocide, because of army and guerrilla activity. From a tourist's perspective, security is no longer a serious concern, but given the region's proximity to the DRC it would still be wise to make enquiries before heading off the beaten track.

RUHENGERI

Location, they say, is everything, and on this score Ruhengeri is privileged indeed. As the closest town to the Volcanoes National Park, it is a most convenient base from which to track mountain gorillas in the Virungas, and is

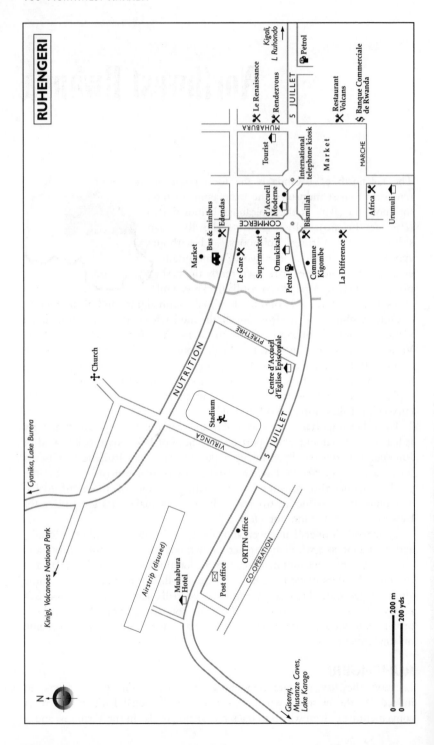

RUHENGERI

probably the busiest tourist centre in Rwanda (granted, all this means at present is that on a busy day there is a fair chance of bumping into a few other travellers here). Not only do the Virungas harbour the world's only extant population of mountain gorillas, but their distinctive volcanic outlines provide an otherwise workaday town with a memorably stirring backdrop, at least in clear weather.

For all its strategic importance, Ruhengeri is an inherently unremarkable small African town, sprawling amorphously from the tight grid of pot-holed roads that surround the central market. Fortunately, it does make for a very agreeable travel base: the mood is friendly and free of hassle, there are good facilities for budget travellers (an assertion which might be disputed by anybody who arrives hoping to exchange travellers' cheques), and the temperate mid-altitude climate is difficult to fault. The market is lively and worth a visit, and there are some pleasant strolls around town. Because it lies so close to the border, Ruhengeri seems to have attracted quite a number of Ugandans, which means that English is more widely spoken than in most parts of Rwanda.

Getting there and away
The main minibus-taxi stand is on Avenue de la Nutrition, at the edge of the compact town centre, within five minutes' walk of the more popular budget hotels.

To/from Kigali
Kigali and Ruhengeri are linked by a 96km surfaced road. The road is in fair condition, though the combination of outrageous bends, the occasional pot-hole, and some seriously manic local drivers makes it advisable to take things relatively slowly. Even the most cautious drivers should cover the distance in 90 minutes (Kigali residents who go gorilla tracking often drive up early in the morning.)

Regular minibus-taxis connect Kigali (Nyabugogo bus station) and Ruhengeri, leaving in either direction when they have a full complement of passengers. Tickets cost about US$2 and the trip takes around 90 minutes.

To/from Gisenyi
The 62km drive between Ruhengeri and Gisenyi follows a fairly good (and by Rwandan standards unusually straight) surfaced road, and should take no longer than an hour. Minibus-taxis between the two towns leave regularly and cost US$1.50.

To/from Uganda
The border crossings between Uganda and Rwanda are covered more fully on page 28. Coming to Ruhengeri straight from Kampala, the most efficient option is to catch a bus or minibus heading directly to Kigali, where you can pick up a minibus-taxi to Ruhengeri.

Coming from the west of Uganda, you will have to pass through Kabale, from where you can either cross directly in Rwanda at the Katuna border post, or else continue within Uganda to Kisoro and cross at the Cyanika border post. If you have private transport, or are visiting Kisoro anyway, then the Cyanika route is the best option. Kisoro and Ruhengeri lie approximately 40km from each other along a mostly tarred road. On public transport, you'll have to change vehicles at the border, and can expect to pay around US$0.75 for each leg.

Otherwise, given the poor state of the road between Kabale and Kisoro (as well as the limited amount of public transport), the most circuitous route between Kabale and Ruhengeri on paper is almost certainly the most efficient in practice: that is to catch a minibus-taxi from Kabale to Kigali (you might need to change vehicles at the border), from where you can pick up another to Ruhengeri. A variation on this would be to stop at Byumba on the Kabale–Kigali road, then travel along the back road to Base on the Ruhengeri–Kigali road, but this will almost certainly entail spending a night in Byumba (see page 184).

Where to stay

Ruhengeri boasts an unusually good selection of affordable accommodation. The most upmarket option is the **Hotel Muhabura** (BP 118; tel/fax: 546296), which lies on the outskirts of town along Avenue du 5 Juillet in the direction of Gisenyi. Set in compact green grounds, this is a very pleasant and reasonably priced hotel, with two types of room available: large self-contained doubles with hot bath and shower for US$14 and larger suites, also with hot shower and bath, for US$20. A good bar and restaurant are attached to the hotel. But watch out for the scam about having to pay for an expensive room because the standard ones are 'all full' – it isn't necessarily true, as one of the authors discovered to her cost.

Of the cheaper places scattered around the town centre, the pick is the **Home d'Accueil Moderne** (BP 121, tel: 546525, fax: 546904), situated on Avenue du 5 Juillet diagonally opposite the market and only two minutes' walk from the minibus stand. Clean, freshly painted double or twin rooms with nets and en-suite toilet and hot shower cost US$7.50. The staff here are very friendly and helpful, safe parking is available, and it's no problem if you arrive with US dollars only. The courtyard bar/restaurant serves chilled drinks and decent meals, while the television ensures it is popular with locals in the evenings.

Not quite so central, but still only a few minutes on foot from the minibus stand, the **Centre d'Accueil de l'Eglise Episcopale** is set in large church grounds on Avenue du 5 Juillet near the junction with Rue de Pyrèthre. Basic but clean rooms, some with nets, cost US$3.50 per person, making it particularly good value for solo travellers. The welcome is friendly, the communal ablutions are clean and have hot showers, and a limited selection of meals are available. Camping is normally permitted in the church grounds for a nominal charge.

Back in the town centre, on Rue de Muhabura, the new **Tourist Resthouse** is a relative of the popular Skyblue Hotel in Kabale (Uganda), which means the staff speak more English than in most places in Rwanda. The clean but cramped rooms (singles only) are adequate, and at US$7 they would be considered good value in many parts of Africa, but they seem relatively overpriced in Ruhengeri.

The same goes for the **Hotel Urumuli** (aka Hotel Urumuri), which lies on a back road close to the market, and charges just short of US$10 for a small, scruffy self-contained double with flaking paint and no hot water. For the truly perverse, however, nothing will match up to the **Omukikaka Inn**, a run-down dump which charges US$7.50 for a dirty double facing on to an uncomfortably chaotic courtyard.

In addition to the places listed above, there is accommodation within 20km of Ruhengeri at Kinigi (Volcanoes National Park), Lake Karago and Lake Ruhondo (see sections later in chapter).

Where to eat and drink

As with hotels, there is plenty of choice when it comes to eating out in Ruhengeri. The most extensive and expensive menu, inevitably, is at the **Muhabura Hotel**. The food is pretty good here – a selection of grills, stews and mild curries at around US$5–7 for a heaped plate – and so is the ambience on the semi-shaded balcony. Beers and other drinks are only slightly more expensive than at the local bars and restaurants in town.

The **Home d'Accueil Moderne** has a popular courtyard restaurant serving a fair selection of grilled and fried meals in the US$2–3 range (great fish and chips). The courtyard restaurant in the **Hotel Urumuli** was our favoured place to eat in Ruhengeri; the whole tilapia (a freshwater fish), chicken and goat kebabs are all recommended and excellent value. The **Tourist Hotel** also has an inviting menu, dominated by stews rather than grills.

Scattered around town are at least a dozen local restaurants serving local food (mostly gristly stews with boiled potatoes) for around US$1 per plate – the **Bismillah Restaurant** is one of the best. If you're into do-it-yourself meals there are plenty of grocers with a range of cans, jars, packets, bottles and so forth.

Other practicalities
Foreign exchange

If you are coming from Kigali, try to exchange all the money you will need for Ruhengeri there: the only banking facilities in Ruhengeri are at the **Banque Commerciale du Rwanda** behind the market; it doesn't accept travellers' cheques, and by its own admission offers a lousy rate for cash.

Travellers fresh across the border from Uganda will probably need to change some foreign currency in Ruhengeri. With US dollars, this shouldn't be a problem: most of the hotels will sort you out at a rate fractionally lower than the street rate in Kigali, which is probably a safer bet than trying to change money on the street or in the market. If you don't have US dollars, you've no option but to use the bank

ORTPN

The ORTPN office (tel: 546645 or 085 19874) is on the first floor of the municipal buildings on Avenue du 5 Juillet; look out for the signpost on the opposite side of the road to the Hotel Muhabura and Centre d'Accueil de l'Eglise

Episcopale, and about halfway between them. This is the base from which gorilla trekking is organised: travellers who arrive in Ruhengeri with a pre-booked permit and their own transport can simply pitch up on the day at around 7.30am, while those who arrive without a permit or without transport are advised to pop in the afternoon before they want to go trekking to make arrangements.

There is another ORTPN office in Kinigi, on the slopes of the Virungas about 12km from Ruhengeri, but for the time being the office in town is more useful to most travellers.

One might reasonably expect the ORTPN office in Ruhengeri to serve as a more general tourist office, and to be a good source of leaflets and information about other tourist sites in Rwanda. This is not the case at the time of writing but improvements are planned.

Communications
There are no email or internet facilities in Ruhengeri at the time of writing, though if the trend in neighbouring countries is anything to go by, that is bound to change sooner or later. The best place for telephone calls and faxes, local or international, is the kiosk in front of the Home d'Accueil Moderne.

Excursions from Ruhengeri
Most people who visit Ruhengeri see it purely as a base from which to track gorillas (see the section *Volcanoes National Park*) and very few explore the surrounding area further. But several local points of interest make for worthwhile day or overnight excursions from Ruhengeri, notably the little-visited Lakes Karago, Burera and Ruhondo, and, within walking distance of the town centre, the highly accessible Musanze Cave and Natural Bridge. If rushed for time, you could conceivably visit Gisenyi (on Lake Kivu) as a day trip from Ruhengeri.

Musanze Cave and Natural Bridge
A good pretext for stretching your legs while in Ruhengeri, and an interesting goal in its own right, Musanze Cave lies in the grounds of a school about 2km from the town centre off the Gisenyi road. The main cave, reportedly 2km long, has an entrance the size of a cathedral, and is home to an impressive bat colony. The large ditch out of which the cave opens is littered with pockmarked black volcanic rubble, and at the opposite end there is a natural bridge which was formed by a lava flow from one of the Virunga volcanoes.

Legend has it that Musanze Cave was created by a local king, and that it has been used as a refuge on several occasions in history. More recently, the cave was reportedly the site of a massacre during the genocide, and until recently it was still littered with human remains. Local schoolchildren say that with a good torch you can follow the cave for its full 2km length to a second entrance further along the Gisenyi road, though I would definitely want to verify that before attempting it myself.

To get to Musanze Cave from the town, follow Avenue du 5 Juillet past the Hotel Muhabura towards Gisenyi. Just short of 2km from the town centre, you'll see the large steel *Entrepots Opravia Musanze* to your left. Turn right directly opposite this building, following a curved dirt track which after about 100m leads to a football field and school. The cave lies in a ditch on the opposite side of the football field; any of the schoolchildren will point it out to you (and the rest will follow you down anyway!).

If you want a longer stroll, have a wander in the residential area opposite the Muhabura Hotel – some charities have their offices there, and there's a rough cross marking a genocide burial site.

Lake Karago

This small lake is less impressive than the two larger lakes which lie to the east of Ruhengeri, but it is also a lot more accessible on public transport, and sufficiently attractive that it served for years as the site of the President of Rwanda's holiday home. Lake Karago makes for a pleasant rustic excursion from Ruhengeri, with the main attraction being the characteristically mountainous Rwandan landscape around the lake and a set of rapids along the river that runs into the lake. There were also quite a few birds around when we visited, notably pelicans and herons.

Lake Karago lies 1.5km from Mukamiira, a small junction town on the main road between Ruhengeri and Gisenyi. Regular *matatus* cover the 20km between Ruhengeri and Mukamiira, where you need to turn left at the main junction towards Ngororero. The walk from Mukamiira to the first viewpoint over the lake takes about 15 minutes. From here, several footpaths lead to the shore, a 10–20-minute descent, depending on how muddy it is and which path you use.

Although Lake Karago can easily be visited as a day trip out of Ruhengeri, there is a basic but welcoming guesthouse in Mukamiira should you feel moved to spend the night. The guesthouse, which appears to be anonymous, is signposted *Bar Restaurant Chambres*, and it lies alongside the Gisenyi road about 500 from the Ngororero junction. Single rooms cost US$2.50 (a fair reflection of the quality of the accommodation); hot bucket showers are provided, meals are prepared to order, and the fridge is stocked high with beers and sodas.

Lake Burera

The largest and most beautiful of the lakes in the vicinity of Ruhengeri, Burera has until now been almost entirely neglected by travellers. With a private vehicle, however, the dirt road that loops around Burera's eastern shore makes for a superb day outing, while adventurous backpackers could happily spend several days exploring the lake using a combination of motorcycle-taxis, boats, and foot power. No formal accommodation exists anywhere on the lake shore, but the area is dotted with small villages where it shouldn't be a problem to ask permission to pitch a tent.

Lake Burera is visually reminiscent of Uganda's popular Lake Bunyonyi – not too surprising when you realise that these two bodies of water lie no more than 20km apart as the crow flies. Burera's eccentric shape is defined by the

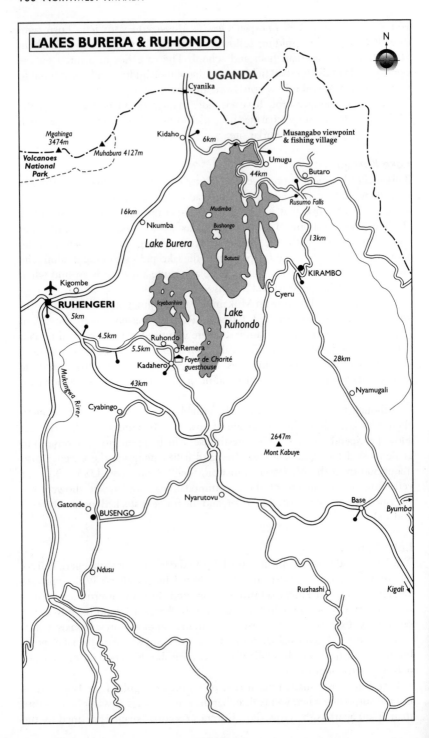

LAKES BURERA & RUHONDO

incredibly steep hills that enclose it. The slopes which fall towards the lake are densely terraced and intensively cultivated: very little natural vegetation remains among the fields of plantains, potatoes, beans and other crops, while the most common tree is the Australian eucalyptus. The stunning and distinctive scenery around the lake is enhanced by the outlines of the Virunga Mountains, the closest of which towers 10km away on the western horizon.

For travellers with their own transport, the circuit around the lake is straightforward enough. The road is mostly in good shape, and likely to present no problems provided that your vehicle has reasonable clearance (a 4x4 would be advisable during the rainy season). The full round trip from Ruhengeri covers about 150km, 90km of which are on dirt, and realistically takes a minimum of five hours to complete. Better, arguably, to leave after breakfast, carry a picnic lunch, and make a day of it, stopping along the way to enjoy the views and rustic villages.

To follow the circuit, head out of Ruhengeri along the road towards Cyanika for about 15km until you reach Kidaho, where you need to turn right into an unsignposted dirt road. After about six relatively flat kilometres along this track, the lake becomes visible to the right: on the shore you'll see a small fishing village (so far as we could ascertain, this is also called Kidaho) and dozens of small boats used to ferry locals around the lake. A few hundred metres past this village, a side road leads around the small Musangabo peninsula, offering stunning views in all directions.

The largest centre on the eastern shore of the lake is Butaro, which maps would suggest is only about 10km from Musangabo. In reality, the two are divided by a spectacular 44km stretch of road which hugs the cultivated contours about 100–200m above the lake shore. En route, the road passes through the small market village of Umugu. Butaro itself lies a couple of kilometres off the main road; about 50m from the junction, the attractive Rusumo Falls (not to be confused with their namesake on the Tanzania border) tumble over a cliff to the fields next to the lake.

After Butaro, the road veers away from the lake, and the views are few and far between, which leaves you with the option of returning the way you came (65km of which 50 are on dirt) or pushing on to complete the circuit (85km of which 41 are on dirt). Assuming that you decide to sally forth, the next main settlement you will reach, after 13km, is Kirambo (also referred to as Cyeru, the district for which it is the headquarters). Here, you can either turn left along a side road which leads to the village of Ruyange in a cultivated river valley at the southern tip of Lake Burera (a 20km round trip), or else continue straight ahead towards Base on the main Kigali–Ruhengeri road. Base lies 28km past Kirambo, and is almost equidistant between Kigali and Ruhengeri.

For travellers without a vehicle, the absence of public transport along parts of this circuit make it inaccessible or challenging, depending on how you see these things. For a day trip to Burera, it is easy enough to get as far as Kidaho – any Cyanika-bound minibus-taxi can drop you there, though you will probably be expected to pay the full fare of around US$0.75 – from where a motorcycle-taxi to Musangabo peninsula will cost less than US$1. With an early start, you should also have time to catch a boat-taxi from the fishing village next to the peninsula to the lake shore below Butaro and the Rusumo Falls, and to return the same way. The boat taxi takes 30–60 minutes in either direction, and costs around US$1.25. It should also be straightforward and affordable to hire a boat privately, either to go to the falls, or else just to explore the lake.

Keen walkers might also think about exploring the area over a few days. I've not heard of anybody doing this, so it would be uncharted territory, and would probably be practical only if you have a tent and are prepared to ask permission to camp at the many villages and homesteads along the way. It would probably be advisable to carry some food (though fish and potatoes should be easy to buy along the way). It is difficult to imagine that any serious security concerns are attached to hiking in this Uganda border area; you'll come across loads of local pedestrians for company, and travellers are still something of a novelty in this rural area.

The road to the east of the lake can effectively be viewed as an unusually wide hiking trail: it offers great views the whole way, is used by very few vehicles, and follows the contours for most of its length. The most beautiful stretch for hiking is the 44km between Musangabo and Butaro (which can also be covered by boat), and you would be forced to walk the 13km between Butaro and Kirambo. From Kirambo, there is a limited amount of public transport to Base, where it is easy to find a lift on to Ruhengeri or Kigali.

Lake Burera could also be explored more extensively by boat, once again an option suitable only for those with a tent and a pioneering spirit. The obvious place to start a trip of this sort would be Musangabo, though boats are the main form of transport throughout the area, so it should be easy enough to hire a boat and paddler anywhere. In addition to Rusumo Falls, there are at least four large islands in the southern half of the lake: Mudimba, Munanira, Bushongo, and Batutsi. In theory, it should be possible to boat to the south of Lake Burera, hike across the narrow strip of hilly terrain that separates it from Lake Ruhondo, and then pick up another boat to the Foyer de Charité on the southern shore of that lake (see *Lake Ruhondo* below). We've never heard of a traveller who attempted anything like this, so drop us a line to let us know how it goes!

Lake Ruhondo

Separated from Lake Burera by a 1km-wide strip of land (thought to be an ancient lava flow from Mount Sabinyo), Lake Ruhondo is, like the more northerly lake, an erratically shaped body of water whose shore follows the contours of the tall, steep hills that characterise this part of Rwanda. In common with Lake Burera, Ruhondo's shores are densely cultivated, and little natural vegetation remains, but it is nevertheless a very beautiful spot, offering dramatic views across the water to the volcanically formed cones of the Virunga Mountains looming on the horizon. Ruhondo is also an easy target for an overnight excursion, since good accommodation is available.

The lake is most accessible from the southwest, where the **Foyer de Charité** guesthouse (BP 53 Ruhengeri; tel: 085 10659) has a superb location on a hilltop overlooking the lake, with sweeping views across to the volcanoes in the northwest, and potentially stupendous sunsets. Established as a religious retreat in 1968, the mission was renovated in 1995 after it had been damaged during the genocide, and, although it remains first and foremost a religious retreat, lay visitors are very welcome. More than 40 comfortable guest rooms are available, at a charge of US$12/18 single/double (considerably cheaper for church visitors), as are communal hot showers, solid meals (around US$2 for breakfast and US$5 for lunch or dinner) and cold beers and sodas. It is advisable to phone in advance, as the mission occasionally closes to lay visitors for special religious events.

The best route to the Foyer de Charité starts on the main Kigali road about 5km south of Ruhengeri. Coming from Ruhengeri, you need to turn left along a dirt road signposted for Remera which initially leads through a marshy area dotted with traditional brick-making urns, before following a cultivated river valley. After 2.8km, take a left fork, then almost 2km after that turn right to cross a bridge over the river. The road is flat until this point, but now it starts to ascend gently, with the lake becoming visible to the left about 2.5km past the bridge. Several footpaths lead from this viewpoint to the lake shore, an easier ascent than the one from the Foyer de Charité. Beyond the viewpoint, the road continues to climb for 3km to the village of Kadahero, where a left turn leads after about 200m to the mission.

This is all straightforward enough provided that you have a vehicle, ideally a 4x4, and that – if driving along the tar from Kigali – you don't inadvertently take an earlier road signposted for Remera (this road does lead to the mission, but it's longer and rougher). There is no public transport, however, and hitching might prove to be frustrating. One option would be to catch public transport towards Ruhengeri as far as the turn-off to Remera, then to walk the final 10km to the mission (the last 6km would be steep going with a rucksack). The alternative is to hire a motorcycle taxi from Ruhengeri – the going rate is around US$3–4 one-way – and arrange to be collected at a specified time.

There is little in the way of formal entertainment at the mission – the beautiful singing at evening mass might qualify I suppose – but it's a lovely place to relax for a couple of days, and there's plenty of room for exploration on the surrounding roads. Several footpaths lead down the steep slopes below the mission to the lake shore, a knee-crunching descent and lung-wrenching ascent. At the lake, it is easy to negotiate a fee to take a pirogue to one of the islands, or to the hydroelectric plant on the opposite shore, where a small waterfall connects Lake Ruhondo with Lake Burera. Curio-hunters might be tempted to fork out around US$5 for an *iningire* – the traditional stringed instrument with which hawkers greet all *wazungu* visitors to the Foyer de Charité, a somewhat dirge-like rendition of *Frère Jacques* being the local favourite!

THE VOLCANOES NATIONAL PARK

This 13,000-hectare national park (in French *Parc des Volcans*) protects the Rwandan sector of the Virunga Mountains (also known as the Birungas), a range of six extinct and three active volcanoes which straddles the border with Uganda

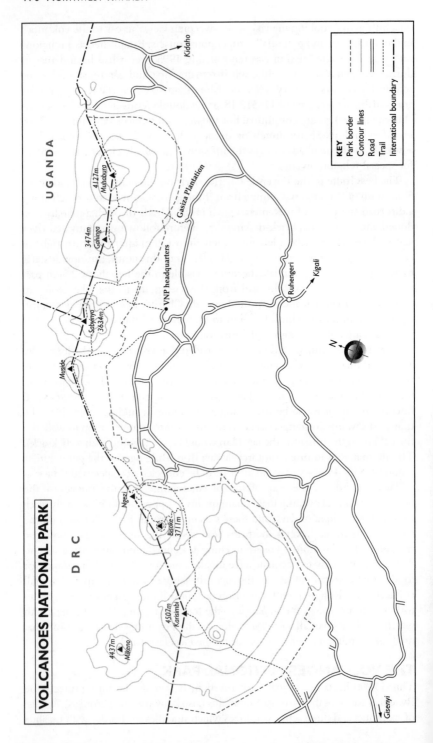

and the DRC. The Volcanoes Park forms a contiguous conservation unit with the Virungas National Park and Mgahinga National Park, which respectively protect the DRC and Ugandan sectors of the Virungas. The three national parks are managed separately today (that's if the word 'managed' can be applied to any park in the DRC at the time of writing). Prior to 1960, however, the Volcanoes and Virungas Parks together formed the Albert National Park.

Under Belgian colonisation, the Albert National Park was established by the decree of April 21 1925, in the triangle (considered a gorilla sanctuary) formed by the Karisimbi, Mikeno and Visoke volcanoes. At the time of its creation it was the first national park in Africa to be known as such. The *Institut du Parc National Albert* was created by decree on July 9 1929. A further decree on November 12 1935 determined the final boundaries of the Albert National Park, then covering 809,000 hectares. About 8% of the park lay in what is now Rwanda and today constitutes the Volcanoes National Park, while the rest was in the Congo. At the time of independence, Rwanda's new leaders confirmed that they would maintain the park (the gorillas were already well known internationally), despite the pressing problem of overpopulation.

Ranging in altitude from 2,400m to 4,507m, the Volcanoes National Park is dominated by the string of volcanoes after which it is named. This chain of steep, tall, free-standing mountains, linked by fertile saddles which were formed by solidified lava flows, is one of the most stirring and memorable sights in East Africa. The tallest mountain in the chain, and the most westerly part of the national park, is Karisimbi (4.507m) on the border with the DRC. Moving eastwards, the other main peaks are Visoke or Bisoke (3,711m), also on the DRC border; Sabinyo (3,634m) at the juncture of Rwanda, Uganda and the DRC; and Gahinga (3,474m) and Muhabura (4,127) on the Uganda border.

The altitudinal vegetation zones of the Virungas correspond closely with those of other large East African mountains, although the Afro-montane forest which once flourished below an altitude of 2,500m has been almost entirely sacrificed to make way for agriculture. Between 2,500m and 3,500m, where an average annual rainfall of 2,000m is typical, bamboo forest is interspersed with stands of tall hagenia woodland. Higher altitudes support a cover of Afro-alpine moorland, grassland and marsh, a landscape dominated by other-worldly giant lobelia and senecio plants similar to those found on Kilimanjaro and the Ruwenzoris.

The Volcanoes National Park is best known to the outside world as the place where, for almost 20 years, the American primatologist Dian Fossey

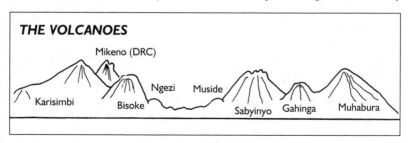

THE VOLCANOES

Mikeno (DRC)

Karisimbi   Bisoke   Ngezi   Muside   Sabyinyo   Gahinga   Muhabura

MOUNTAIN GORILLAS – THE MOVIE

A forerunner – long ago – to the making of *Gorillas in the Mist* was possibly the work of a Briton, Ben Burbridge, who spent some time in Rwanda during the late 1920s in order to, as he put it, 'take moving pictures' of the mountain gorillas.

This, to his great satisfaction and after considerable patience, he apparently achieved, and commented that this was a far better way of 'capturing' the creatures than doing so physically.

A team of local bearers had to lug all his film-making paraphernalia over the rough ground and through dense vegetation, and were baffled as to why he should go to all this trouble instead of simply shooting the gorillas, as they would have done.

Because of his experience in tracking them, he was later asked to capture some gorillas for the zoo in Tervuren, Belgium, so that the Belgian public could see at first hand the exotic wildlife native to their Trust Territory.

Burbridge seems to have felt deep admiration and respect for his 'subjects', which (he complained) tended to be visible only until he had assembled his film-making equipment, at which point they perversely vanished; and he treated them well, in contrast to many earlier colonials who had few qualms about slaughtering wildlife 'in the interests of science'.

undertook her pioneering studies of mountain gorilla behaviour. It is largely thanks to Fossey's single-mindedness that poaching was curtailed while there were still some gorillas to save. For her dedication, Fossey would pay the ultimate price: her brutal – and still unsolved – murder at the Karisoke Research Centre in December 1985 is generally thought to have been the work of one of the many poachers with whom she crossed swords in her efforts to save her gorillas.

Three years after her death, Fossey's life work was exposed to a mass audience with the release of *Gorillas in the Mist*, a cinematic account of her life filmed on location in the Volcanoes Park. *Gorillas in the Mist* drew global attention to the plight of the mountain gorilla, and generated unprecedented interest in the gorilla tourism programme which had been established in the park some ten years earlier. In 1990, the Volcanoes Park was the best organised and most popular gorilla sanctuary in Africa, and gorilla tourism was probably Rwanda's leading earner of tourist revenue.

The wheels came off in February 1992, when the park headquarters were attacked, two park employees were killed, and the research centre established by Dian Fossey had to be evacuated. The park reopened to tourism in June 1993, but it was evacuated in April 1994 due to the genocide. In late 1995, it once again reopened to tourism, only to close again a few months later. Gorilla tracking was finally resumed on a permanent basis in July 1999, since when the number of tourists visiting the Virungas every month has shot up from about 30 to 150, a figure that is likely to increase further over the next couple of years. More details of gorillas and gorilla tracking follow later in this section. Also see page 90 for details of the current activities of the Dian Fossey Gorilla Fund International.

In addition to gorilla tracking, a network of day and overnight hiking trails used to transect the Virungas. These included a relatively gentle day walk to Lake Ngezi (2,865m), as well as more challenging day hikes to the peaks of Sabinyo and Visoke, and overnight trails to the higher peaks of Karisimbi and Gahinga. All these trails were closed during the civil war, and some reports suggest that they may have been planted with land mines. According to the park management there are no plans to reopen them in the foreseeable future. Given the Rwandan government's sensitivity to international opinion and eagerness to re-establish a tourist industry, it can be assumed that, should the trails open during the lifespan of this edition, they will be safe. Check with ORTPN and/or tour organisers in Kigali (see pages 112–13) for the latest information on this.

Gorillas aside, little information is available regarding the current status of large mammals in the park, but some 76 mammal species have been recorded in Uganda's neighbouring Mgahinga National Park, and it seems reasonable to assume that most of these animals also occur in the larger Rwanda section of the Virungas. Surprisingly, monkeys are poorly represented by comparison with other forests in Rwanda and western Uganda. The only one likely to be encountered by tourists is the golden monkey, a beautiful and distinctive bamboo-associated race of the blue monkey, endemic to the Albertine Rift, and according to some reports unlikely to number more than 1,000 across its limited range. A small number of silver monkey, a more widespread race of blue monkey, also occur in the forest of the Virungas. Elephant and buffalo are still quite common, judging by the amount of spoor we encountered, but are very timid and infrequently observed. Also present are giant forest hog, bushpig, bushbuck, black-fronted duiker, spotted hyena, and several varieties of small predator. Recent extinctions, probably as a result of deforestation, include the massive yellow-backed duiker and leopard.

In 1980, roughly 180 bird species had been recorded in the park, though it is possible that several rainforest specialists have since vanished. A local speciality is the vulnerable Grauer's swamp warbler, while at least 13 Albertine Rift endemics are present, including handsome francolin, Ruwenzori turaco, Ruwenzori batis, strange weaver, dusky crimson-wing, Shelley's crimson-wing and Archer's ground robin. Until such time as the walking trails in the park reopen, the birding opportunities in the Volcanoes Park will be somewhat limited.

Getting there and away

The normal base for visiting the Volcanoes Park is Ruhengeri, which can easily be reached on public transport from Gisenyi, Kigali or Uganda. With a private vehicle, it is perfectly possible to drive to Ruhengeri from Gisenyi or Kigali on the day you track (you need to be at the ORTPN office in Ruhengeri by 08.00), but this isn't a reliable option using public transport. There is no public transport between Ruhengeri and the park headquarters at Kinigi. Details of arranging transport to tie in with gorilla tracking are included under the gorilla tracking section below.

Where to stay and eat

Most travellers stay in Ruhengeri, and some in Gisenyi, on the night before they go gorilla tracking. Another option is the **Asoferwa Tourist Village** (BP 656 Kigali; tel: 86394; fax: 84413), a spanking new development on the site of the former national park camping and chalet site next to the ORTPN headquarters at Kinigi. The tourist village lies some 13km from Ruhengeri, in a cultivated area close to the base of Mount Sabinyo, and has an attractive, almost Alpine façade and comfortable communal areas. Unfortunately, the self-contained double rooms are rather dingy and are already showing signs of sloppy workmanship (leaky toilets, enigmatic hot water supply, cupboards that don't close properly), which makes them poor value at US$50. Camping, too, is costly by comparison with a budget hotel room in Ruhengeri.

Gorillas and gorilla tracking

The most celebrated resident of the Virunga Mountains is the mountain gorilla, distinguished from other forms of gorilla by several adaptations to its high altitude home, most visibly a longer and more luxuriant coat. Approximately 300 mountain gorillas live in the Virungas, with their total range of 420km^2 spread across three countries: Rwanda, Uganda and the DRC. Current estimates place Rwanda's gorilla population at around 140–150, about half of which move in two large groups of between 30 and 40 individuals, and the remainder in five or six groups of between five and 15 animals.

While the lowland races of gorilla were first described by European biologists in the mid-18th century, the mountain gorilla was unknown to Western science until 1902, when two individuals were shot in the Virunga Mountains by Oscar van Beringe. The first detailed study of wild mountain gorilla behaviour was undertaken in the 1950s by George Schaller, whose pioneering work formed the starting point for the more recent and better publicised study done by the late Dian Fossey in Rwanda.

Mountain gorillas are on average bulkier than other races of gorilla, weighing up to 200kg, though the heaviest individual gorilla on record is a 210kg eastern lowland gorilla measured in Zaire. Like other

DEATH ON KARISIMBI

In February 1907 a German geologist named Kirchstein (who was later the first European to climb Visoke) had a sad experience when descending Karisimbi with a group of porters.

We had safely traversed the first half of the moor when we were suddenly assailed by an extraordinarily violent shower of hail which came down from an almost bright sky, whilst a dense fog gathered at the same time. The temperature sank to zero, and then a snowstorm of such fury set in that, if I had not myself been a witness of it, I should have deemed it impossible in equatorial Africa. My carriers had scarcely perceived the snow when they threw away their loads, lay down on the ground, and with wails declared that the gods had decreed that they must die. It was in vain that I urged them to pursue the march ... I fought my way, wading up to my knees in icy cold water, accompanied by my two Askari and a very few followers, through the storm and snow to the edge of the crater. Arrived there we contrived to erect a temporary camp in the shelter of the trees and made a fire. Time after time, accompanied only by the two Askari, I penetrated the pathless swamp, and so brought one hapless native after the other to the warm camp fire. I ordered my men to leave the loads where they were so long as they rescued the people. But even our own strength failed at last ... and the closing darkness, too, made any further attempt at rescue hopeless...

Absolutely drenched through, without any tent, limbs shivering from emotion and cold, and wrapped in a blanket only – that is how we spent the sleepless night round the camp fire, only to have to resume our work of exhumation again with the first grey light of morning. *Exhumation*, not rescue, for what remained to be rescued was heartrendingly little. Very few of the luckless ones showed any trace of life. All the rest, twenty in number and nearly half my caravan, lay corpses in the snow. Frozen under a tropical sun!'

In the Heart of Africa, Cassell, 1910

gorillas, they are highly sociable, moving in defined troops of anything from five to 50 animals. A troop typically consists of a silverback male (the male's back turns silver when he reaches sexual maturity at about 13 years old), his three or four wives and several young animals. Unusually for mammals, it is the male who forms the focal point of a troop; when he dies, the troop normally disintegrates. A silverback will start to acquire his harem at about 15 years of age, normally by attracting a young sexually mature female from another troop. He may continue to lead a troop well into his forties.

Female gorillas reach sexual maturity at the age of eight, after which they often move between troops several times. However, once a female has successfully given birth, she will normally stay with the same silverback until he dies, and she will even help defend him against other males (if a male takes over a troop, he will kill any nursing infants which are not his, a strong motive for a female to help preserve the status quo). A female gorilla has a gestation period similar to that of a human, and if she reaches old age she will typically have raised up to six of her offspring to sexual maturity. A female's status within a troop is based on the length of time she has been with a silverback: the longest-serving member of the harem is normally the alpha female.

Mountain gorillas have a primarily vegetarian diet, and are known to eat 58 different plant species. Gorillas also eat insects, with ants being a particularly popular protein supplement. A gorilla troop will spend most of its waking hours on the ground, but it will generally move into the trees at night, when each member of the troop builds itself a temporary nest. Gorillas are surprisingly sedentary creatures, typically moving less than 1km in a day, which makes tracking them on a day-to-day basis relatively easy for experienced guides. A troop will generally move a long distance only after a stressful incident, for instance an aggressive encounter with another troop.

Gorillas have few natural enemies and they often live for up to 50 years in the wild, but their long-term survival is critically threatened by poaching, deforestation, and increased exposure to human-borne diseases. Unlike their lowland cousins, mountain gorillas have never been reared successfully in captivity. Dian Fossey's *Gorillas in the Mist* (see *Further Reading*) is a good starting point for anybody who wants to know more about mountain gorilla behaviour.

Conservation and tourism

Until recently lumped together as one race (see box *Gorilla taxonomy*, page 178–9), the mountain gorilla and Bwindi gorilla are the only representatives of the world's largest primate to occur east of the Albertine Rift. Although both races number about 300 in the wild, the Bwindi gorilla is probably the more secure of the two, since it is confined to one forest in Uganda where it is protected in the Bwindi-Impenetrable National Park. The mountain gorilla, by contrast, has a range that straddles three countries. While national parks in all these countries afford some protection to the mountain gorilla, the volatility of this area in recent years has repeatedly forced researchers and rangers to evacuate one or other of the parks.

Poaching and deforestation have certainly taken a heavy toll since 1902, but it is difficult to say how many mountain gorillas lived in the Virungas before that – given their restricted range, it seems unlikely that the total population would have exceeded a couple of thousand. During the two decades following the 'discovery' of mountain gorillas, it is known that at least 50 gorillas were captured or killed in the Virungas, prompting the Belgian government to create Africa's first national park there.

The gorilla population of the Virungas is thought to have been reasonably stable in 1960, when the gorilla researcher George Schaller estimated it to be around 450. By 1980, however, that number had plummeted to 250, a decline caused by several factors: the splitting of the Albert National Park into its current Rwandan and Zairian components, the ongoing political instability caused by fighting between local Hutus and Tutsis, the handing over of more than 40% of the gorillas' habitat to local farmers in 1957 and to a European-funded agricultural scheme in 1968, and a grisly but profitable tourist trade in poached gorilla heads and hands – the latter used by some sad individuals as ashtrays!

In 1978, the first gorilla tourism project was initiated in the Volcanoes Park; it integrated tourism, education and anti-poaching measures with remarkable success. By the middle of the 1980s, gorilla tourism was raising up to US$10 million annually, making it Rwanda's third highest earner of foreign revenue. At the end of that decade, the Virunga gorilla population had increased by almost 30% to 320 animals. The mountain gorilla had practically become Rwanda's national emblem, and it was considered by the government to be the country's most important renewable natural resource. To ordinary Rwandans, the gorillas were a source of great national pride: living gorillas ultimately create far more work and money than poaching had ever done.

Gorilla tourism in Rwanda came to an abrupt halt in 1991, when the country erupted into a civil war which culminated in the genocide of 1994. The civil war also raised considerable concern about the survival of the gorillas. Researchers and park rangers were twice forced to evacuate the Volcanoes Park, land mines were planted by various military factions, and the Virungas were used as an escape route by thousands of fleeing refugees. Remarkably, however, when researchers were finally able to return to the park, it was discovered that only four gorillas could not be accounted for. Two of the missing gorillas were old females who most probably died of natural causes; the other two might have been shot, but might just as easily have succumbed to disease. It is also encouraging to note that the war has had no evident effect on breeding activity, a strong indication that it was less disruptive to the gorillas than had been feared.

While concern about the fate of a few gorillas might seem misplaced in the context of a war which claimed a million human lives, it is these self-same gorillas which give Rwanda a real chance of rebuilding the lucrative tourist industry that was shattered by the war. It will do this in an environment in which increasing concern is being voiced about the ramifications of habituating gorillas for tourists. There is, for instance, the issue of health: humans and gorillas are genetically close enough for there to be a real risk of a tourist passing a viral or bacterial infection to a habituated gorilla, which might in turn infect other members of its group, potentially resulting in all their deaths should they have no resistance to the infection.

Another concern is that habituating gorillas to humans increases their vulnerability to poachers. During 1995, seven habituated gorillas died as a result of poaching: four members of Bwindi's Kyaguliro Group were speared

GORILLA TAXONOMY

The gorilla is a widespread resident of equatorial East and Central African rainforest. Recent estimates indicate a global population of perhaps 100,000 wild gorillas, mainly concentrated in the Congo Basin (Gabon and the DRC). Until recently, all gorillas were classified as one species (*Gorilla gorilla*), with three races recognised: the western lowland gorilla (*G. g. gorilla*) of the Congo Basin, the eastern lowland gorilla (*G. g. graueri*) of the DRC immediately west of the Albertine Rift, and the mountain gorilla (*G. g. beringei*) of the Virunga and Bwindi ranges on the eastern side of the Albertine Rift.

This conventional classification of gorillas has recently been shattered by advances in DNA tests and fresh morphological studies. It is now known that the western and eastern gorilla populations have almost as many genetic differences as humans and chimpanzees, which means they should almost certainly be regarded as distinct species tentatively assigned as *G. gorilla* (west) and *G. beringei* (east).

The status of the western gorilla is reasonably secure, since it is far more numerous in the wild than its eastern counterpart, and has a more extensive range. DNA research has, however, resulted in the Cross River gorilla *G. g. dielhi* of the Cameroon–Nigeria border area being recognised as a distinct race of western gorilla. The Cross River gorilla has the dubious distinction of being placed on a shortlist of the world's 25 most endangered primate morphs, and it fulfils the IUCN criteria for a listing of 'Critically

to death, while in what was then Zaire, the famous silverback Marcel was shot dead, together with one adult female. In both cases, an infant was removed: the one captured at Bwindi is now assumed to be dead; the one taken from the Volcanoes Park was confiscated at the Ugandan border and returned to the troop from which it was taken. These incidents were thought to be linked to one dealer's attempts to acquire an infant gorilla, and did not appear to signal the start of a trend. Nevertheless, the very fact that habituated gorillas were targeted highlights their relative vulnerability to poachers.

Given the above, a reasonable response might be to query the wisdom of habituating gorillas in the first place. The problem facing conservationists is that gorillas cannot be conserved in a vacuum. At current prices, the authorities can potentially earn US$12,000 daily in tracking permits alone, much of which can be pumped back into the protection and management of the Volcanoes Park. There are also the broader benefits of job creation through tourism in and around the Virungas. And even in terms of pure conservation, habituation has many positive affects, allowing researchers and rangers to monitor the gorillas on a daily basis, and to intervene when one of them is ill, injured or in a snare. As one gorilla researcher based in Ruhengeri put it, tourism for all its negatives is probably the only thing that will save the Volcanoes Park – and by default save the gorillas.

Endangered', as it lives in five fragmented populations, only one of which is protected, and which together total no more than 200 individuals.

Although at least 15,000 eastern gorillas remain in the wild, all but 600 of them are assigned to the lowland race. The remaining 600 are generally classified as mountain gorillas, which – like their Cross River counterparts – are listed among the world's 25 most endangered primate morphs. There is, however, growing consensus among primate researchers that this conventional assignation needs to be revised. It was previously thought that the approximately 300 gorillas resident in Uganda's Bwindi-Impenetrable Forest, though they live at a lower altitude and have a thinner coat, were racially identical to the mountain gorillas of the Virungas – a not unreasonable assumption given that the montane forests of the Virungas and Bwindi were linked by a corridor of mid-altitude forest until about 500 years ago. But DNA tests indicate that the Bwindi and Virunga gorillas are discrete races, and that the two montane forests have supported isolated breeding populations of gorillas for many millennia.

Esoteric stuff, perhaps, but the bottom line is that a mere 300 mountain gorillas remain in the wild, the entire population is confined to the Virunga Mountains, and approximately half of them are resident in Rwanda's Volcanoes Park. Neither the mountain gorilla nor the Bwindi gorilla has been bred successfully in captivity, and both races should probably be regarded as 'Critically Endangered' – one criterion for this classification being that fewer than 250 mature adults remain in the wild.

For post-genocide Rwanda, however much it may struggle to re-establish a reputation as a viable tourist destination, its case would be ten times worse without the mountain gorillas. It is the gorillas that will bring back the tourists, who will also spend money in other parts of the country, thereby generating foreign revenue and creating employment well beyond the immediate vicinities of the mountain gorilla reserves. Tourism is probably integral to the survival of the mountain gorilla; the survival of the mountain gorilla is certainly integral to the growth of Rwanda's tourist industry. This symbiotic situation motivates a far greater number of people to take an active interest in the fate of the gorillas than would be the case if gorilla tourism were to be curtailed.

Visiting the gorillas

Mountain gorilla tracking in the Virungas is a peerless wildlife experience, and one of Africa's indisputable travel highlights. It is difficult to describe the simple exhilaration attached to first setting eyes on a wild mountain gorilla. These are enormous animals: the silverbacks weigh about three times as much as the average man, and their bulk is exaggerated by a shaggily luxuriant coat. And yet despite their fearsome size and appearance, gorillas are remarkably peaceable creatures, certainly by comparison with most primates – gorilla tracking would be a considerably more dangerous pursuit if these gentle giants had the temperament of vervet monkeys, say, or baboons (or, for that matter, humans).

More impressive even than the gorillas' size and bearing is their unfathomable attitude to their daily human visitors, which differs greatly from that of any other wild animal. Anthropomorphic as it might sound, almost everybody who visits the gorillas experiences an almost mystical sense of recognition: we regularly had one of the gorillas break off from chomping on bamboo to study us, its soft brown eyes staring deeply into ours, as if seeking out some sort of connection.

Equally fascinating is the extent to which the gorillas try to interact with their visitors, often approaching them, and occasionally touching one of the guides in apparent recognition and greeting as they walk past. A photographic tripod raised considerable curiosity in several of the youngsters and a couple of the adults – one large female walked up to the tripod, stared ponderously into the lens, then wandered back off evidently satisfied. It is almost as if the gorillas recognise their daily visitors as a troop of fellow apes, but one too passive to pose any threat – often a youngster would put on a chest-beating display as it walked past us, safe in the knowledge that we'd accept its dominance, something it would never do to an adult gorilla. (It should be noted here that close contact with humans can expose gorillas to fatal diseases, for which reason the guides try to keep their tourists at least five metres away – but the reality is that there is little anybody can do to stop the gorillas from flouting rules of which they are unaware.)

The magical hour with the gorillas is relatively expensive and getting there – have no illusions – can be hard work. The hike up to the mountain gorillas' preferred habitat of bamboo forest involves a combination of steep slopes, dense vegetation, slippery underfoot conditions after rain, and high altitude. For all that, the more accessible gorilla groups can be visited by reasonably fit adults of any age, and in 15 years of African travel we have yet to meet anybody who has gone gorilla tracking and regretted the financial or physical expense.

Permits

A gorilla tracking permit costs US$250, and can be bought in advance through the ORTPN office in Kigali, or bought on the day at the ORTPN office in Ruhengeri. Either way, it is advisable to visit or ring the ORTPN office in Ruhengeri on the afternoon before you intend to go tracking in order to make arrangements. At the time of writing, advance booking is rarely necessary, but that might easily change during the lifespan of this edition. Also check how payment is to be made – you may need to hand over your $250 in cash.

Eight permits per day are issued for each of the habituated groups in the Volcanoes Park. At the time of writing, two habituated groups stay within tracking range on a permanent basis, while two others spend most of their time in the Volcanoes Park but occasionally cross the border into Uganda or the DRC. Depending on the movement of the gorillas, this means that between 16 and 32 permits can be issued daily.

Above Baby mountain gorilla, Volcanoes National Park

Left L'Hoest's monkey, Nyungwe Forest Reserve

Below left Angola colobus monkey, Nyungwe Forest Reserve

Below right Mountain gorilla, Volcanoes National Park

Above Street store selling crafts, Kigali
Right Tea picker, Byumba
Below Traditional brick-making site

The more difficult to reach of the two permanent groups is the **Susa Group**, which lives on the slopes of Mount Karisoke. Consisting of 33 individuals, including two silverbacks and several youngsters, this is the second largest group of mountain gorillas in the world (there is a larger research group) and it was the one originally studied by Dian Fossey. A visit to the Susa Group is delightfully chaotic and totally unforgettable, with gorillas seemingly tumbling out of every bush and bamboo stand. The Susa Group is the first choice of most fit visitors, but be under no illusions about the severity of the hike. The ascent from the car park to the forest boundary is gaspingly steep, and will take the best part of an hour. On a good day, it will take no more than 20 minutes to reach the gorillas from the boundary; on a bad day you might be looking at two hours in either direction (the record from the previous day will give an indication of how deep in the gorillas are, as they generally don't move too far in one day).

A far less strenuous prospect is the **Sabinyo Group**, whose permanent territory lies within the Volcanoes Park, on a lightly forested saddle between Mount Sabinyo and Mount Gahinga. Depending on exactly where the gorillas are, the walk from the car park to the forest boundary is flat to gently sloping, and will typically take 20–30 minutes. Once in the forest, the gorillas might take anything from ten minutes to an hour to reach, but generally the slopes aren't too daunting. The Sabinyo Group consists of 12 individuals, again with two silverbacks, and a youngster born in July 2000. Although it is less numerically impressive than the Susa Group, the Sabinyo Group does seem more cohesive and one gets a clearer impression of the group structure and interaction.

Group Thirteen spends most of its time on the same saddle as the Sabinyo Group, but its territory does cross into neighbouring countries, so it is not permanently in the Volcanoes Park. When it is around, however, it is normally just as easy to reach as the Sabinyo Group. Group Thirteen's name dates to when it was first habituated, and numbered 13 gorillas, but today it is a small group of seven. As with the Sabinyo Group, this means you get a good feel for group structure and interaction. Group Thirteen seems to be a favourite of many of the guides, probably because its silverback is more relaxed and approachable than those in other groups.

Finally, there is the **Amahoro Group**, which lives on the slopes of Mount Visoke. This group of 19 animals is reasonably habituated, but the silverbacks are jumpy and cannot be approached as closely as in other groups. There is some debate about whether this group should be fully habituated for tourists or not, but it seems likely that economics will win out over other considerations. I have not visited this group personally, but the hike is intermediate in difficulty between the Susa and Sabinyo.

Transport

No public transport connects Ruhengeri to any of the points where one enters the forest to go gorilla tracking, all of which lie about 10–15km from town. At the time of writing, the ORTPN people in Ruhengeri were usually happy to squeeze single permit-holders or couples into the vehicle they use to transport the guides and trackers, but this is likely to change as Rwanda catches on with travellers.

For larger groups, the only option is to hire a vehicle and driver for the morning. In the rainy season, a 4x4 will probably be necessary. The going rate for a 4x4 is around US$50–70 for the round trip. The ORTPN office in Ruhengeri can put you in touch with reliable drivers and vehicles, though you might get a better price if you ask around yourself. In the dry season, an ordinary taxi should be adequate, and will cost about half of what a 4x4 would charge. Before doing this, however, consider that the cost of hiring a vehicle is minimal relative to the cost of a gorilla permit: should you make private arrangements and the vehicle breaks down or isn't sturdy enough for the roads, you risk not being able to use your permit!

Travellers with private transport will need to be directed to the appropriate entry point to go gorilla tracking (the best place to enter the forest is different for each group, and can change from one day to the next). Normally, one of the guides will accompany your vehicle from the ORTPN office in Ruhengeri (or, if you prefer, the office in Kinigi) to show you the way.

Physical preparation

Depending on which group you visit, and your own level of fitness, the trek to see the gorillas will be at best taxing and at worst exhausting (the guides told us they have on occasion had to carry tourists down, and we met one Dutch woman who was too exhausted by the hike up to the forest to continue on to see the gorillas). One reason for this is the steep slopes that characterise the Virungas, particularly en route to the Susa Group. Once in the forest, the slopes aren't as steep, and the pace is slower, but bending and crawling through the thick vegetation can be tiring, particularly after rain when everything is muddy underfoot.

Don't underestimate the tiring effects of being at high altitude. The trekking takes place at elevations of between 2,500m and 3,000m above sea level, not high enough for altitude sickness to be a concern, but sufficient to knock the breath out of anybody – no matter how fit – who has just flown in from a low altitude. For this reason, visitors who are spending a while in Rwanda might think seriously about leaving their gorilla tracking until they've been in the country a week or so, and are better acclimatised. Most of Rwanda lies at above 1,500m, and much of the country is higher – a couple of days at Nyungwe, which lies above 2,000m, would be good preparation for the Virungas. Likewise, if you are coming from elsewhere in Africa, try to plan your itinerary so that you spend the few days immediately before you go gorilla tracking at medium to high altitude: to give one example, were you flying in from Kenya, a few days in Nairobi (2,300m) or even the Masai Mara (1,600m) would be far better preparation than time at the coast.

If you are uncertain about your fitness, don't visit the Susa Group, but rather opt for Group Thirteen or the Sabinyo Group, both of which are reached by reasonably easy hikes on flattish terrain. Once on the trail, take it easy, and don't be afraid to ask to stop for a few minutes whenever you feel tired. Drink plenty of water, and carry some quick calories – biscuits and chocolate can both be bought at supermarkets in Ruhengeri. The good news is that in 99% of cases, whatever exhaustion you might feel on the way up will vanish with the adrenalin charge that follows the first sighting of a silverback gorilla!

What to wear and take

Whichever group you visit, you may have to walk a long distance in steep, muddy conditions, possibly with rain overhead, before you encounter any gorillas. Put on your sturdiest walking shoes. Ideally, wear thick trousers and a long-sleeved top as protection against vicious stinging nettles. It's often cold when you set out, so start off with a sweatshirt or jersey (which also help protect against nettles). The gorillas are thoroughly used to people, so it makes little difference whether you wear bright or muted colours. Whatever clothes you wear to go tracking are likely to get very dirty as you slip and slither in the mud, so if you have pre-muddied clothes you might as well wear them. When you're grabbing for handholds in thorny vegetation, a pair of old gardening gloves are helpful.

Carry as little as possible, ideally in a waterproof bag of some sort. During the rainy season, a poncho or raincoat might be a worthy addition to your daypack, while sunscreen, sunglasses and a hat are a good idea at any time of year. You may well feel like a snack during the long hike, and should certainly carry enough drinking water – at least one litre, more to visit the Susa Group. Bottled water is sold in Ruhengeri. Especially during the rainy season, make sure your camera gear is well protected – if your bag isn't waterproof, seal your camera and films in a plastic bag (for further details about photographing gorillas see the box *Photographic tips* on pages 66–8).

Binoculars are not necessary to see the gorillas. In theory, birdwatchers might want to carry binoculars, though in practice only the most dedicated are likely to make use of them – the trek up to the gorillas is normally very directed, and walking up the steep slopes and through the thick vegetation tends to occupy one's eyes and mind.

Regulations and protocol

Tourists are permitted to spend no longer than one hour with the gorillas, and it is forbidden to eat or smoke in their presence. It is also forbidden to approach within less than 5m of the gorillas, a rule that is difficult to enforce with curious youngsters (and some adults) who often approach human visitors.

Gorillas are susceptible to many human diseases, and it has long been feared by researchers that one ill tourist might infect a gorilla, resulting in the possible death of the whole troop should they have no immunity to that disease. For this reason, you should not go gorilla tracking with a potentially airborne infection such as flu or a cold, and are asked to turn away from the gorillas should you need to sneeze in their presence.

To the best of my knowledge, no tourists have ever been seriously hurt by habituated gorillas, but there is always a first time. An adult gorilla is much stronger than a person, and will act in accordance with its own social codes.

Therefore it is vital that you listen to your guide at all times regarding correct protocol in the presence of gorillas.

BYUMBA

The small but sprawling town of Byumba lies about 3km off the main road between Kigali and Kibale (Uganda), and is likely to be visited only by travellers who want to cut across from the Kibale–Kigali road to Base on the Ruhengeri road. Byumba has nothing in the way of tourist attractions, though the surrounding countryside is rather pretty (Byumba lies at the heart of a major tea-growing area) and the dirt road to Base is one of the most scenic in the country.

There is plenty of transport to Byumba from Kigali and the Gatuna border with Uganda. The 42km road between Byumba and Base, notable for spectacular views of the tea estates around Base, is serviced by at least one bus daily, leaving Byumba in the early morning and returning from Base later in the day. There don't seem to be any minibus-taxis along this route, but hitching isn't impossible. On the Kigali–Byumba road about 10km outside Kigali is the rather surprising Highland Flowers Rose Farm, growing high-quality roses for sale locally and for export to Europe.

The most convenient place to stay in Byumba is **Ikaze Bagenzi Bar Restaurant Amacumbi**, which has basic singles for around US$3, a room sleeping four in bunk beds for US$6.50, and a self-contained double for US$10. There are showers, running water and flush toilets. The guesthouse lies about 300m from the bus station, and can be reached by walking downhill past the Banque de Kigali and bakery, turning right when you reach an open area used as a market, then left at the next junction. The smarter-looking **Kurumuri Guesthouse** was closed for renovations when I looked in, but was scheduled to open some time in late 2000. It lies about 2km from the bus station along the Base road (no signpost but look out for the blue gate), which is rather inconvenient for travellers dependent on public transport.

Travellers coming from Uganda will be pleased to know that the well-organised Banque Commerciale du Rwanda, 100m from the bus station, changes US dollars cash and travellers' cheques.

GISENYI

The most northerly port on the Rwandan part of Lake Kivu, Gisenyi is well worth a visit, especially as it lies little more than an hour by road from the gorilla tracking base of Ruhengeri. Gisenyi is split into an upper and lower town, the former an undistinguished grid of busy roads centred around a small market area, the latter a more spacious and atmospheric conglomeration of banks, government buildings, old colonial homesteads and hotels lapped by the waters of Rwanda's largest lake. The waterfront, with its red sandy beaches, pleasing mismatch of architectural styles, and shady palm-lined avenues, has the captivating air of a slightly down-at-heel tropical beach resort. Indeed, Gisenyi could be easily be mistaken for a sweaty West African or Indian Ocean backwater, except that the relatively high altitude of 1,500m means it has a refreshing climate at odds with its tropical appearance.

In 1907, the Duke of Mecklenburg wrote:

> Kissenji possesses an excellent climate, for by virtue of its 1,500
> metres above sea level all enervating heat is banished. The natural
> coolness prevalent in consequence makes a visit there a very agreeable
> experience. The man who has this place allotted to him for his sphere
> of activity draws a prize. In front are the swirling breakers of the most
> beautiful of all the Central African lakes, framed in by banks which
> fall back steeply from the rugged masses of rock; at the rear the stately
> summits of the eight Virunga volcanoes.

Gisenyi today offers little in the way of formal sightseeing, but its singular atmosphere, combined with an excellent range of affordable accommodation, makes it the sort of town which you could easily settle into for a few days. It's a interesting place to wander around, too, whether your interest lies in the prolific birds that line the lake shore, the fantastic old colonial buildings that dot the leafy suburban avenues, lazing around on the beach, or mixing in to the hustle and bustle of the market area. Further afield, the 6km walk or *matatu* drive to Rubona port offers some lovely lake views, while at Rubona itself you can easily arrange to explore the immediate vicinity in a dugout canoe or pirogue.

A couple of touching genocide stories linger in the mind. At a secondary school here, a group of teenaged girls were ordered to separate themselves into Tutsis and Hutus. When they refused, saying that they were all Rwandans, they were all killed together. Then there was a Catholic lay worker, a Hutu, who helped many hunted people to flee across the border even when she knew the military were aware of her action. When the *interahamwe* finally came to her house, 30 refugees were there. One by one they were shot in front of her, after which she asked to be killed too, so that they might stay together in death as in life. Before shooting her, the militia leader asked her to pray for his soul.

Gisenyi is home to the Imbabazi orphanage (tel: 540740), originally started in December 1994 by Rosamond Halsey Carr at her plantation in nearby Mugongo to shelter some of the many genocide orphans and displaced children, and shifted to its present site in 1998. Several of these children have since been reunited with their families, but new, post-genocide orphans have taken their place. The current total is somewhere over 100. This is a positive and heartwarming project, which gave love and security to at least some of the genocide's younger victims, and now provides a home for other orphans. See *Appendix 3*, page 224.

Getting there and away

All buses and minibus-taxis leave from the bus station next to the market in the old town centre. The main port for Gisenyi is at Rubona, about 6km south of town; the two are connected by regular minibuses.

To/from Kigali and Ruhengeri

Gisenyi lies approximately 60km from Ruhengeri by road, and 160km from Kigali. The road is sealed and mostly in good condition, though some caution

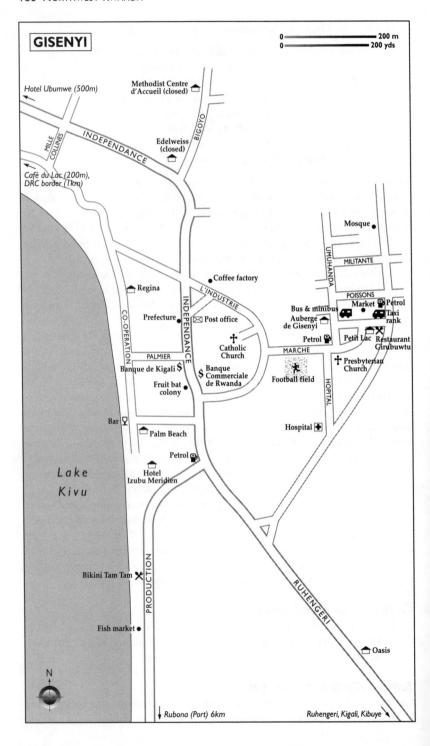

GISENYI

0 ——— 200 m
0 ——— 200 yds

Hotel Ubumwe (500m)

Methodist Centre
d'Accueil (closed)

BIGOYO

MILLE COLLINES

INDEPENDANCE

Edelweiss
(closed)

Café du Lac (200m),
DRC border (1km)

Mosque

UMUHANDA

MILITANTE

Coffee factory

L'INDUSTRIE

POISSONS

Regina

CO-OPERATION

INDEPENDANCE

Prefecture

Post office

Bus & minibus

Market

Petrol

Auberge
de Gisenyi

Taxi
rank

PALMIER

Petrol

Petit Lac

Restaurant
Girubuwtu

Banque de Kigali $

Catholic
Church

MARCHE

Banque
Commerciale
de Rwanda

Presbyterian
Church

Fruit bat
colony

Football field

HOPITAL

Bar

Palm Beach

Lake
Kivu

Petrol

Hotel
Izubu Meridien

Hospital

Bikini Tam Tam

PRODUCTION

Fish market

RUHENGERI

Oasis

N

↓ Rubona (Port) 6km

Ruhengeri, Kigali, Kibuye ↘

is recommended. The direct drive from Kigali should take no longer than three hours. Regular minibus-taxis connect the three towns: the fare to Ruhengeri is around US$1.50 and to Kigali US$3.

To/from Kibuye and Cyangugu

To drive from Gisenyi to Kibuye, you first need to head out along the Ruhengeri road for 10km, before turning right at a poorly signposted junction on to a 78km dirt road which brings you out at Commune Mabanza on the surfaced road between Kigali and Kibuye. It's a drive of about 110km in all, and the dirt stretch is in variable condition, so three to four hours should be allowed. Although the dirt road runs parallel to Lake Kivu, it offers disappointingly few glimpses of the lake, though this is compensated for by some spectacular mountain scenery and relic patches of Gishwati Forest. From Kibuye, it's another 100km to Cyangugu, a three-to-four-hour drive, mostly along dirt roads.

Public transport along the road between Gisenyi and Kibuye is rather less frequent than along the surfaced road heading east from Gisenyi, but a few minibus-taxis cover the route daily at a fare equivalent to US$2.50. You'll need to change vehicles at Kibuye if you are heading on to Cyangugu; with an early start this should be do-able in a day.

In theory, the most appealing means of transport between the various lake ports is by boat. The lake ferry which once covered this route hasn't operated in years, but small cargo boats do run between the three ports and will take passengers for a negotiable fare (expect to pay around US$2.50). This is an informal arrangement, dependent on what boats are leaving and when, but, as far I as could ascertain, boats head south from Rubona port on most days. Typically, they leave in the mid-afternoon, and take about six to eight hours to travel to Cyangugu, half that time to Kibuye. The boats we saw had no cover, so make sure you have sunblock and a hat, as well as plenty of water and food. Owners of private motor-boats may also be willing to make the trip, at least to Kibuye, but it won't work out cheap no matter how skilfully you bargain, so is probably only worth considering if you're in a group of three or four.

Where to stay

Upper and mid-range

Gisenyi has a range of accommodation to suit most tastes and budgets, and prices are generally very reasonable for what you get. Most of the accommodation is on the lake front, about 15 minutes on foot from the bus and minibus-taxi stand; travellers who don't want to walk down will find a few taxis lined up at the petrol station next to the bus stand. There are a couple of cheap guesthouses close to the bus station, but on the whole it is more pleasant to stay on the lake.

Top of the range in Gisenyi is the **Hotel Izubu Meridien** (BP 252; tel/fax: 61319), a large modern monolith set in lovely wooded gardens running down to the lake shore. The Meridien is close to international standards in quality and appearance; well maintained, clean, and boasting a good restaurant and comfortable bar. The large carpeted rooms are as blandly comfortable as you could ask for (a criticism in another context, but in Rwanda an occasional dose of bland comfort is welcome), and they all have satellite television, telephone, fridge, private balcony and hot bath – exceptional value for money at around US$50/60 single/double (you'd pay three time as much for similar rooms in many African countries).

Next door to this, the **Palm Beach Hotel** (BP 347; tel: 085 00407) is a smaller and more idiosyncratic set-up with an art-deco façade, stylish decor, and a light airy ambience to the interiors. Large self-contained doubles with private balcony and en-suite hot bath cost US$30, while smaller rooms range in price from US$20 to US$25. The restaurant is very atmospheric, with a distinctly European feel in pleasing contrast to the equally likeable beachfront bar.

Falling in the same price range, the **Oasis Guesthouse** (tel: 085 01732) lies about 500m out of town along the Ruhengeri road. This is a very pleasant little hotel, with a variety of rooms, ranging from spacious self-contained doubles with sofa, balcony, television and hot bath at US$30 to self-contained singles at US$15. The restaurant looks good and is very affordable. Negatives are the distance from the beach and town centre, and the lack of character by comparison with several other hotels in Gisenyi.

Budget

Situated on the beachfront, the wonderful **Hotel Regina** would easily make my nomination list for Africa's best budget hotel. Built in the colonial era, and still largely fitted in period style, the Regina exudes tropical languor, being sufficiently run-down to fit in the budget category, but not so much that you could fairly describe it as run-down. The wide veranda overlooks a tangled garden and the lake, while the bar and restaurant, with their high ceilings and wooden floor, could be a movie set. Large, airy self-contained doubles cost around US$18, while rooms using communal hot baths and toilets cost US$10/14 single/double. The food is acceptable and affordable, but the service is appropriately lethargic.

A few hundred metres further from the town centre, also overlooking the lake, the **Café du Lac** is another atmospheric and affordable gem. It consists of a well-maintained old colonial house in which two upstairs double rooms are rented out at around US$12 per night (shared bathroom). The wooden floors, slatted windows and whitewashed appearance create plenty of period character, and the interior has a spacious, airy feel. Meals and drinks are served in the ground-floor restaurant or on the large lawn.

By comparison with all the above, the **Hotel Ubumwe** (BP 39, tel: 085 06647) is a bit of a non-starter: reasonably comfortable but otherwise undistinguished rooms with en-suite hot showers and toilets at an uncompetitive US$15/20 single/double. The location, too, is less than ideal: a good 20-minute walk from the town centre, and set back a block from the lake.

Cheaper rooms are available at two places close to the bus station. The better of these is the friendly **Auberge de Gisenyi**, a standard local guesthouse with clean but cramped self-contained rooms (cold running water, hot buckets on request) at US$10/12 single/double. The rooms are centred around a green open courtyard which doubles as a bar, and there is a small restaurant attached. The cheapest rooms in Gisenyi – around US$5/7 single/double – are to be found at the grubby **Logement Petit Lac**, an option recommended only to those who are seriously short of cash.

Incidentally, you could spend merry hours in Gisenyi chasing phantom hotels. The **Hotel Edelweiss**, signposted all over town and still alluded to in several travel guides, is in fact an overgrown shell which presumably ceased to function during the genocide. So far as we could establish, signposts to the Methodist Church's **Centre d'Accueil** can also be ignored with impunity (the building is in good nick but nobody's home), as can references in several travel guides to the more central **Centre d'Accueil** once run by the Presbyterian Church (another victim of the genocide). Also likely to be disappointed are any campers who are lured to the **Bar-Restaurant Bikini Tam-Tam** on the basis of signposts suggesting that it doubles as a campsite – it doesn't.

Where to eat and drink

The best places to eat are generally the hotels. The restaurant at the **Palm Beach Hotel** is probably the best in town, with attractive decor and good Belgian cuisine in the US$5–7 range, and the beachfront bar is a great place to indulge in the tradition of sundowners. The food at the **Hotel Izubu-Meridien** is also very good, though more expensive, and you can eat well at the **Hotel Regina** for comfortably under US$5.

Another good spot for sundowners – indeed for a drink at any time of day – is the **Bar-Restaurant Bikini Tam-Tam**, which has a perfect lakefront position marred only slightly by the smell from the fish market next door. A limited selection of snacks and grills are available in the US$1–5 range.

Foreign exchange

Any of the three banks marked on the map will change US dollars cash at rates considerably lower than those on the street. The Banque de Kigali also changes travellers' cheques, but only if they are shown proof of purchase (ie: the receipt that is supposed never to be carried with your travellers' cheques).

Excursions from Gisenyi
Rubona

Set on an attractive peninsula 6km from the town centre, Rubona is the main harbour for Gisenyi and the site of Rwanda's largest brewery. It is connected to the town centre by a surfaced road and regular minibus-taxis, a scenic route which would make for a pleasant stroll in one or other direction. Rubona is a bustling little satellite town, and fun to stroll around, but it is mainly of interest to travellers who want to go out on to the lake, whether for a short paddle on one of the hundreds of small fishing pirogues or dugout canoes that dot the harbour, or for a ride on a motorised cargo boat connecting Gisenyi to the more southerly ports of Kibuye and Cyangugu.

About 500m from the harbour and the Bralirwa brewery there is a new and attractively situated lakefront restaurant; this was under construction when we visited and scheduled to open before the end of 2000. There is no formal accommodation in Rubona, but the owner of the new restaurant, Odette Nyiramungi, told us that travellers were welcome to pitch a tent on the site for a small fee; you can give her a ring at 085 24293 to confirm this.

Goma
At the time of writing, it is possible to go across to the town of Goma in the DRC, for a day trip, on Sundays only. No visa is required, but a fee equivalent to US$5 is levied. The border post lies on the edge of Gisenyi town, a few hundred metres from the Hotel Ubumwe, and there is plenty of transport along the 20km road to Goma on Sundays. How long this arrangement will persist is anybody's guess, but it would be worth checking the current situation if a flit across to the former Zaire takes your fancy.

Gishwati Forest Reserve
In the early 20th century, Gishwati was the second-largest tract of indigenous forest in Rwanda, stretching along the western rift escarpment from the Virungas halfway down Lake Kivu. The forest has since become heavily fragmented: by 1989 it consisted of two main stands covering a combined 28,000 hectares, about a quarter of its extent 100 years earlier, and today little if anything of Gishwati remains. Maps of Rwanda still show a substantial Gishwati Forest Reserve to the east of Gisenyi, clipping the main roads to Ruhengeri and to Kibuye.

We tried to explore the forest from the Ruhengeri road, driving southwards from a recently settled refugee camp below a sheer outcrop called Bigogwe Rock, approximately 13km west of Mukamiira. This area appears to have been forested until recently, since a few isolated indigenous trees still stand between the terraced cultivation, but nothing that could be called a forest remains. After 8km of driving along very rough roads we came out at what locals seem to call Gishwati: the rolling grassland of a former presidential farm, not forest by any stretch of the imagination, but remarkable all the same for being perhaps the only unprotected natural grassland we saw anywhere in Rwanda – an almost surreal reminder of what much of the country must have looked like a couple of centuries ago.

More hearteningly, we did see some relic forest patches when we drove along the main dirt road between Gisenyi and Kibuye. How extensive these are, I cannot say: we saw no sign of an eastward road along which the area could be explored, nor did we encounter any forest wildlife.

Eastern Rwanda

East of Kigali, the highlands of the Albertine Rift descend towards the western rim of the Lake Victoria Basin, a relatively flat and low-lying region marked by a distinctly warmer and more humid climate than the rest of Rwanda. Geographically, the most significant feature of eastern Rwanda is probably the Akagera River, which forms the border with Tanzania, and feeds the extensive complex of lakes and marshes protected within Akagera National Park.

For tourists, Akagera National Park is undoubtedly the most important attraction in eastern Rwanda. Although the park was recently reduced in area and has suffered heavily from poaching during the last decade, it remains Rwanda's only conventional safari reserve. The untrammelled savannah of Akagera is home to typical plains animals such as lion, elephant, buffalo, zebra and giraffe, while its lakes and marshes support large numbers of hippo and crocodile, as well as a multitude of water birds. At present, Akagera is not an easily accessible destination for those without private transport, nor is there any accommodation within its boundaries, but it makes for a highly alluring overnight safari out of the capital – provided that you have access to a vehicle, and are prepared to camp, or to stay at a hotel in a nearby town.

Akagera aside, the east of Rwanda lacks any major tourist attractions. The handful of towns that dot the region are uniformly dull; they are fine to use as a base, but have little inherent charm, although some have lively markets. Other landmarks include the Rusumo Falls on the Tanzania border and Lake Muhazi, both of which are diverting enough if you are in the area, but not really worth making a major effort to reach. The area of rolling hills and cattle farming in the far northeast near the Uganda border offers extensive views – but again this is an area for strolling and people-watching rather than any great excitement.

The main roads through eastern Rwanda are surfaced and covered by the usual proliferation of minibus-taxis. Accommodation options are limited by comparison with those in other parts of the country, but all the main towns have at least one reasonably comfortable – and reasonably priced – hotel. Because it lies at a lower altitude than the rest of the country, the Tanzania border area is the one part of Rwanda where malaria is a major rather than a minor risk, particularly during the rainy season.

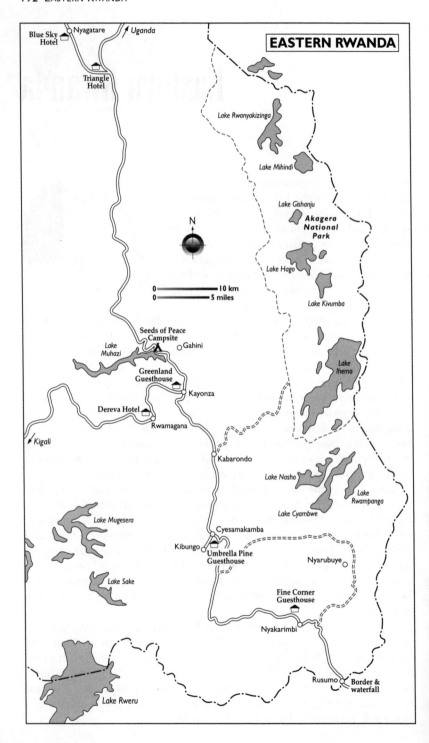

EASTERN RWANDA

Blue Sky Hotel
Nyagatare
Uganda
Triangle Hotel

Lake Rwanyakizinga

Lake Mihindi

Lake Gishanju

Akagera National Park

Lake Hago

N

Lake Kivumba

0 ⟶ 10 km
0 ⟶ 5 miles

Seeds of Peace Campsite
Gahini

Lake Muhazi

Greenland Guesthouse
Kayonza

Lake Ihema

Dereva Hotel
Rwamagana

Kigali

Kabarondo

Lake Nasho

Lake Rwampanga

Lake Mugesera

Lake Cyambwe

Cyesamakamba
Kibungo
Umbrella Pine Guesthouse

Lake Sake

Nyarubuye

Fine Corner Guesthouse

Nyakarimbi

Lake Rweru

Rusumo
Border & waterfall

RWAMAGANA

One of several unremarkable small towns in eastern Rwanda, Rwamagana is of interest to travellers primarily as a base from which to explore Lake Muhazi and Akagera National Park, though it does boast a couple of marginally interesting colonial buildings including a large church. The town lies about 60km from Kigali, no more than a hour's drive along a good surfaced road covered by regular minibus-taxis, some of which are 'express' while others also serve villages nearby. In Kigali they leave from the Nyabugogo bus station and call at Remera bus station en route. On your return you may also be dropped off at Kigali's central bus station in Avenue de Commerce.

The **Dereva Hotel** (BP 126; tel: 67244), set in large green grounds alongside the main road, offers what are probably the most commodious lodgings in this part of Rwanda, and is very reasonably priced at around US$12/17 for a suite-sized single/double with hot showers. The attached restaurant serves large meals in the US$3–5 range. If the Dereva is full you could try the **Ikambere** (tel: 67372).

In common with so many other parts of Rwanda, Rwamagana is benefiting from foreign aid to repair and reconstruct after widespread damage during the genocide. For example, Luxembourg is financing the rehabilitation of the hospital and a new dormitory for the School of Nursing. The hospital narrowly escaped a major massacre; the RPF army arrived just as those singled out for death were being marched away by the *interahamwe*. But already a number of other staff and patients had been killed and the hospital damaged. Teachers and students at the School of Nursing also had a fortunate escape as the *interahamwe* harrassing them seemed (unusually) more interested in looting than killing. Elsewhere in the area, thousands died.

The nearby Cyaruhogo rice scheme, on 680 hectares, was established in 1978 with aid from China and now provides almost 4,000 jobs.

KAYONZA

This small, rather scruffy settlement is situated 78km from Kigali, at the junction of the main north–south road connecting Kagitumba on the Rwanda border to Rusumo on the Tanzania border. Kayonza is, if anything, even less remarkable than Rwamagana, though once again it serves as a possible base for exploring Lake Muhazi and Akagera National Park and is readily accessible from Kigali on public transport (minibuses leave from Nyabugogo bus station). The **Greenland Guesthouse** is a decent local place offering small but clean rooms for US$7/12 single/double, and it serves tasty inexpensive local food.

LAKE MUHAZI

In common with most lakes in Rwanda, Muhazi is an erratically shaped body of water whose shores follow the contours of the surrounding hills. It is a pretty spot, though not as beautiful as the lakes around Ruhengeri, but – at least for travellers dependent on public transport – it has the virtue of being highly accessible. The eastern tip of Lake Muhazi lies beside the surfaced

THE ORIGIN OF 'RWANDA'

According to the historian Alexis Kagame, the name 'Rwanda' is derived from the verb *kwanda* which, in the local language, means literally 'to enlarge, to grow'. Oral tradition identifies Rwanda, at around the middle of the 14th century, as a tiny kingdom just a few square kilometres in size, named 'Royaume (kingdom) de Gasabo' or '*Rwanda* de Gasabo'. Its capital was said to be on the banks of Lake Muhazi. Again according to oral tradition, once Rwanda had been created by the mythical Gihanga, successive rulers of this tiny kingdom enlarged – hence the name – its borders in all directions by war and conquest.

Kagitumba road, about 8km north of Kayonza. Here, opposite the turn-off to the small hillside town of Gahini, the **Seeds of Peace Centre** (tel: 67422) has an attractive position overlooking the lake, and serves a variety of meals and drinks (no alcohol). For those wanting to eat or drink outside on the shore of the lake, staff carry trays hazardously up and down the steep grassy slope, somehow or other spilling very little. A couple of traditional homes have been reconstructed here and are open to visitors; also there is a small beach below the centre, and boats are available for hire. Camping is permitted at a rather steep US$12 per tent, and rooms should be available by early 2001.

Further along the road towards Rwamagana is the **Jambo Pleasure Beach**, a similar (but currently smaller) lakeside resort. More tourist development beside Muhazi seems likely. Watching the sun on the water and Rwandan families enjoying the pleasant surroundings, I recalled with a shiver that a friend spent three days hiding here during the genocide, before escaping to safety. There's no hint of the horror now.

Lake Muhazi also has a population of otters; recent research is described in the journal *Mammalia*, Vol 54 no 1, January 1990.

Back in the olden days, this was a lake much studied by the Germans as they explored their new territory. Writing in 1907, a Doctor Mildbraed rather crossly commented:

> The west end of Lake Mohasi terminates in a papyrus swamp, and therefore promised rich spoils for zoological treasure-hunters. We were all the more keenly disillusioned to find the fauna far more meagre in character in this great water basin – the first we had explored in Africa – than we had been led to suppose in Germany. In spite of the luxurious vegetation at this part of the lake, the most diligent search was needed before we found a few sponges and polypi attached to some characeous plants.

I can't answer for the contents today but I guess there's rather more man-made waste than Doctor Mildbraed will have encountered.

NYAGATARE

The far northeastern tip of Rwanda is a wide-open area of rolling landscapes and cattle, stretching to the hills of Uganda in the distance. The vegetation is much the same as that of Akagera National Park: fresh and gently green at moister times of year, parched and tinder dry just before the rainy season, with weary cattle – mostly the long-horned Ankole – plodding from clump to clump of bristly scrub. There's a slightly pioneering feel about the hamlets and villages here; they squat defiantly, surrounded by the empty plains. As you drive up from Kigali you'll also notice patches of new housing, built (often with foreign funds) to accommodate the returning refugees. These are the houses of a child's pictures, plain and single-storeyed, with a small square window on either side of the front door. In fact they're dotted all over Rwanda, but the open landscapes here make them more visible.

Nyagatare is a small, scattered town and administrative centre – and, if you want a wholly un-touristy experience, you could consider spending a night there. Minibuses run from Kigali's Nyabugogo bus station, and it's handy for the Uganda border if you're travelling on.

The **Blue Sky Hotel** (BP108 Nyagatare; tel: 65244) has five en-suite doubles/twins with mosquito nets for around US$13, and 20 more rooms with shared facilities (clean) at US$5 single, US$8 double. Electricity is from a generator so don't plan too much reading in bed. At present the hotel is used mostly by government staff and officials on business in the area. In the evenings the bar is companionably busy with local people and the restaurant isn't bad – although breakfast is a touch spartan. There are a couple more small restaurants in the main street serving the usual *mélanges* of meat, rice and vegetables. In late 2000 another hotel was being renovated nearby – it looked larger and smarter – and 5km or so from Nyagatare as you turn off from the main Kigali-Uganda road there's also the **Triangle Hotel** (20 small bare

RWANDA, MY COUNTRY

A M, who was exiled in Uganda during the 1970s and 1980s, returned to Rwanda after the genocide and now lives and works in Nyagatare.

God created you with care and concern, source of big rivers like the Nile, with moderate rainfall throughout the year and enough sunshine, both to support the vegetation. Life is convenient. The undulating landscape of hills and mountains in the northwest is covered with forests and harbours different species of wildlife, especially the famous gorillas that cause curiosity because of their scarcity worldwide. Here in Umutara region in the east the savannah land is fitting for livestock; domestic life neighbours a national park called Akagera, dotted with a good number of lakes, where you can find different types of fine birds on the shores and wild animals deep in the woodland. Lastly but not least, the gentleness, hospitality and faithfulness of your indigenous people will bring many from far away to visit you.

rooms, mosquito nets, US$8 double, basic shared facilities, no phone or restaurant but probably OK if you're stuck or broke).

The tiny main street offers – surprisingly – a photo laboratory, post office, dry cleaners, barber, general store and a sign-writer who also sells local paintings (rather gaudy, judging by the selection I saw).

What you can do from Nyagatare is walk – ask (and take note of) local permission and advice, fill up your water-bottle and then just stroll off across fields, plains, hillsides… It's a wonderfully clear, open panorama (unlike in much of the rest of Rwanda with its jutting hills and intensive cultivation) and if you crave occasional shade you can head for trees or bushes. I was there during a drought when there was little vegetation to attract wildlife, but local farmers told me that they often find antelope and zebra grazing peacefully among their cattle. Also, in Nyagatare as in all of Rwanda, you can while time away pleasantly by people-watching and engaging in conversation. (Have you remembered how to ask 'What's your name'? I'll remind you. It's *Witwandé?*)

KIBUNGO

The largest town in the southeast of Rwanda, Kibungo lies about 25km south of Kayonza junction and 100km from Kigali. It is the most convenient base from which to explore Akagera National Park (though Rwamagana, only slightly further from the park entrance, does have a smarter hotel) and the obvious springboard for a day trip to the Rusumo Falls. Otherwise, it is no more distinguished than other towns in this part of Rwanda: a small grid of roads lying 3km west of the altogether more bustling junction town of Cyesamakamba. Regular minibus-taxis connect Kibungo to Kigali and Rusumo.

It's the administrative centre of Kibungo prefecture, in a region suffering not only from the aftermath of the genocide (much still needs to be reconstructed, both physically and mentally) but also from the unkindness of nature; at the time of writing it depends on external food aid, as the autumn rains were both too late and too little.

The only accommodation we could find was the **Umbrella Pine Guesthouse** (tel: 66269 or 72567), which is situated in Cyesamakamba (aka Cyamakamba) on the main road towards Rusumo about 200m past the turn-off to Kibungo proper. This cosy little local hotel, centred around a large courtyard bar and restaurant, has clean but rather gloomy rooms with en-suite hot shower and nets for US$7/12 single/double. Good, inventive meals cost around US$5. The Christmas tree in the courtyard, evidently decorated all year round, comes complete with a terrifying gadget that tinkles the opening bars of *Santa Claus is Coming to Town* all day through. It might be worth mentioning that after a couple of hours of this torture, we turned off the switch and it remained off for the rest of our stay.

A couple of other bars and restaurants are dotted around the junction, serving chilled beers, goat kebabs and other local fare – the food isn't comparable with that of the Umbrella Pine, but it is a lot cheaper.

RUSUMO FALLS

The Rusumo border with Tanzania, 60km southeast of Kibungo, is also the site of Rwanda's most impressive waterfall. Rusumo Falls isn't particularly tall, and it couldn't be mentioned in the same breath as the Victoria or Blue Nile Falls, but it is a voluminous rush of white-water nevertheless, as the Akagera River surges below the bridge between the two border posts. The Rwandan officials don't appear to have any objection to tourists wandering on to the bridge to goggle at the spectacle, though it's a moot point whether the falls actually justify the two-hour round trip from Kibungo.

It's here at Rusumo that the German Count von Götzen, later to become Governor of German East Africa, entered Rwanda in 1894. He then travelled across the country to Lake Kivu, visiting the Mwami at Nyanza en route. Later, in 1916, when the Belgians were preparing to wrest the territory from the Germans, Belgian troops dug a trench and mounted artillery at the spot where one can see the falls today, in order to dislodge the German troops ensconced on the other bank who were guarding the only negotiable crossing.

If you are heading this way, it's definitely worth stopping at **Nyakarimbi**, a large village straddling the Kibungo road about 20km from the Rusumo border crossing. This part of Rwanda is noted for its distinctive cow-dung 'paintings' – earthy, geometric designs which are mostly used to decorate the interiors of houses. In Nyakarimbi, however, a couple of the houses have cow-dung paintings on their outer walls, and one – unsignposted but easily recognised by the black-and-white whorled pattern facing the main road – serves as a craft co-operative. This is where most of the geometric paintings and pottery you see in Kigali originate from, but it's more fun (and cheaper) to buy them at source, especially as the people who run the co-operative aren't at all pushy. To the north of Nyakarimbi, a powerfully evocative genocide memorial at Nyarubuye commemorates the many thousands who died in this area.

So far as travel practicalities go, the surfaced road between Kibungo and Rusumo is in reasonable condition, and can be covered in an hour. Regular minibus-taxis service the route. The closest accommodation to the border is the **Fine Corner Guesthouse**, which lies alongside the main road one or two kilometres from the Nyakarimbi co-operative in the direction of Kibungo. Clean but basic double rooms cost US$3.50 (bucket showers only) and meals are available.

AKAGERA NATIONAL PARK

Named after the river which runs along its eastern boundary, Akagera National Park is Rwanda's answer to the famous savannah reserves of anglophone East and southern Africa. In contrast to the rest of the country, Akagera is relatively warm and low-lying, and its undulating plains support a cover of dense, broad-leafed woodland interspersed with lighter acacia woodland and patches of rolling grassland studded evocatively with stands of the superficially cactus-like *Euphorbia candelabra* shrub. To the west of the plains lies a chain of low mountains, reaching elevations of between 1,600m

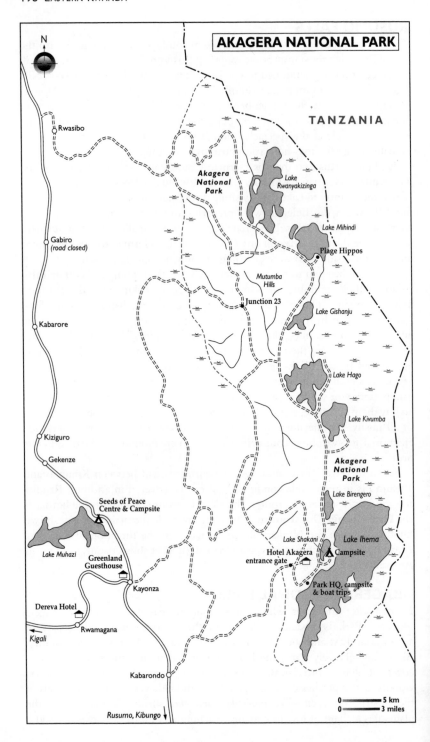

AKAGERA NATIONAL PARK

and 1,800m. The eastern part of the park supports an extensive network of wetlands: a complex of a dozen lakes linked by extensive papyrus swamps and winding water channels fed by the mighty Akagera River.

In terms of game viewing, it would be misleading to compare Akagera to East Africa's finest savannah reserves. Poaching has greatly reduced wildlife populations in recent years, and what was formerly the north of the park has been settled by returned refugees. The intense human pressure on Akagera is reflected in the fact that much of the northern and western territory was de-gazetted in 1998, reducing its total area by almost two-thirds from 250,000 to 90,000 hectares. Even after this concession to local land requirements, the lakes that remain within the national park are dotted with local fishing camps, and routinely used to water domestic cattle (the distinctive long-horned Ankole cow is far and away the most commonly seen large mammal in Akagera). The pollution and garbage around the park headquarters underscore an abiding sense of lawlessness, which – while it has no effect on the security of tourists – has to raise serious concerns about Akagera's long-term prospects.

For all that, Akagera is emphatically worth visiting. There are plenty of animals around, and they aren't as skittish as one might expect. To give some idea, over the course of three game drives, we saw a total of 20 mammal species, ranging from elephant and buffalo to the tiny elephant-shrew and bushbaby. The lakes support some of the highest concentrations of hippo you'll find anywhere in Africa, as well as numerous large crocodiles, while lion, leopard and possibly black rhino are still present in small numbers. And the birdlife is phenomenal: not only the sort of rarities that will have ardent birdwatchers in raptures, but also some of Africa's most impressive concentrations of big waterbirds.

As big an attraction as the animal life is the sensation of being in a genuinely off-the-beaten-track chunk of bush: this is one African game reserve where you can still drive for hours without passing another vehicle, never knowing what wildlife encounter might lie around the next corner. Akagera is also among the most scenic of savannah reserves, with its sumptuous forest-fringed lakes, tall mountains, and constantly changing vegetation.

Akagera is a good game reserve. It could, with improved management and a bit of time, once again become a truly great one. Equally, it could well be that Akagera will simply not be able to withstand the clamour for land from outside its already reduced boundaries. Which way it goes, one senses, will depend largely on its ability to generate serious tourist dollars and employment opportunities. Rwanda's population has doubled in the last 20 years and it is set to double again over the next 20. The pressure on Akagera will only increase with time, yet in the context of this rapid population growth, forsaking 90,000 hectares of not particularly arable game reserve to cultivation and grazing will at best alleviate a short-term problem. It will not address the heart of the land issue.

The survival of Akagera is not simply an esoteric conservation concern, but one that has implications for the country's development as a whole. Prior to the civil war, Rwanda's fledgling tourist industry was one of its three main

AKAGERA'S HISTORY

The Belgian colonisers were concerned about nature conservation. From 1920 onwards (and earlier, in the Congo) conservation measures were put into practice and became the object of various legislative and administrative decrees. It was the decree of November 26 1934 that created the *Parc National de la Kagera*, on about 250,000 hectares. The park included – which was extremely rare before 1960 – a Strict Natural Reserve and an adjoining area where certain human activities were tolerated. It came under the jurisdiction of the *Institut des Parcs Nationaux du Congo Belge et du Ruanda-Urundi*, which was also responsible for the three parks (Albert, Garamba and Upemba) in the Belgian Congo. (In fact 8% of the Albert Park was also in Rwanda; now representing the Volcanoes Park in the northwest.) Kagera was renamed Akagera after independence, when the new Republic's leaders announced their intention of maintaining the park (and the Volcanoes Park) despite population pressure. Akagera's borders were altered – a few thousand hectares were retroceded to local communities while almost 20,000 hectares of the lacustrine zone to the south were incorporated. Several dozen elephants were transported, first by helicopter and then by truck, from Bugesera, which was to be developed for agriculture. In November 1984, Rwanda held an official celebration of the park's 50th anniversary.

sources of foreign revenue. If Rwanda is to rebuild that industry, and to develop a self-contained tourist circuit of its own, then it desperately *needs* Akagera. For, without a savannah reserve of Akagera's ilk, the country seems destined to attract nothing but pit-stop cross-border gorilla tourism, tourists spending one or two nights in one small part of the country as an extension of a safari elsewhere in East Africa.

If you visit Akagera, you won't regret it – it's a lovely, untrammelled slice of African bush. No less important, perhaps, you'll be doing Rwanda a favour.

Natural history

Akagera is notable for protecting an unusually wide diversity of habitats within a relatively small area. Prior to the civil war, it was regarded as one of the few African savannah reserves to form a self-sustaining ecological unit, meaning that its resident large mammals had no need to migrate seasonally outside of the park boundaries. Whether that is still the case today is an open question, as roughly two-thirds of the original park was de-gazetted in 1998, and, while some of this discarded territory is still virgin bush today, it is probably only a matter of time before it will all be settled, putting further pressure on Akagera's diminished wildlife populations.

The modern boundaries of the park protect a 90,000ha area, which stretches from north to south along the Tanzania border for approximately 60km, and is nowhere wider than 30km from east to west. The eastern third of the park consists of an extensive network of wetlands, fed by the Akagera River, and dominated by a series of small-to-medium-sized lakes. Lake Ihema, the most southerly of the lakes to lie within the revised park boundaries, is also the largest body of open water, covering about 100km^2. The lakes are connected by narrow channels of flowing water and large expanses of seasonal and perennial papyrus swamps. The eastern wetlands are undoubtedly the most important of the habitats protected within the park: not only do they provide a permanent source of drinking water for the large mammals, but they also form an important waterbird sanctuary while harbouring a number of localised swamp dwellers.

Akagera's dominant terrestrial habitat is broad-leafed woodland, though pockets of acacia woodland also exist within the park, while some of the lake fringes support a thin belt of lush riparian woodland. Ecologically, the savannah of Akagera is in several respects unique, a product of its isolation from similar habitats by the wetlands to the east and mountainous highlands of central Rwanda to the west. The flora shows strong affinities with the semi-arid zones of northern Uganda and Kenya, but the fauna is more typical of the Mara-Serengeti ecosystem east of Lake Victoria. Akagera's geographical isolation from similar habitats is emphasised by the natural absence of widespread plains animals such as rhino and giraffe, both of which were subsequently introduced and (at least until the civil war) have thrived in their adopted home. Much of the bush in Akagera is very dense, but there are also areas of light acacia woodland and open grassland, notably on the Mutumba Hills and to the northeast of Lake Rwanyakizinga.

Mammals

While Akagera's considerable scenic qualities and superb birdlife are largely unaffected by the recent years of turmoil, the large mammal populations have suffered badly at the hands of poachers. Having said that, we arrived at Akagera expecting the worst, and were pleasantly surprised at how much wildlife there still is. It is the classic 'bad news, good news' scenario. The populations of all large mammals (except perhaps hippo) are severely depleted by comparison with ten years ago, while a few high-profile species, if not already locally extinct, appear to be heading that way. The good news, however, is that most large mammals are still sufficiently numerous to form a viable breeding population; furthermore, with adequate protection, these numbers are likely to be supplemented by animals crossing into the park from unprotected parts of neighbouring Tanzania which still support plenty of big game. Akagera, in short, is a damaged but salvageable game reserve.

Extirpated species include the **African wild dog**, probably a victim not of poaching but, in common with many other African reserves, of a canine plague which would have been introduced into the population through contact with domestic dogs. **Black rhino**, introduced in 1954, might well be extinct and are certainly very vulnerable, though it would not be surprising if the thick bush still held a few individuals (two unverified rhino sightings were reported by visitors over the year before we visited the park).

ANTELOPE OF AKAGERA

The 11 antelope species in Akagera range from the eland, the world's largest antelope, through to the diminutive common duiker. The most common, however, is the **impala** *Aepeceros melampus*, a slim handsome antelope which bears a superficial similarity to the gazelles, but belongs to a separate family. Chestnut in colour, the impala has diagnostic black and white stripes running down its rump and tail, and the male has large lyre-shaped horns. It is one of the most widespread antelope species in east and southern Africa, normally seen in large herds in woodland habitats, and common in the woodland around and between the lakes of Akagera.

The **Defassa waterbuck** *Kobus ellipsiprymnus defassa* is a large, shaggy brown antelope with a distinctive white rump. The male has large lyre-shaped horns, thicker than those of the impala. Waterbuck inhabit practically any type of woodland or grassland provided that it is close to water, and they are probably the most common large antelope after impala in the far south of Akagera.

Very common in the north of the park and in the Mutumba Hills, the **topi** or **tsessebe** *Damaliscus lunatus* is a large, slender dark-brown antelope

Defassa waterbuck

Topi

Impala

with striking yellow lower legs. It has a rather ungainly appearance, reminiscent of the hartebeest and wildebeest, to which it is closely related, and is often seen using an anthill as a sentry point. Oddly, the herds of topi we saw in northern Akagera are far larger than those found in the Serengeti ecosystem.

Similar in size to a topi, but far more handsome, the **roan antelope** *Hippotragus equinus* has, as the Latin name suggests, a horse-like bearing, The uniform fawn-grey coat is offset by a pale belly, and it has short decurved horns and a light mane. Recent reports suggest that roan are now rare in Akagera.

Much larger still is the **common** or **Cape eland** *Taurotragus oryx*, which attains a height of up 1.75m and can weigh as much as 900kg. The common eland is light brown in colour, with faint white vertical stripes, and a somewhat bovine appearance accentuated by the relatively short horns and large dewlap. In Akagera, small herds are most likely to be seen on the open grassland of the Mutumba Hills, where is it quite common.

continued overleaf

Roan antelope

Common eland

Klipspringer

Oribi

Reedbuck

A trio of smaller antelope are also mainly confined to the Mutumba Hills. The largest of these is the **Bohor reedbuck** *Redunca redunca*, a light fawn animal with moderately sized rounded horns; reedbucks are almost always seen in pairs, and in Akagera are rather skittish. The smaller **oribi** *Ourebia ourebi* is a tan grassland antelope with short straight horns and a small but clearly visible circular black glandular patch below its ear. It is the commonest antelope on the Mutumba Hills, typically seen in parties of two or three, and has a distinctive sneezing alarm call. The **klipspringer** *Oreotragus oreotragus* is a goat-like antelope, normally seen in pairs, and easily identified by its dark, bristly grey-yellow coat, slightly speckled appearance and unique habitat preference. Klipspringer means 'rockjumper' in Afrikaans and it is an apt name for an antelope which occurs exclusively in mountainous areas and rocky outcrops.

The only small antelope found in thicker bush is the **common duiker** *Sylvicapra grimmia*, an anomalous savannah representative of a family of 20-plus small hunchbacked antelopes associated with true forests. Generally grey in colour, the common duiker has a distinctive black tuft of hair

Common duiker

Bushbuck

sticking up between its small straight horns. It is common in all bush areas, though it tends to be very skittish.

A widespread resident of thick woodland and forest, the pretty **bushbuck** *Tragelaphus scriptus* is a medium-sized, rather deer-like antelope. The male is dark brown or chestnut, while the much smaller female is generally pale red-brown. The male has relatively small, straight horns, while both sexes have pale throat patches, white spots and sometimes stripes. The bushbuck tends to be secretive, but might be seen anywhere in Akagera except for open grassland.

Similar in appearance to the bushbuck, and a close relation, the semi-aquatic **sitatunga** *Tragelaphus spekei* is a widespread but infrequently observed inhabitant of west and central African swamps. The male, with a shoulder height of up to 125cm (much taller than a bushbuck) and a shaggy fawn coat, is unmistakable, while the smaller female might be mistaken for a bushbuck except for its more clearly defined stripes. The status of the sitatunga within Akagera is uncertain; they are almost certainly still present, but uncommon and restricted to inaccessible swampy areas.

Spotted hyena

Of the larger predators, **spotted hyena** and **leopard** are still around, but infrequently observed (though you might well come across hyena spoor, particularly the characteristic white dung). The future of the park's **lion** – many of which have been poisoned by cattle herders – hangs in the balance. A solitary female was seen in the north of the park in early 2000, and a few months later a female with three cubs was sighted in the same area. Probably this was the same female, and she must have found a male lion somewhere – given the tenacity of these regal felines, and their tendency to wander long distances, this is one species which could naturally replenish itself through individuals crossing over from Tanzania.

Leopard

Smaller predators are well represented. Most likely to be encountered by day are various **mongooses** (we saw dwarf, banded and black-tailed mongooses), while at night there is a chance of coming across viverrids such as the lithe, heavily-spotted and somewhat cat-like **genet**, and the bulkier black-masked **civet**. Also present, but rarely seen, are the handsome spotted **serval cat** and the dog-like **side-striped jackal**.

Banded mongoose

One of the most common terrestrial mammals is the **buffalo**, and while the population is nowhere near the estimated 8,000 that roamed the park in the 1980s, it is probably still measurable in thousands. **Hippo**, too, are present in impressive numbers: we saw pods of between 40 and 50 animals on all of the lakes, and on some of the lakes there must be at least a dozen pods. The park's formerly prodigious **elephant** herds have suffered badly from poaching, but a viable population estimated at around 60 survives, centred around Lake Hago. Small herds of **Burchell's zebra** are regularly encountered in open areas, while the population of 30 **Masai giraffe**, descendants of a herd introduced from Kenya in 1975, tend to stick to patches of acacia woodland.

African buffalo

The handsome **impala** is probably the most common and habitat-tolerant large mammal in the park, and of the 11 antelope species which occur in Akagera (see box *Antelope of Akagera* on pages 202–5), only the aquatic **sitatunga** is immediately endangered and unlikely to be seen by visitors. Also very common are three savannah primates: the dark, heavily built **olive baboon**, the smaller and more agile **vervet monkey**, and the tiny wide-eyed **bushbaby** (the latter a nocturnal species likely to be seen only after dusk). The forest-dwelling **silver monkey**, although listed for Akagera, is probably now very rare, possibly even extirpated, due to habitat loss following the reduction in the park's area. For the same reason, it is debatable whether Africa's largest swine, the **giant forest hog**, still occurs in Akagera. The smaller **bushpig**, a secretive nocturnal species, is present but rarely encountered, while the **warthog**, a bolder diurnal pig, is very common throughout.

Warthog

Birds

Akagera is, after Nyungwe, the most important ornithological site in Rwanda. What's more, these two fine birding destinations complement each other to such an extent that our lists for them probably had less than 20% of species in common. In addition to being the best place in Rwanda to see a good selection of savannah birds and raptors, Akagera is as rich in waterbirds as anywhere in East Africa, and one of the few places where papyrus endemics can be observed.

Among the more colourful and common of the savannah birds are the gorgeous lilac-breasted roller, black-headed gonalek (easily picked up by its jarring duets), little bee-eater, Heuglin's robin-chat and brown parrot. Less colourful, but very impressive, are the comical grey hornbill and noisy bare-faced go-away bird. The riparian woodland around the lakes hosts a number of specialised species, of which Ross's turaco, a bright-purple, jay-sized bird with a distinctive yellow mask, is the most striking.

A notable feature of Akagera's avifauna is the presence of species such as crested barbet, white-headed black chat and Souza's shrike, all of which are associated with the *brachystegia* woodland of southern Tanzania and further south, but have colonised the mixed woodland of Akagera at the northernmost extent of their range. Also worthy of a special mention is the red-faced barbet, a localised endemic of savannahs between Lake Victoria and the Albertine Rift. Finally, the savannah of Akagera is one of the last places in Rwanda where a wide range of large raptors is resident: white-backed and Ruppell's griffon vultures soar high on the thermals, the beautiful bateleur eagle can be recognised by its wavering flight pattern and red wing markings, while brown snake eagles and hooded vultures are often seen perching on bare branches.

Most of the savannah birds are primarily of interest to the dedicated birder, but it is difficult to imagine that anybody would be unmoved by the immense concentrations of water-associated birds that can be found on the lakes. Pelicans are common, as is the garishly decorated crowned crane, the odd little open-bill stork, and the much larger and singularly grotesque marabou stork. Herons and egrets are particularly visible and well-represented, ranging from the immense goliath heron to the secretive black-capped night heron and reed-dwelling purple heron. The lakes also support a variety of smaller kingfishers and shorebirds, and a prodigious number of fish eagles, whose shrill duet ranks as one of the most evocative sounds of Africa.

On a more esoteric note, the papyrus swamps are an excellent place to look for a handful of birds restricted to this specific habitat: the stunning and highly vocal papyrus gonalek, as well as the more secretive and nondescript Caruthers's cisticola and white-winged warbler. Akagera used to be regarded as one of the best places in Africa to see the shoebill, an enormous and unmistakable slate-grey swamp-dweller whose outsized bill is fixed in a permanent Cheshire-cat smirk. Placed in a monospecific genus, the secretive and localised shoebill is among the most sought-after of African birds, and its continued presence in Akagera would do much to boost Rwanda's status as an avi-tourism destination. Unfortunately, we were unable to establish whether the civil war and subsequent reduction in the park's area had any impact on the shoebill's habitat – judging by the blank looks that our questioning and frantic pointing at the field guide drew from everybody we spoke to, the prognosis is less than fantastic!

Reptiles

The **Nile crocodile**, the world's largest reptile and a survivor from the age of the dinosaurs, is abundant in the lakes. Some of the largest wild specimens you'll encounter anywhere are to be found sunning themselves on the mud-banks of Akagera, their impressive mouths wide open until they slither menacingly into the water at the approach of human intruders. Not unlike a miniature crocodile in appearance, the **water monitor** is a type of lizard which often grows to be more than a metre long and is common around the lakes, tending to crash noisily into the bush or water when disturbed. Smaller lizards are to be seen all over, notably the colourful rock agama, and a variety of snakes are present but, as ever, very secretive.

Dangerous animals

Although it is technically forbidden to leave your vehicle except at designated look-out points, the guides in Akagera seem to enforce this rule somewhat whimsically. Bizarrely, the guides we used were very nervous about approaching elephant and buffalo in a vehicle (the former might sometimes go for a car, the latter only in freak instances), but were in our opinion dangerously blasé about trying to sneak up on elephants by foot. So it's probably worth noting that, whatever your guide might say, it is extremely foolhardy to leave the vehicle in the presence of elephant, buffalo or lion.

Hippo and crocodile are potentially dangerous, and claim far more human lives than any terrestrial African animal. For this reason, you should be reasonably cautious when you leave the car next to a lake, particularly at dusk or dawn or in overcast conditions, when hippos are most likely to come out of the water to graze. The danger with hippos is getting *between* them and the water; you have nothing to worry about when they are actually in the water. Special caution should be exercised if you camp next to a lake – don't wander too far from your site after dark, and take a good look around should you need to leave your tent during the night (if there are hippo close by, you'll almost certainly hear them chomping at the grass). Crocs are a real threat only if you are daft enough to wade into one of the lakes.

The most dangerous animal in Akagera is the malaria-carrying anopheles mosquito. Cover up after dark – long trousers and thick socks – and smear any exposed parts of your body with insect repellent. Many tents come with built-in mosquito netting. This will protect you when you sleep, provided that you don't hang a light at the entrance to your tent, which will ensure that a swarm of insects enter it with you. Incidentally, never leave any food in your tent: fruit might attract the attention of monkeys and elephants, while meat could arouse the interest of large predators.

Not so much a danger as a nuisance are tsetse flies, which are quite common in dense bush and can give a painful bite. Fortunately, the pain isn't enduring (though people who tend to react badly to insect bites might want to douse any tsetse bite in antihistamine cream) and there is no risk of contracting sleeping sickness during a short stay in Akagera. Insect repellents have little effect on these robust little creatures, but it's worth noting that they are attracted to dark clothing (especially blue).

Further information

A useful fold-out colour map is sold at the ORTPN office in Kigali. This map was accurate before the civil war, and it remains so for the southern part of the park. However, it does still show the old park boundaries, and details in the north are rather historical. The numbered junctions shown on the map help with navigation, though only about half of the junctions are still numbered on the ground. The map costs around US$2.50 and includes some descriptive material about the park on the flip.

Getting there and away

In a private vehicle, Akagera can be reached from Kigali in a long two hours, and from Kibungo or Rwamagana in about one hour. The only usable entrance gate, 500m from the disused Hotel Akagera, is reached via a 27km dirt road which branches from the main surfaced road at Kabarondo,15km north of Kibungo. This dirt road is in fair condition – passable in any vehicle except perhaps after rain – and all intersections are marked with fading green signposts for the Hotel Akagera. Within the park, however, a 4x4 is advisable, though any vehicle with good clearance should be okay in the dry season.

Reaching Akagera on public transport is more problematic. Any minibus-taxi travelling between Kayonza and Kibungo can drop you at the junction, from where the only realistic option is a motorbike-taxi (assuming that you can find one). At the time of writing, travellers are permitted to go as far as Lake Ihema on a motorbike, but once there the options are limited: no walking is permitted with or without a guide, and no vehicle is available for game drives.

Where to stay

The **Hotel Akagera**, perched on a rise overlooking Lake Ihema, has been closed since 1994. The large modern-looking building, once managed by Sabena, serves as something of a reminder of the tourist boom experienced by Rwanda prior to the civil war, and it remains in remarkably good condition. There is some talk of the hotel reopening over the next few years, although, with the national park being so reduced in area, it's debatable whether this vast monolith would ever receive the volume of tourists for which it was designed. Another casualty of the civil war is **Gabiro Lodge** in the north of the park, which has been seconded to the military. This means that no accommodation is available within the park at the time of writing, though it seems likely that the situation will change within the lifespan of this edition. The ORTPN office in Kigali is the obvious place to seek updated information.

Camping is permitted at the staff headquarters on the shore of Lake Ihema, though the combination of scavenging baboons, abundant litter and human racket make this a less than enticing prospect. A far better place to pitch a tent is Lake Shakani, a small forest-fringed body of water which lies about 4km from Lake Ihema. This is a great spot, but facilities are limited to a couple of small shelters, so campers would need to be fully self-sufficient with drinking water, food, firewood and pretty much anything else they need. Facilities aside, Lake Shakani is a tremendously attractive spot, with plenty of crocs, hippos and birds to keep you amused. Deeper in the park, camping is permitted at designated sites on Lake Hago and in the Mutumba Hills; once again you would need to be entirely self-sufficient to contemplate doing this. We were told by one ranger that camping costs US$3.50 per person, and by another that it is free provided that you have paid your entrance fee. Either way, it's a small price to pay for your own private slice of African bush!

For most visitors, however, a more realistic option will be to base themselves at one of the nearby towns. Kibungo is the closest town of any size, only 40km from the entrance gate, and it has a decent hotel. See page 196. The alternative is Rwamagana, which has a smarter hotel but is about 20km further from the park entrance.

Fees

An entrance fee equivalent to about US$9 per person is charged. So far as we could establish, this is a genuine entrance fee as opposed to a daily fee – in other words, you only pay when you enter, no matter how long you spend in the park.

Boat trips

In theory, boat trips are available on Lake Ihema. When we visited, however, the park's boat wasn't working, and we were taken on a boat operated by the military. You'll have to check the situation when you arrive, but, assuming that a boat is available, it's a worthwhile trip. Close encounters with outsized crocodiles and large pods of hippo are all but guaranteed, and you'll also pass substantial breeding colonies of African darter, cormorant and open-bill stork along the way. Other waterbirds are abundant: the delicate and colourful African jacana can be seen trotting on floating vegetation, fish eagles are posted in the trees at regular intervals, jewel-like malachite kingfishers hawk from the reeds, while pied kingfishers hover high above the water to swoop down on their fishy prey. Of greater interest to enthusiasts will be the opportunit) to spot marsh specialists such as blue-headed coucal and marsh flycatcher. On a less positive note, you won't fail to notice the thick, dirty foam that laps the lake's shores (evidence of a high level of pollution).

Game drives

Game drives are available only to those with a private vehicle, ideally a 4x4. Guides can be provided at no extra charge (though a tip will be expected) and, while most of them have limited knowledge, they will help you to find your way around and will probably be better at picking up game in the thick bush. The game-viewing circuit is in essence limited to one main road running northwards from the park headquarters at Lake Ihema. Most of the lakes are passed by this road, or can be approached using a short fork. North of Lake Hago, the road branches into two main forks, one of which heads west into the Mutumba Hills, the other continuing along the lake route. These roads reconnect at Lake Rwanyakizinga.

The possibilities for game drives are restricted by the fact that the park can only be entered near Lake Ihema at the defunct Akagera Hotel. In a long half-day, you could realistically travel from the entrance as far north as the Mutumba Hills and back. To head further north requires the best part of a day, with the option of using the exit-only route north of Lake Rwanyakizinga emerging on the main tar road to the Uganda border. The tracks in the far north are very indistinct, and should be attempted only in the company of a guide. Once back on the main road, the guide can be dropped at Kayonza or Kabarondo junctions with enough money to make his way back to the headquarters by motorbike-taxi.

Starting from the entrance gate, a hilly road through very thick scrub leads over about 5km to **Lake Ihema**. Defassa waterbuck are resident in this area, as are some reportedly aggressive buffaloes. The park headquarters at the lake are worth stopping at to look for hippos, crocodiles and waterbirds. Baboons hang around the headquarters, and a pair of the localised white-headed black chat is resident. This is also where boat trips can be arranged.

About 4km north of Lake Ihema, a road forks through more thick scrub to the small **Lake Shakani**, a scenic camping spot and home to large numbers of hippo. The bush here is rattling with birdlife (look out for the brilliant red chest of the black-headed gonalek) and impala are rather common. Unfortunately the lake is also a popular place to water cattle. About 8km north of this, **Lake Birengiro** is a shallow, muddy body of palm-fringed water which supports huge numbers of waterbirds, notably pelicans, storks and the odd long-toed plover. The best of the lakes for general game viewing, however, is **Lake Hago**, about 15km further north and encircled by a decent track. This is where elephant are most likely to be seen, as well as small herds of buffalo and zebra, and it must support several hundred hippo.

South of Lake Hago, the vegetation is mostly very dense, and animals are difficult to spot, though you can be reasonably confident of seeing baboons, vervet monkeys and impala. This all changes when you turn left at Junction 23, to ascend towards the **Mutumba Hills** through an area of park-like woodland whose large acacias are favoured by giraffe. Eventually the woodland gives way to open grassland and easily the best game viewing in the park. Here, you can be certain of seeing the delicate oribi and reedbuck, as well as the larger topi. With luck, you'll also encounter eland, zebra and (in the wet season) large herds of buffalo.

North of the Mutumba Hills, the vegetation is again very thick, and animals can be difficult to spot, though impala, buffalo and zebra all seem to be present in significant numbers. The papyrus beds around **Lakes Gishanju** and **Mihindi** form the most accessible marshy areas in the park, and are worth taking slowly by anybody who hopes to see papyrus-dwellers. The **Plage Hippos** (Hippo Beach) on Lake Mihindi was, oddly, about the one place in Akagera where we stopped next to open water and *didn't* see any hippos, but it's a pretty spot, and would make for an ideal picnic site.

Heading further north, **Lake Rwanyakizinga** is another favoured spot with elephants, and the open plains to the west of the lake are excellent for plains animals such as warthog, zebra, and herds of 50-plus topi. This little-visited part of Akagera is one that is inhabited by lion – and possibly rhino. Having looked around this area, your options are either to head back the way you came, or to head cross-country out of the park along the route mentioned earlier in this section.

Epilogue

Janice Booth

When I returned to Kigali after exploring Rwanda – as I hope you have been doing through the pages of this book, since reading the *Prologue* – there was a message for me from the former headmaster. He had located Peter's brother – the one who had been with him in Uganda – who had returned to Rwanda after the genocide and was working in the north of the country.

I was preparing to travel up there by minibus the next day, when another message came, to tell me that Peter's youngest sister (she had been one of the two girls in the photo) was working in Kigali and I could phone her. Suddenly shaking, I dialled the number, remembering my attempted phone call to Peter's workplace almost six years before. A gentle voice answered, speaking good French. We talked a little. 'When he was still with us' was the phrase she used to convey that Peter had died. The next day she came to my hotel – and I saw that the awkward teenager in the family photo had become a poised, stylish and beautiful young woman. Of the five siblings (including Peter) in the photo, she and one brother had survived.

Peter and his wife, with their baby who was only a few days old, had been killed quickly in the street, together with one of Peter's brothers who was visiting them during his university vacation. This was at least better than the lingering death endured by many. Unknowingly, I had walked in the area while I was in Kibuye. It was assumed that they had been buried in Kibuye's mass grave. I discovered – he hadn't told me this, perhaps thinking that I would disapprove – that Peter also had a daughter born in 1990, before he (and the baby's mother) were imprisoned, and the mother died in jail. At the time Peter had written: 'So many died, of the hunger and the beatings.' This little girl survived horrors during the genocide and is now cared for by the surviving brother from the photo – her smile, they tell me, is just like her father's.

I have visited Peter's daughter at home and during my last visit she was able to move to a good private school nearby, as the local state school was proving too stressful. She enjoys learning English and her best subject is maths, for which she got 75 out of 90 in her last exams. I've been twice to visit the brother from Uganda, working in the north; he has a government job at present (he's a civil engineer) and is also building up a cattle farm. And I'm closely in touch with Peter's sister, chatting with her by email every week. She missed out on further education because of the genocide, so now she's just starting at college (I feel privileged to be able to help with the cost) in order to gain better qualifications. So – I seem to have acquired a new family, and I couldn't be happier about it.

At the end of my first visit something happened which stretches coincidence to its limits. Peter's sister phoned, four days before I was due to leave, to say that some bodies had been found near to the place where he had been killed. (This happens – some bodies were just hurriedly and roughly buried.) His wife's sister was going over to see if she could identify them by their clothing. And yes – the bodies turned out to be those of Peter, his wife, their baby, his brother and a friend. Six years after the genocide, and at exactly the moment when I was in Rwanda, they had been found and could be reburied, and I could give his sister some money to pay for flowers on my behalf. The story was complete.

But – then in fact it continued, with the publication of this book which, I hope, will encourage travellers to visit the country that Peter loved, and to boost its economy with their foreign exchange. He would have been so proud and pleased to be a part of this, and I – and his family too – can take comfort in the fact that his otherwise tragic and pointless death has, in the end, proved not to be completely wasteful. When I read his sister's happy emails (she is enjoying college) and remember his daughter's smile, I can feel his pleasure and approval.

And, if Peter had not written to me all those years ago from Uganda, you would not be holding this book in your hands today!

Appendix 1

LANGUAGE

Words in Kinyarwanda are spelt phonetically here, to make their pronunciation easy. The letters 'r' and 'l' (and their sounds) are often interchanged, also sometimes 'b', 'v' and 'w'. When a word ends in 'e', pronounce it as the French 'é'. Pronounce 'i' as 'ee' rather than 'eye'.

English	French	Kinyarwanda
Courtesies		
good day/hello	*bonjour*	*muraho*
good morning	*bonjour*	*mwaramutse*
good afternoon	*bonjour*	*mwiriwe*
good evening	*bonsoir*	*mwiriwe*
sir	*monsieur*	*bwana*
madam	*madame*	*mubyeyi*
how are you?	*ça va?*	*amakuru?/bitese?*
I'm fine, thank you	*ça va bien, merci*	*amakuru/meza/égo*
please	*s'il vous plaît*	*mubishoboye*
thank you	*merci*	*murakoze*
excuse me	*excusez moi*	*imbabazi*
goodbye (morning)	*au revoir*	*mwiliwe*
goodbye (afternoon)	*au revoir*	*mwilirwe*
goodbye (evening)	*au revoir*	*muramukeho*
goodbye (for ever)	*au revoir/adieu*	*murabeho*

Basic words		
yes	*oui*	*yégo*
no	*non*	*oya*
that's right	*c'est ça*	*ni byo*
maybe	*peut-être*	*ahali*
good	*bon*	*byiza*
hot	*chaud*	*ubushyuhe*
cold	*froid*	*ubukonje*
and	*et*	*na*

Questions		
how?	*comment?*	*bite?*

English	French	Kinyarwanda
how much?	*combien?*	*angahe?*
what's your name?	*quel est votre nom?*	*witwande?*
when?	*quand?*	*ryali?*
where?	*où?*	*hehe?*
who?	*qui?*	*nde?/bande?*

Food/drink

beans	*haricots*	*ibihyimbo*
beer	*bière*	*byeri*
butter	*beurre*	*amavuta*
bread	*pain*	*umugati*
coffee	*café*	*ikawa*
eggs	*oeufs*	*amagi*
fish	*poisson*	*amafi*
meat	*viande*	*inyama*
milk	*lait*	*amata*
potatoes	*pommes de terre*	*ibirayi*
rice	*riz*	*umuceli*
salad	*salade*	*salade*
soup	*potage*	*isupu*
sugar	*sucre*	*isukali*
tea	*thé*	*icyayi (chai)*
tomatoes	*tomates*	*inyanya*
drinks	*boissons*	*ibinyobura*
water	*eau*	*amazi*

Shopping

bank	*banque*	*ibanki*
bookshop	*librairie*	*isomero*
chemist	*pharmacie*	*farumasi*
shop	*magazin*	*iduka*
market	*marché*	*isoko*
battery	*pile/batterie*	*bateri*
film	*filme*	*filime*
map	*carte*	*ikarita*
money	*argent*	*amafaranga*
soap	*savon*	*isabuni*
toothpaste	*dentifrice*	*umuti w'amenyo*

Post

post office	*poste (PTT)*	*iposta*
envelope	*enveloppe*	*ibahasha*
letter	*lettre*	*urwandiko*
paper	*papier*	*urupapuro*
postcard	*carte postale*	

English	French	Kinyarwanda
stamp	*timbre*	*tembri*

Getting around

bus	*bus*	*bisi*
bus station	*gare routière*	*aho bisi ihagarara*
taxi	*taxi*	*tagisi*
car	*voiture*	*imodoka*
petrol station	*station d'essence*	*aho kunyweshereza essence*
plane	*avion*	*indege*
far	*loin*	*kure*
near	*près*	*hafi*
to the right	*à droit*	*i buryo*
to the left	*à gauche*	*i bumoso*
straight ahead	*tout droit*	*imbere*
bridge	*pont*	*ikiraro*
hill	*colline*	*agasozi*
lake	*lac*	*ikiyaga*
mountain	*montagne*	*umusozi*
river	*fleuve*	*uruzi*
road	*route*	*umuhanda*
street	*rue*	*inzira*
town	*ville*	*umudugudu*
valley	*vallée*	*umubanda*
village	*village*	*akadugudu*
waterfall	*chute*	*isumo*

Hotel

bed	*lit*	*igitanda*
room	*chambre*	*icyumba*
key	*clef/clé*	*urufunguzo*
shower	*douche*	*urwiyu hagiriro*
bath	*baignoire*	*urwogero*
toilet/WC	*toilette*	*umusarane*
hot water	*l'eau chaude*	*amazi ashushye*
cold water	*l'eau froide*	*amazi akonje*

Miscellaneous

dentist	*dentiste*	*umuganga w'amenyo*
doctor	*médecin*	*umuganga*
embassy	*ambassade*	*ambasade*
tourist office	*bureau de tourisme*	*ibiro by ubukererarugendo*

Time

minute	*minute*	*idakika*
hour	*heure*	*isaaha*

day	*jour*	*umunsi*
week	*semaine*	*icyumweru*
month	*mois*	*ukwezi*
year	*an/année*	*umwaka*
now	*maintenant*	*ubu/nonaha*
soon	*bientôt*	*vuba*
today	*aujourd'hui*	*none*
yesterday	*hier*	*ejo hashize*
tomorrow	*demain*	*ejo hazaza*
this week	*cette semaine*	*iki cyumweru*
next week	*semaine prochaine*	*icyumweru gitaha*
morning	*matin*	*igitondo*
afternoon	*après-midi*	*ni munsi*
evening	*soir*	*umugoroba*
night	*nuit*	*ijoro*
Monday	*lundi*	*ku wa mbere*
Tuesday	*mardi*	*ku wa kabili*
Wednesday	*mercredi*	*ku wa gatatu*
Thursday	*jeudi*	*ku wa kane*
Friday	*vendredi*	*ku wa gatanu*
Saturday	*samedi*	*ku wa gatandatu*
Sunday	*dimanche*	*ku cyumweru*
January	*janvier*	*Mutarama*
February	*février*	*Gashyantare*
March	*mars*	*Werurwe*
April	*avril*	*Mata*
May	*mai*	*Gicuransi*
June	*juin*	*Kamena*
July	*juillet*	*Nyakanga*
August	*août*	*Kanama*
September	*septembre*	*Nzeli*
October	*octobre*	*Ukwakira*
November	*novembre*	*Ugushyingo*
December	*décembre*	*Ukuboza*

Appendix

CONTACT ADDRESSES

Aid to Displaced Persons (see page 88) 35 Rue du Marché, 4500 Huy, Belgium; tel: 085 213481; fax: 085 230147; email: aidepersdepl.huy@proximedia.be

Association pour la Promotion de l'Education et de la Culture or **APEC** (see page 81) in Tumba, near Butare: contact via Aid to Displaced Persons, above

Centre for the Formation of Art (see page 89) Kigali; contact the Reverend Dennis Mungabo on mobile 08533697

Centre Presbytérien d'Amour de Jeunes (see page 81) BP 56 Kigali; tel/fax: 76929

Communauté des Autochtones Rwandais or **CAURWA** (see page 75) BP 3809 Kigali; tel/fax: 7640; email: CAURWA@rwandatel1.rwanda1.com

Forest Peoples' Project (see page 88) 1c Fosseway Centre, Stratford Rd, Moreton-in-Marsh GL56 9NQ, England; email: info@fppwrm.gn.apc.org

Dian Fossey Gorilla Fund International (see page 90) 800 Cherokee Av, SE, Atlanta, Georgia 30315, USA; tel: 1 800 851 0203; email: 2help@gorillafund.org; web: www.gorillafund.org

Forum for African Women Educationalists or **FAWE** (see page 77) FAWE Rwanda Chapter, BP 622 Kigali; tel: 82514; email: fawerwa@rwanda1.com

Imbabazi orphanage (see page 185) BP 98 Gisenyi; tel: 540740

Kigali Institute of Science, Technology & Management (see page 104) Av de l'Armée, BP 3900 Kigali; tel: 74696; email: info@kist.ac.rw; web: www.kist.ac.rw

Kigali Public Library (see page 87) c/o Beth Payne, American Embassy Kigali, 2210 Kigali Place, Washington DC, 20521-2210, USA; email: kigalilibrary@aol.com

National University of Rwanda (see page 127) BP56 Butare; tel: 530122; fax: 530121; email: nurcc@nur.ac.rw; web: www.nur.ac.rw

Nyamata Vocational School Project (see page 86) via RUGO (below)

Office Rwandais du Tourisme et des Parcs Nationaux (see page 49) Av de l'Armée, BP 905 Kigali; tel: 76514/5, 73396; email: ortpn@rwandatel1.rwanda1.com

Rwanda United Kingdom Goodwill Organisation or **RUGO** (see page 85) c/o Ernest Sagaga, RUGO Secretary, 158A Harrow View, Harrow, Middlesex HA1 4TL; tel: 020 8427 3186; or Mike Hughes tel: 01252 861059; web: www.rugo.org

Rwanda Privatisation Secretariat (see page 91) BP 158 Kigali; tel: 75383/70989/70991/70992; fax: 75384; email: pvs@rwandatel1.rwanda1.com

Rwandan Women's Network (see page 79) Tel: Peter on mobile 08511050

World Sponsorships (see page 88) via Aid to Displaced Persons, above

Voluntary Service Overseas (see page 89) 31 Putney Bridge Rd, London SW15 2PN; tel: 020 8780 7200; web: www.vso.org.uk

Appendix

FURTHER READING
Historical background

Reader, John *Africa: A Biography of the Continent* Hamish Hamilton, 1997
This award-winning book, available as a Penguin paperback, provides a compulsively readable introduction to Africa's past, from the formation of the continent to post-independence politics — the ideal starting point for anybody seeking to place their Rwandan experience in a broader African context.

Fegley, Randall (compiler) *Rwanda – World Bibliographical Series volume 154* Clio Press, 1993
This selective, annotated bibliography contains over 500 entries covering a wide range of subjects including Rwanda's history, geography, politics, literature, travellers' accounts, flora and fauna. Its preface and introduction give a condensed but useful (although somewhat dated) overview of Rwanda from early times until just before the genocide.

Kagame, Alexis *Un abrégé de l'ethno-historie du Rwanda* and *Un abrégé de l'histoire du Rwanda de 1853 à 1972*, Editions Universitaires du Rwanda, Butare, 1972 and 1975.
These very comprehensive works are now out of print (and there are no English translations) but the seriously interested should try to track down secondhand copies. Drawing on oral tradition, Kagame describes the country and its people from several centuries before the arrival of the Europeans (in the first book) through to the first decade of colonisation (in the second).

Natural history
Field guides (mammals)

Kingdon, Jonathan *The Kingdon Field Guide to African Mammals* Academic Press, 1997
This is my first choice: the most detailed, thorough and up-to-date of several field guides covering the mammals of the region. The author, a highly respected biologist, supplements detailed descriptions and good illustrations of all the continent's large mammals with an ecological overview of each species. An essential purchase for anybody with a serious interest in mammal identification.

Stuart, Chris & Tilde *The Larger Mammals of Africa* Struik, 1997
This useful field guide doesn't quite match up to Kingdon's, but it's definitely the best of the rest, and arguably more appropriate to readers with a relatively casual interest in African wildlife. It's also a lot cheaper and lighter!

Stuart, Chris & Tilde *Southern, Central and East African Mammals* Struik 1995
This excellent mini-guide, compact enough to slip into a pocket, is remarkably thorough within its inherent space restrictions. Highly recommended for one-off safari-goers, but not so good for forest primates, which limits its usefulness in Rwanda.

Dorst, J & Dandelot, P *Field Guide to the larger mammals of Africa* Collins, 1983
Haltenorth, T & Diller, H *Field Guide to the Mammals of Africa including Madagascar* Collins, 1984
Formerly the standard field guides to the region, these books are still recommended in many travel guides and other resources. In my opinion, they have largely been superseded by subsequent publications, and now come across as very dated and badly structured – with mediocre illustrations to boot.

Estes, Richard *The Safari Companion* Green Books (UK), Russell Friedman Books (SA), Chelsea Green (USA)
This unconventional book might succinctly be described as a field guide to mammal behaviour. It's probably a bit esoteric for most one-off visitors to Africa, but a must for anybody with a serious interest in wildlife.

Field guides (birds)

Van Perlo, Ber *Illustrated Checklist to the Birds of Eastern Africa* (Collins, 1995)
No modern field guide overtly covers the birds of Rwanda, but Van Perlo's guide is the next best thing, since it illustrates and provides a brief description of every species recorded in Uganda and Tanzania, along with a distribution map. So far as I'm aware, this makes it comprehensive for Rwanda (I don't know of any bird found in Rwanda but not in Tanzania or Uganda), and I found that distribution details can normally be extrapolated from the maps of neighbouring countries. If you buy only one bird field guide for Rwanda, this should certainly be it, but be aware that the descriptive detail is very succinct and many of the illustrations are misleading.

Williams, J & Arlott, N *Field Guide to the Birds of East Africa* (Collins, 1980)
As with the older Collins mammal field guides, Williams' was for years the standard field guide to the region, and is still widely mentioned in travel literature. Unfortunately, it feels rather dated today: less than half the birds in the region are illustrated, several are not even described, and the bias is strongly towards common Kenyan birds.

Zimmerman et al *Birds of Kenya and Northern Tanzania* (Russell Friedman Books, 1996)
This monumentally handsome hardback tome is arguably the finest field guide to any African territory in print. The geographical limitations with regard to Rwanda barely need pointing out, but while this book cannot be

recommended as a primary field guide outside of the region it specifically covers, its wealth of descriptive and ecological detail and superb illustrations make it an excellent secondary source within Rwanda. A lighter and cheaper but less detailed paperback version was published in 1999.

Others
Fossey, Dian *Gorillas in the Mist* Hodder & Stoughton, 1983
Enjoyable and massively informative, Fossey's landmark book is recommended without reservation to anybody going gorilla tracking in the Parc Des Volcans.

Goodall, Jane *Through A Window* Houghton Mifflin, 1991
Subtitled *My Thirty Years with the Chimpanzees of Gombe*, this is one of several highly readable books written by Jane Goodall about the longest ongoing study of wild primates in the world. Set in neighbouring Tanzania, this is nevertheless obvious pre-trip reading for anybody who intends to track chimps in Nyungwe.

Kingdon, Jonathon *Island Africa* Collins, 1990
This highly readable and award-winning tome about evolution in ecological 'islands' such as deserts and montane forests is recommended to anybody who wants to place the natural history of Nyungwe and the Virungas in a continental context.

Mowat, Farley *Woman in the Mists* Futura, 1987
An excellent biography of the controversial Dian Fossey, one which leans so heavily on her own journals that parts are almost autobiography.

Stuart, Chris & Tilde *Africa's Vanishing Wildlife* Southern Books, 1996
An informative and pictorially strong introduction to the endangered and vulnerable mammals of Africa, this book combines coffee-table production with an impassioned and erudite text.

Background to the genocide
Prunier, Gérard *The Rwanda Crisis – History of a Genocide* Hurst & Company, London, 1998
This detailed and painstakingly researched history of the Rwandan genocide, full of personal anecdotes and individual stories, describes with icy clarity the composition of the time bomb that began ticking long before its explosion in 1994. Prunier presents the genocide as part of a deadly logic, a plan hatched for political and economic motives, rather than the result of ancient hatred. An Africa scholar, journalist and French political analyst, he helps the reader to understand not only Rwanda's genocide but also the complexities of modern conflict in general.

Melvern, L R *A People Betrayed – the Role of the West in Rwanda's Genocide* Zed Books, London & New York, 2000
Linda Melvern's investigative study of the international background to Rwanda's genocide contains a full narrative account of how the tragedy

unfolded. Documents held in Kigali, and previously unpublished accounts of secret UN Security council deliberations in New York, reveal a shocking sequence of events, and the failure of governments, organisations and individuals who could – had they opted to do so — have prevented the genocide. Understanding of this aspect of Rwanda's tragedy is crucial to the prevention of other such occurrences in the future. Melvern also recounts the all-too-often forgotten heroism of those who stayed on in Rwanda and did what they could in deteriorating conditions.

Gourevitch, Philip *We wish to inform you that tomorrow we will be killed with our families* Picador, 1998
Subtitled 'Stories from Rwanda', this winner of the *Guardian* First Book Award is war reporting of the highest order. Blending starkly factual narrative with human anecdotes and observations, Gourevitch paints on a broad canvas and the picture he creates is unforgettable. In this very accessible book he shows us 'little people' caught up in unstoppable horrors – and reaching great heights of heroism.

Rwanda – Death, Despair and Defiance African Rights, London, 1995
This 1,200-page compilation by the UK organisation African Rights is a painfully thorough and detailed account of the genocide and its effect on Rwanda's people – the careful preparations, the identities of the killers and their accomplices, the massacres, the attacks on churches, schools and hospitals, and the aftermath. Victims tell their own stories and those of their families, and the horror and immensity of the slaughter are highlighted by the simplicity of their narratives. The impact is powerful, sometimes overwhelming. The index enables the reader to discover easily what happened in any particular area or village.

Keane, Fergal *Season of Blood – a Rwandan Journey* Penguin, 1995
Keane's prose – sometimes so precisely balanced that it verges on poetry — is always impeccable. Here he blends factual narrative and analysis with spontaneous emotion in such a way that the reader is both moved and informed in a single phrase. As a BBC correspondent, he was travelling around Rwanda – among the killers and among the victims — as the genocide spread countrywide. His reports at the time brought home the extent of the human tragedy and their essence is preserved in this book, which won the 1995 Orwell Prize.

Murphy, Dervla *Visiting Rwanda* Lilliput Press, Dublin, 1998
The author visited Rwanda early in 1997 intending to trek alone in the mountains. Finding this inadvisable, she instead travelled around the country talking to people, observing, asking questions, and acquiring her own independent view of post-genocide Rwanda. She describes the survivors facing the herculean task of recovery, and considers the options for a barely functioning judicial system faced with the biggest work-load in its history. Also she traces the political background to the genocide and its aftermath. Murphy displays little optimism about Rwanda's future, but she writes with her usual skill and gives the reader much food for thought.

Kamukama, Dixon *Rwanda Conflict – its Roots and Regional Implications*
Fountain Publishers, Kampala, 1993, updated 1997
In this short book the history of Rwanda up to 1960 and the analysis of
political events are brisk but sometimes too black-and-white. However, there
is a useful appendix giving chronological 'Highlights in Rwanda Conflict'
from May 1990 until June 1996.

Rwandan fairy tales and legends
Well why not! These are culled from oral tradition and often demonstrate
social attitudes. Nothing exists in English, but French-speakers could try:

Rugamba, Cyprien (compiler) *Contes du Rwanda* Edicef, Conseil International
de la Langue Française, Paris, 1983
Traditional tales, such as 'The Rat and its Cows', 'The Hare and the Old
Woman'. The book also has a good introduction (for adults) describing the
background to the stories.

Kanyungo, M, Gakwaya, F & Nizeymana, M *Bakamé, le lièvre futé, et autres
histoires du Rwanda* Editions Bakamé, Kigali, 1999
First produced in Kinyarwanda in 1996, then translated into French, the three
stories in this book were collected by a small publishing company concerned
that the custom of telling tales to children is dying out in this modern age and
the books available to them are too westernised. The comments about this in
the 'Postface' are as interesting to adult readers as the stories themselves.

Miscellaneous
Lewis, Jerome & Knight, Judy *The Twa of Rwanda* World Rainforest
Movement (UK), 1996
The Twa are the smallest 'ethnic' group in Rwanda. This report, published
by the World Rainforest Movement in co-operation with the International
Work Group for Indigenous Affairs (Denmark) and Survival International
(France), traces their history, highlights their current impoverished
situation, quotes their opinions about their past and future, and allows them
to express their fears and aspirations. It also shows the dilemma faced by
African governments as they try to build national unity while still respecting
cultural diversity.

Halsey Carr, R & Howard Halsey, A H *Land of a Thousand Hills* Viking, 1999
Rosamond Halsey Carr moved to Rwanda as a young bride in 1949 and has
stayed for over 50 years. She watched the decline of colonialism, the problems
of independence and the growing violence. When the genocide started she was
evacuated by the American Embassy but returned four months later, and
began turning an old pyrethrum drying house on her flower plantation into a
home for genocide orphans, which – now relocated near Gisenyi – still
functions today. This very readable and moving book chronicles the
extraordinary life of an extraordinary woman, in the country she loved and
made her home.

WEBSITES

For practical information, the two most comprehensive websites on Rwanda are **www.rwandemb.org** (set up by the Rwandan Embassy in Washington DC) and the official Rwanda government website **www.rwanda1.com**. These have numerous links and cover a wide range of topics, including Rwanda's history, geography, politics, development, genocide trials, economy, business potential and tourism. On the whole they are kept up to date although some sections haven't been touched for a while at the time of writing. The website of the National University of Rwanda has useful information about the country as a whole, plus various links: **www.nur.ac.rw**. The KIST site (see page 104) is also helpful: **www.kist.ac.rw**.

For up-to-the-minute news reports from the Great Lakes countries and elsewhere in Africa try **www.reliefweb.int/IRIN**; another source of African news is **www.africanews.org**. The business-oriented website of MBendi Information Services gives a brisk overview of the country plus the current rate of the Rwandan franc against the US dollar: **www.mbendi.co.za**. The Rwanda News Agency site looks potentially promising as long as it is kept up to date: **www.ari.rna.com**. Rwandanet, a site run privately by a Rwandophile, gives useful news, background details and practical information, but some of the addresses and contact details need updating: **http://rwanda.free.fr**.

Conditions in Rwanda – as in other African countries – may change, so, as a matter of security before you travel, do check either the Foreign Office website **www.fco.gov.uk**, or else that of the US Department of State **http://travel.state.gov/travel_warnings.html**.

The site of the UN International Criminal Tribunal for Rwanda, **www.ictr.org**, has details of the current status of genocide criminals and the trials in progress. Human Rights Watch on **www.hrw.org** carries news of Rwanda and you can purchase its publications online. At the time of writing it is advertising a detailed 800-page report on the genocide, *Leave None to Tell the Story*.

Finally, just doing a general internet search under 'Rwanda' will give you a number of possibilities for browsing – some sites are up-to-date and reasonably helpful while others haven't been updated for seven years or so, and weren't very accurate even then. By the time you read this, new ones will certainly have been added – including, possibly, one for the Rwandan Embassy in London.

Index

Page numbers in bold indicate main entries, those in italics show maps.

accommodation 55
Aid to Displaced Persons 88
AIDS/HIV 46, 74, 81
air tickets, cheap 27
airlines 25–7
airport departure tax 27, 35
Akagera National Park 192, **197–212**, *198*
Albert National Park 171, 200
altitude 2, 36, 182
antelope 202–5
APROSOMA party 13
Arboretum, Ruhande 127–8
archaeology 5
Art, Centre for the Formation of 89–90, 110
Arusha Accord 17, 19
Astrida 15, 122

banana beer/wine 57, 129
banks *see* money
bargaining 59–60
Base 58, 167, 168
beaches 153, 184
begging 61
Belgian colonisation 10–15
bicycle-taxis 54
bilharzia 43–5
birdwatching 4, 139, 145, 152, 199, 207–8
Bizimungu, Pasteur 18, 19
boats, lake transport 53, 149, 155, 168, 187, 189
boat-trips 157, 168, 189, 210
bookshops 49, 109, 127
border crossings 28–9
    Burundi 28
    DRC 28
    Tanzania 29
    Uganda 28, 161–2
Brewery, Bralirwa 189–90
bribery 62
budgeting 36
Bugarama Hot Springs 151–2
Bugesera 200
Bukavu (DRC) 151
buses 54
Butare 122–127
    cathedral 128
    genocide 122
    hotels/guesthouses 125–6
    National Museum 128–9

Butare *continued*
    National University 127
    Ruhande Arboretum 127–8
    town plan *124*
Butaro (Lake Burera) 167
butterflies 140, 145
Bwindi Forest (Uganda) 131
Byumba 184

camping 32, 55, 190, 194, 210
cattle 5, 7, 195, 199
CAURWA 75–7
Centre Culturel d'Echanges Franco-
    Rwandaises 107, 109
charities 85–90
chiefs, traditional 8
chimpanzees 136–7, 145, 152
Classé, Bishop Léon 12
climate 25
clothing 33, 61, 183
cow-dung paintings 197
credit cards 35, 51
currency *see* money
Cyamakamba 196
Cyamudongo Forest 152–3
Cyangugu 146–51, *148*
Cyanika 161–2
cyber cafés, Kigali 105
Cyesamakamba 196

Dairy, Ikivuguto National 121
dance, Batwa 76–7
dance, Intore 72–3
Dian Fossey Gorilla Fund 90
distances 52
drink 56–7
driving licence, international 30

ebola 46
embassies, foreign in Rwanda 62–3
embassies, Rwandan abroad 30–1
entertainment 66, 107

famines 10–11
FAR 20
FAWE 77–9
fax 65
female travellers 61
food 55–6

forced labour 11
foreign exchange *see* money
Forest Peoples' Project 88–9
Fossey, Dian 90, 171–2, 181, 222
Foyer de Charité 169

Gacaca 19, 20, **22–3**
Gahini 194
genocide 17–19
genocide memorials
    Kibuye 153, 157
    Kigali 107
    Murambi 129–30
    Ntarama 114
    Nyamata 114
    Nyarubuye 197
Genocide Survivors' Fund 21
genocide trials 22–3
German East Africa 9–10
Gikongoro 129
Gisakura Tea Estate 144–5
Gisenyi 159, **184–9**, *186*
Gishwati Forest Reserve 131, 190
Gitarama 14, **115–17**
Goma (DRC) 99, 190
Goodall, Jane 137, 222
Gorillas in the Mist 172, 222
gorillas *see* mountain gorillas
gorilla-viewing permits 36

Habyarimana, Juvenal 15–17
Halsey Carr, Rosamond 185, 224
handicrafts 73, 77, 89–90, **109–10**, 197
Harroy, Jean-Paul 13
hippos 199, 206, 208
hitch hiking 53
hospitals 37, 46
hot springs, Bugarama 151–2
hotels/guesthouses 55
Hutu Manifesto 13
Hutus (Bahutu) 5, 7, 9–10, 73–4

identity cards 12–13
Imana 69
Imbabazi Orphanage 185
immunisations 37–8
inflation 21
insect repellent 39
insurance, travel 41
interahamwe 17, 19, 130
International Criminal Tribunal 19, 225
internet/email 65
Intore dancers 72–3, 119
investing in Rwanda 90–1

Kabgayi 117–18
Kagame, Alexis 6, 220
Kagame, Paul 15, 16–17, 18, 19
Kamageri's Rock 118
Kamembe *see* Cyangugu
Kamiranzovu Marsh 137
Karamba (Nyungwe) 145

Karisoke Research Centre 172
Kayibanda, Grégoire 13, 14, 15, 117
Kayonza 193
Keane, Fergal 223
Kibeho 130
Kibungo 196
Kibuye 153–5, *154*
Kidaho (Lake Burera) 167
Kigali 95–111
    central, map *98*
    environs, sketch-map *108*
    hotels/guesthouses 97–102
    nightlife 103
    restaurants 102–3
Kigali Public Library 87
King's Palace (Nyanza) 119–20
kingdoms, ancient 6
Kisoro 161–2
KIST 104–5

Lake Burera 165–7, *166*
Lake Ihema 201, 210, 211
Lake Karago 165
Lake Kivu 146–7, 153, 157, 185
Lake Muhazi 193–4
Lake Ruhondo 168–9, *166*
lakes, Akagera Park 210–12
language 57–8, 215–18
League of Nations 10
life expectancy 74
literature 70
Logiest, Guy 14, 117
Lusaka Agreement 19

malaria 38–9
maps 36, 96, 209
markets 118, 110–11, 118
MDR party 15
Mecklenburg, Duke of 9, 31, 185
Mgahinga National Park (Uganda) 171, 173
minibus-taxis 54, 113
missions, religious 9, 11
mobile phones 65, 106
monarchy 6, 8
money 35, 50–1, 103–4
money-changers 50–1, 104
monkeys 132–5, 173
motorbike-taxis 54
Mount Karisimbi 171, 175
mountain biking 53
mountain gorillas 174–81
    conservation 176, 178
    habituated groups 181
    permits 180
    regulations 183–4
    taxonomy 178–9
    tourism 176–7
    tracking 174–6, 178–81, 182–3
MRND party 15
MSM party 14
MTN RwandaCell 64–5
Mukamiira 165, 190

Murambi 129–30
Murphy, Dervla 223
Musanze Cave 164
Museum, Geological 107
Museum, Kabgayi 117–18
Museum, National (Butare) 128–9
Museveni, Yoweri 16
music 71–2
musical instruments 109, 110
Mutumba Hills 210, 211
Muvunyi, Tharcisse 122
Mwami Musinga 11
Mwami Rudahigwa Mutara III 11, 13, 14, 119
Mwami Rwagubiri 9

National Ballet (Intore) 72–3, 119
National Museum of Rwanda 128–9
National University of Rwanda 127
Ndaba Falls 157
newspapers 63
Nyabisindu see Nyanza
Nyagatare 195–6
Nyakabuye 152
Nyakarimbi 197
Nyanza 118–21
Nyungwe Forest 4, 115, **130–45**, *138*
    camping/guesthouses 141, 142
    coloured trails 143–4
    entry fees 142

OAU 19
Obote, Milton 16
Office Rwandais du Tourisme et des Parcs
    Nationaux see ORTPN
Operation Turquoise 18, 19, 130
ORTPN 49, **92**, 107, 163–4

Parc des Volcans see Volcanoes National Park
PARMEHUTU party 14
pharmacies 37, 66
photography 66–8
Plage Hippos 212
poaching 172, 177–8, 199
population 2
post/mail 65
post office, Kigali 105
prisoners 22–3, 156–7
privatisation 91
public holidays 49

quotas, introduction of 15

RADER party 13
radio and TV 66
railways 53
rainy seasons 2, 26
RANU party 16
refugees 24
religion, traditional 69–70
Remera (Lake Ruhondo) 169
Royal Drum 7, 8
RPF 16, 18

RRWF party 16
Ruanda-Urundi 9, 95
Rubona (Gisenyi) 185, 189–90
RUGO 85–7
Ruhango 118
Ruhengeri **159–64**, *160*, 173–4
Rusizi Falls 151
Rusumo Falls (Lake Burera) 167
Rusumo Falls (Tanzania border) 197
Ruwenzori colobus 132
Rwamagana 193
Rwanda Tourist Board see ORTPN
Rwandan Patriotic Front see RPF
Rwigema, Fred 16–17
Ryangombe 70

safety 48, 60–1
self-drive 51–2
Sons of Chiefs, school for 9, 12
Stanley, Henry (explorer) 8
street children 79–81

taxis 54, 96
telephone 65, 105–6
theft 60–1
tour operators (international) 29–30
tour operators (Kigali) 112–13
travel clinics 39–41
travel insurance 41
travellers' cheques 35, 50
tsetse flies 43, 209
Tumba, primary school 81, 88
Tutsis (Batutsi) 5, 7, 9–10, 73–4
Twa (Batwa) 5, 7, 9–10, 75–7, 224
Twagiramungu, Faustin 18

ubuhake 7, 8, 13
uburetwa 11
UNAMIR 18
UNAR party 14
United Nations Organisation 10, 13
Unity and Reconciliation Commission 20, 78
Uwasenkoko Marsh 137
Uwinka 141, 143–4

Virgin Mary, apparitions 130
Virunga Mountains 169–71
Virungas National Park (DRC) 171
visas 30
volcanoes 171
Volcanoes National Park 4, 169–83, *170*
volcanoes, hiking trails 173
Voluntary Service Overseas see VSO
von Götzen, Gustav Adolf 9, 197
VSO 77, 89

waragi 57, 156
Waterfall Trail (Nyungwe) 143–4
watersports 155
websites 225

yellow fever 30, 37